Twisted Memories

Kinoshita Yūji

TWISTED MEMORIES

木下夕爾 『ねじれた記憶』

Collected Poetry

of

Kinoshita Yûji

1993

DEDICATION

These translations I gratefully dedicate to

BEN BEFU

別府勉先生に捧げる
for reasons he knows best

Manufactured in the United States of America
Printed on acid–free paper by
Thomson–Shore, Inc., Dexter, MI 48130–0305

Kinoshita [family] Yûji [given] (1914–1965)
      [Poems. English. 1993]
      Twisted Memories : Poetry / Kinoshita Yûji;
      translated from the Japanese

      280 pp.   15 x 23 cm.
      Chronology, Notes, English and Japanese Indexes
      ISBN 1–880276–25–9

Library of Congress Catalog Card Number: **93–060299**

Available from **YAKUSHA**
Post Office Box #666, Stanwood, WA 98292–0666
$30.00 (postpaid—U.S. currency only) Hardcover

C O N T E N T S

I N T R O D U C T O R Y

T H E P O E T R Y

S U P P L E M E N T A R Y

UNESCO COLLECTION OF REPRESENTATIVE
WORKS
JAPANESE SERIES

The poetry of Kinoshita Yûji has been accepted by
the Japanese National Commission of
The United Nations Educational, Scientific, and Cultural Organization

UNESCO

Kinoshita Yûji in 1938 (at 24)
Graduation from the Nagoya School of Pharmacy

二十四歳の木下夕爾・昭和十三年

PREFACE

Since the Meiji Restoration more than a century ago, a radical movement for modernization through Europeanization has affected every part of Japan. To most effectively implement this movement, a centralized political system led by a powerful bureaucracy was established in Tokyo—which then became not only the center of political power but also of cultural development.

Tokyo's influence in education, journalism, publishing, and art grew until it came to be seen as "*Chûô* [the Center]," a term that suggests its privileged superiority vis–à–vis the provinces. Painters, composers, novelists, and poets born outside Tokyo dreamed, and still do, of settling in the capital to attain distinction. That Tokyo was in some sense an enormous window onto the civilization and cultures of Europe and America was an important aspect of its magnetism.

European–style centralization plus the cult of Western ways made of Tokyo a dreamland for successive generations of ambitious intellectuals and artists who then, in this country of little space and many people, became models for others trying to adjust or conform to life in the centralized system.

Kinoshita Yûji was born in a small provincial town in Western Japan, and save for a few years as a student in Tokyo and Nagoya he lived most of his life in his native place—a fact important to remember when reading his poems. He very much wanted to settle in Tokyo, but he could not.

Like many poets of his time, Kinoshita was an eager reader of modern European poetry in translation. Yet his own work remains rooted in the details of everyday life in the small country town of Hiroshima Prefecture where he was born. There, as the resident son responsible for the care of family and family affairs, he passed a succession of what sometimes seemed to him monotonous years. But through those years his keen gaze fastened on and followed the movement and changes about him as well as his own sensibility.

Untouched by trends in Tokyo, he could from a fresh angle catch and fix in words the shifts of wind and cloud, the habits of small animals, the afternoon feeling of a small station where no one gets on or gets off the train, passing encounters with people of the village, a field of withered grass,

11

Japanese vegetables solid on a table, the shape of cakes made from wild fruit.

In his poems, man and nature live in sympathy. And from that sense of natural harmony he wrote, also, beautiful poems for children.

Kinoshita's poems preserve a natural breath and a tranquillity that were already in his time disappearing from Japanese big–city life. Rather than resorting to exaggeration or large–gestured confessions of the modern artist's sense of alienation and the absurd, he worked with firm will to rescue and immortalize the momentary reality of the precious shares with the ancient masters of traditional Japanese waka and haikai (haiku). Living in "*Chihô* [the Province]," far from "*Chûô* [the Center]," he was able to revive in his own quietly modern way a vocation that had been maintained through the centuries by the poets of old.

Indeed Kinoshita was well–known as a haiku poet. The high techniques of crystallization and focus he developed in the practice of that art emerge in his modern verse as a charm of ellipse and suggestiveness, an elegance of simplicity. For this country poet is an elegant poet, one who makes from contemporary Japanese language a very finely textured weaving.

Kinoshita has been fortunate in his translator. Robert Epp's dedication to his work seems also to reflect some older more finely–tuned tradition. Whether in Japan visiting the poet's family and colleagues, eating the regional foods Kinoshita mentions, discussing the poems, or at home revising, Epp's firm will seems to have matched the poet's own. That in the end the translations were satisfactory is attested by the honors they already received.

So there is harmony here between the ways of poet and translator, maker and re–maker. I cannot help but think Kinoshita Yûji would be, is, pleased.

Ôoka Makoto
大岡信

Chôfu, Tokyo
東京都調布市にて

KINOSHITA AS HAIKU POET

K inoshita's contemporary Narise Ôtôshi writes, "The delicate aromas of youth in Kinoshita's haiku drew public attention and high praise."[1] Azumi Atsushi, a fellow haiku poet, asserts, "His haiku are as pure and fresh as his free verse."[2] To grasp the entirety of Kinoshita the poet, we must therefore study his achievements in haiku as well as free verse.

Like most young poets, Kinoshita from the outset was familiar with haiku and tanka, traditional Japanese verse forms.[3] When he began writing haiku at the age of thirty, however, he had already been in the limelight as a promising free–verse poet. What, then, kindled his interest in haiku and what stimulated him to continue writing them till the end of his life? And how did these two forms affect the way he dealt with poetry? The aim of this essay is to answer these questions by chronologically examining selected haiku.

Quirks of fate provide the clue to Kinoshita's transformation. Two fateful events changed him from being a poet of nostalgic, rustic sentiment to a more mature writer pursuing problems like life and death or estrangement and creativity. The first quirk, his stepfather's illness and death, obliged him to take over the family pharmacy in the country; that forced Yûji to give up his dream to become a professional poet or novelist in the city. The second was the outbreak of the Pacific War. The former gradually turned Yûji from a poet merrily "singing" natural beauty to one expressing the pathos of his inner self. The latter stimulated severe thought control measures that forced him to give up writing free verse and turn to haiku.

"I found the realm of haiku beautiful," he wrote, "so I began both reading and writing them, something I'd long avoided."[4] Even strict government censors more or less ignored haiku, which they considered a rather harmless art that mainly portrayed the beauties of nature. Yûji began attending haiku meetings held in his area. He wanted to "bask in the amicable atmosphere of such gatherings so as to forget the fear and fretfulness of those increasingly harsh war–time days."[5]

Haiku's terseness, spontaneity, concreteness, and suggestiveness suited Kinoshita's delicate sensibility. His love of nature and lyrical inclinations also harmonized well with the haiku's mode of expressing feelings or thoughts through natural imagery. He consequently continued writing and submitting haiku to magazines even after the war and government censorship ended. In January 1946 he joined *Shuntô*,[6] the haiku magazine to which he contributed till his death in 1965. *Shuntô* represented one of Japan's strictest traditional haiku schools.[7] Members observed the ancient rules: the fixed 5–7–5 syllable form, the mandatory seasonal term (*kigo*), and also urged occasional *kireji* [literally, "cutting word," one that punctuates a line].

Collected Haiku of Kinoshita Yûji appeared in 1966, one year after his death.[8] This collection includes 561 works organized into four parts: "Before *Enrai* [Distant Thunder]" (1944–45, 20 works), "*Enrai*" (1945–59, 208 works), "*Shunrai* [Spring Thunder] and Others" (1949–65, 147 works), and "After *Enrai*" (1959–65, 189 works).

We find many fine works, even among the early haiku in "Before *Enrai*":

Banked charcoal glows: The blaze died.
dispossessed of every   A sudden darkness also dims
hope.   the light within.

I'm a child again   My bride and I stand close.
tramping down this   Scattered maidenhair leaves...
leaf–scattered path.   dazzling glows.

Though Kinoshita had not been writing haiku long, these are good efforts. We perceive in them the poet's rich sensibility, his sorrow and anger over trying war–time conditions, and joy in his newly–married life. "Late into the night," Kinoshita wrote, "the drone of B–29s and the haiku magazine *Kirara* absorbed my interest. Soon I knew about a hundred poems by heart."[9] These words suggest the gloom of the war's final stage and Yûji's enthusiasm for haiku.

Thanks to war's end, most Japanese felt relieved. No more threats of air raids, no more pitch–dark nights where people must cover every chink or window in the house with dark cloth. The following verses from *Enrai* suggest the acme of Yûji's achievement in haiku:

War has ended!   Evening easterlies
Countless lights glitter   light up houses
in autumn dusk.   one by one....

House after house   Dashing past:
turns on lights the hue   the night train's queue
of daffodils.   of vernal lights.

Kinoshita does not directly express here his delight over the termination of the war. But he effectively communicates deep pleasure through his portrayals of "light." The name *Shuntô* [Spring Light], the haiku group to which he belonged and the title of its journal, implies that light symbolizes relief, delight, and hope. The first haiku he read by Kubota Mantarô, later his mentor, reads:

> Spring still young.
> Sky begins again
> to nurse the moon.

Thinking back on that experience, Kinoshita wrote, "I shall never forget how something tender and warm sparkled my heart, dejected by our defeat." In fact, fourteen of the 108 haiku in *Enrai* deal with light.

Neither Kinoshita's haiku nor his free verse depicts the fear of hunger, poverty or death that other poets often wrote about in the post–war period. He rather deals with natural phenomena, life in a rural milieu, and landscapes. The noted haiku poet Sakuta Kyô writes, "Having matured among the mixed poetic atmosphere of modernism and lyricism, and having savored and conversed with nature, Kinoshita could not become fully acclimated to the nihilistic, illusory, or excessively reality–conscious poets around him."[10] We might claim that Kinoshita expresses his inner voice indirectly through natural figures. Many such images appear in his verse: clouds, wind, rain, thunder, crows, crickets, trees, grain, and the like.

The following also come from *Enrai*:

Spring drizzles
dimple the puddle,
wink at me.

Under the scorching sun
thunderheads chat
like friends.

A distant bolt!
Earrings lying nearby
glitter in its flash.

I felt at one
with the cicada's intent
as it winged to another tree.

Do I imitate
the cricket's constant chirruping
in constantly writing verse?

Silkworm! I wonder if
there's a chilly fall night
inside your cocoon, too.

> So ends my third decade:
> endlessly tamping down soil
> that anchors barley shoots.

Despite belonging to one of the strictest haiku groups in Japan, Kinoshita did not turn into a run–of–the–mill old–fashioned bard. His art did not lean toward depicting and romanticizing or merely reporting nature's observed beauty. He attempted to write modern haiku that might freely express his insights and images, not simply imitate ancient forms. Surrounded by nature, Kinoshita as a matter of course often engaged in dialogue with natural things. His rich imagination allowed immediate empathy, so his verse contains much personification.

"Almost all my poems could be condensed," Kinoshita claims, "into seventeen syllables" without much effort.[11] On the other hand, many of his haiku could easily be converted into free verse by "un–condensing" them. It is true that many works, whether haiku or free verse, have identical themes. He clearly recognized the differences between the styles. And yet works in either genre prove that his attitude toward the objects he wrote about is neither illusive nor fanciful but realistic. His free verse remains as tempered as his haiku. Kinoshita never felt that much distance separated these two types of poetry. He moved rather easily between the two.

Following are examples of such haiku:

A katydid
tracks my attention—
night school in fall.

Primping up:
I my cloak,
the crow its wings.

I picture
a dry fountain spouting water
high into the sky.

Early spring bamboos
resound from my
flung stones.

Kinoshita had long been thinking about and groping for an answer to the problem: "How write haiku like free verse and how write free verse perfectly like haiku?"[12] Over the years he made his free verse more and more concise and suggestive, just as he infused a modern, fresh sense of beauty into the haiku world.

According to Narise Ôtôshi, Kinoshita once said, "A poet is an alchemist of words." Narise points out that haiku poets in those days were so lethargic that they were, so to speak, "boiling herbs in an earthen pot without mastering alchemy."[13] The following haiku, all from *Enrai*, show Yûji's fresh sensibility and craftsmanship.

A woman knits
in a hackney hurrying down
the seashore road.

A shower comes
to trample the gardenias'
fragrance.

The lad—impatient
to have his festival *obi* tied...
bats chasing bugs.[14]

A lightning flash
lets me straighten up some books
this easygoing night.

Similarly, notice these from the "*Shunrai* and Others" section:

Putting on lipstick
this gloomy day in spring...
do you flirt with me?

A squirrel's tail
and a girl wearing a ponytail
melt into a summer grove.

The lingering scent
of perfume attracts and
irritates.

I tell myself
whenever I pass beneath a cross,
I'm a Judas.

Scuffles
over wintering turf—nuns
in wooden shoes.

The lake
mirrored in your eyes...
May's crisp green.

By carefully compressing his thought and feeling into pregnant words, the poet can express himself adequately—even in this extremely brief poetic form. Kinoshita's diction is rather simple, his style plain, yet most of his haiku effectively convey feeling or thought as well as the external situations he describes. Sakuta comments that Yûji "expresses his thought and philosophy not as theory but as sentiment."[15]

In 1959 Kinoshita became chair of the prefectural poets' association and in 1961 presided over the local haiku group *Shunrai*. Following that, both his haiku and free verse turned grave; the former declined, however, while the latter grew more touching. His declining health perhaps began to overshadow his creativity. Aware that his years were numbered, Kinoshita may have wished to be a true poet of free verse rather than a master of haiku. Sakuta Kyô thinks that the more adept Kinoshita's haiku, the more unattractive they became.[16] "After *Enrai*," the last section of the posthumous collection, shows the wane of the haiku poet in him. And yet there are still many above–average pieces:

I feel alone...
though winter trees
crowd close.

A Western cemetery:
shrouded in the glint of blooming
mustard plants.

How cool
the piano to my touch:
bracing May.

My poetry book re–shelved,
its top pages gilt—
ripened wheat!

I'm not yet ready to entrust
these dreams to my son;
fall's mackerel sky.

The cortege can't quite
screen itself behind those
rice–drying racks.

Though he began his career as a free–verse poet, Kinoshita always had a deep interest in the goodness of Japanese tradition and tried to absorb it. To write a good haiku, "you must face the object with a disinterested mind," says the contemporary haiku master Awano Seiho. He added, "you must observe with love until you are deeply impressed."[17] Awano adds, "If you reject nature, you cannot write good haiku."[18] Kinoshita's innocent and sympathetic inclination to love nature matches well with haiku. Moreover, he had the good fortune to study under the excellent haiku masters, Kubota Mantarô and Azumi Atsushi. From them he learned how to develop the proper style and how to lighten his tone by using fewer Chinese graphs and more Japanese syllabary (*kana*)—like using more Anglo–Saxon words in English. They also taught him ways to grasp the sense of the seasons and to maintain consistency and uniformity.[19]

The main features of Kinoshita Yûji's haiku may be summed up as follows: a) he expresses his pent–up feelings or thoughts through natural images; b) as a rule, he observes traditional haiku rules: the fixed 5–7–5 syllable form, a seasonal word, and the occasional punctuating *kireji*; c) his diction is simple and clear, his style and tone gentle; and d) his works are generally rather cheerful and stylish, tender and free, and not in the least self–centered or affected.

He expresses himself through natural images, yet his haiku lack mawkishness. Like his personality, they are moderate and genial, neither too sentimental nor too intellectual. Doubtless Kinoshita contributed much to the haiku world by infusing it with a fresh sense of beauty and wit—fostered in part by his by free verse. At the same time, applying the lessons he learned from haiku made his free verse more concise and suggestive.

Okimoto Jirô
沖本治郎
尾道にて

Former Associate Professor of English
Fukuyama University

NOTES

1. Narise Ôtôshi, "Re–evaluation of Kinoshita Yûji," *Haiku and Essays* (January 1982), p. 51.
2. Azumi Atsushi, "Postscript," *Collected Haiku of Kinoshita Yûji* , ed. by Azumi Atsushi (Tokyo: Bokuyôsha, 1966), p. 226.
3. Tanka, a regular 5–7–5–7–7 syllable verse form—one of the oldest in Japanese poetry—provides the matrix of haiku. In the process of composing *renga* (a *tanka* form of linked verse created through the collaboration of two or more persons in a repartee session), the first 5–7–5 syllable bundle (called *hokku*) became independent in the seventeenth century. In the late nineteenth century, they began calling this bundle *haiku*.
4. Kinoshita Yûji, "My Haiku Training," *My Poetry, My Travels: Collected Essays of Kinoshita Yûji*, ed. by Takata Einosuke (Fukuyama: Naigai In satsu Shuppan, 1985), p. 84.
5. Ibid., p. 57.
6. *Shuntô* is the haiku magazine established in 1946 by Azumi Atsushi and Ômachi Tadasu, with Kubota Mantarô as editor and referee. It continues to publish.
7. In 1946, a noted critic condemned haiku as second–rate art. He said they represented non–individuality, lack of autonomy, old–fashioned values, and a deadeningly negative effect on artistic interest: "Haiku represent accomplishments enjoyed [only] in the special cosmos of the devotee." His criticism became a great stimulus to the development of haiku. See Kuwabara Takeo, *A Secondary Art*, Art and Science Library (Tokyo: Kôdansha, 1946; reprinted 1987), pp. 15–34.
8. Edited by Azumi Atsushi with a Preface by Ibuse Masuji (Tokyo: Bokuyôsha, 1966).
9. Kinoshita, *My Poetry, My Travels*, p. 58.
10. Sakuta Kyô, *Kinoshita Yûji's Haiku* (Tokyo: Bokuyôsha, 1991), p. 169.
11. Kinoshita, *My Poetry, My Travels*, p. 58.
12. Shimizu Bonpei, "Flute Player—A Short Biography of Kinoshita Yûji," *Diffident Poet: Kinoshita Yûji* (Fukuyama: Fukuyama Bunka Renmei, 1976), p. 122. Kinoshita originally wrote this passage for *Shuntô* (December 1954).
13. Narise Ôtôshi, op. cit., p. 51.
14. *Obi* is a very long and broad waistband worn over a kimono to hold it in place; festivals customarily begin after dusk.
15. Sakuta, op. cit., p. 28.
16. Sakuta Kyô scheduled a dialogue between Ibuse Masuji and Kawamori Yoshizô in "Kinoshita Yûji's Free Verse and Haiku," *Haiku and Essays* (January 1982), p. 29.
17. Awano Seiho, *The Spirit of Haiku* (Tokyo: Kadokawa Shoten, 1985), pp. 9, 15.
18. Ibid., p. 10.
19. Sakuta, op. cit., p. 193.

KINOSHITA AND FROST

This brief comparison of some of the themes and poetic characteristics of Kinoshita Yûji and Robert Frost invites a reader to view the unfamiliar in terms of the familiar, a representative of a foreign culture alongside America's perhaps best–known poet. Unfortunately, it leaves much to be desired; inevitably it neglects subtleties of grammar and nuances of sound, so important for both.

Still, enough common ground remains to warrant the attempt: both poets write during the first two–thirds of the twentieth century, create a substantial number of short lyric poems, and frequently turn to external nature for thematic inspiration. This is not to say the poets are very much alike; a comparison in fact suggests quite otherwise. They may start with the same well–nigh universal observation—a group of trees, nature's busyness in spring, the presence of a bird—and end, not only in separate continents, but separate thought–worlds. Or they may, on occasion, convey a similar message, although colored by their own peculiar poetic palette—both virtuosos, both rewarding the reader.

The poems themselves, of course, speak best. Any poet worth his *sushi* turns at some time, perhaps even often, to the theme known in the West as *ubi sunt* ("where are..."), the acknowledgment of fading beauty and the brevity of time: the snows of yesteryear have melted; Helen of Troy's famous beauty has gone to the grave; our mortality is evident—"Nothing Gold Can Stay."

NOTHING GOLD CAN STAY

Nature's first green is gold,
Her hardest hue to hold.
Her early leaf's a flower;
But only so an hour.
Then leaf subsides to leaf.
So Eden sank to grief.
So dawn goes down to day.
Nothing gold can stay.

Frost's deservedly famous poem has a grandly universal sweep in its few lines, from the title pronouncement through the key symbolic words— "green," "gold," "dawn," "Eden"—and the implicit notions of sunset and death. Kinoshita is no stranger to the thought:

AT TABLE

> I strip a month from the calendar
> the way I strip a plaster from my shoulder.
> February already.
> January gone
> in a breath.
> I hear
> a goldfinch singing
> just steps away on withered grass.
> We sit
> speechless,
> like *nikogori* on a plate.

One might notice first that the title of this fine lyric, unlike Frost's asser-
tion, is a seemingly innocuous commonplace "at table." But it locates the
place of nourishment, the source of sustenance—the center from which we
"leaf" and "flower." Kinoshita's blunt beginning jars a reader; the speaker
"strips" a month from the calendar much as he does a Band–Aid from a
once–annoying scratch, an action trivial and habitual until seen as a con-
junction of time and one's own flesh.

The speaker makes the connection and particularizes it further with the
powerful "gone / in a breath." The awareness is as sudden as the image; he
renders time now in that which gives flesh its life. Ironically, we are nor-
mally almost unaware of our breathing; here, we are forced to see our sus-
taining meals and breath in terms of racing time. The goldfinch underscores
the awareness. It too is "doing what comes naturally," singing—but on al-
ready withered grass. By contrast, the partakers in this startling revelation,
the "we" of the poem, are shocked out of any "song"—they are rendered
speechless. Kinoshita's final image, "like *nikogori* on a plate," drives home
the point. The *nikogori*, as the translator's notes indicate, represents cold,
congealed food; the casually treated flesh of the opening lines has become a
lifeless lump.

Frost's universal dictum becomes, in Kinoshita's version, brought home
so to speak; to oversimplify, one could say that the fact that "nothing gold
can stay" has, with Frost's heavy alliteration and repetition, become a love-
ly, and therefore somewhat palatable truth, while for Kinoshita it has en-
tered the intimacy of the family as a stunning and unappetizing shock.

Again, both poets confront the problem of alienation. One might argue that the theme is more persistent for Kinoshita, but surely prominent for Frost, the poet of "walls." Frost's short "Triple Bronze," appearing many years after the classic "Mending Wall," depicts the human penchant for erecting barriers in terms of a three–tiered structure of defense: one's "hide" (cf. the expression, "hidebound"), private fences, and national boundaries. Of the last mentioned, Frost says, concluding his poem, "And that defense makes three / Between too much and me."

Kinoshita's "Once There Was" comes from his last period (1959–1965). It too speaks of alienation:

ONCE THERE WAS

> Once there was a bird's nest
> on that now barren branch tip behind the church.
> A piece of straw that dangled from the nest
> near sparkling young leaves
> tried to keep time with pipe organ and choir.
> I always looked up fondly at that nest,
> picturing little creatures bringing love in,
> smaller ones eagerly awaiting it.
> Once there was a time to love and be loved
> near where stars dot whip–like twigs.
> It's comforting to recall such scenes now
> when I've turned against others and myself,
> when I feel the freeze, the loneliness,
> of being banished from every nest.

Structurally, Kinoshita's poem first offers eight lines which begin with "Once there was a bird's nest" and elaborate on how the speaker saw and re-acted to it. The next two lines summarize or encapsule the meaning of the first eight, repeating the key word "Once." The final four lines stand in con-trast; they delineate the "now" of the alienated present. He returns to the nest image with which he began, but transforms it to the negative—a sign of his rejection.

As with the earlier "Nothing Gold Can Stay," Frost's "Triple Bronze" universalizes: his speaker speaks to the human condition. That "a number of us agree / On a national boundary" slyly states a penchant of Japanese, Americans, Azerbaijani, Serbs, etc. Kinoshita, by contrast, characteristically personalizes: the very specific bird's nest becomes a metaphor for a very personal alienation: "turned against others and myself, / when I feel the freeze...."

Frost is a master of ambiguity. The ambiguous phrase, skillfully placed, lends an air of profundity, provokes interest, and prods a reader toward insight. In "Triple Bronze," the defenses erected are between "too much" and oneself. What is "too much?" One answer is, the opposite of too little: too little communication, too little understanding, too little love—give rise to barriers. The barriers in turn create an ironic switch; excluding others means, ultimately, too much me.

Kinoshita's effectiveness lies elsewhere. He relies not on ambiguity here but on the central nest image and a series of contrasts: then/now, full nest/empty nest, leafy branches/barren, whip–like twigs. The conjunction of "natural" (bird's nest) and "spiritual" (church, choir), deepens the theme; they are the spheres where "love" operates (or ought to). Kinoshita adds a complicating factor near the end; his alienated speaker is doubly so. Whereas Frost's persona acknowledges his part in the universal tendency for barrier–building, Kinoshita's has also turned against himself—inwardly and outwardly "forced from every nest." Frost's speaker at least shares a "human" trait, however wrongheaded; Kinoshita's, by contrast, is an outcast from "every nest," living in a spiritual deep–freeze.

The personalizing touch underscores a major difference in the two poets. An often as not, Frost's speaker is a sage New England rustic commenting on the ambiguities and ironies of the people and nature he observes around him. His "I" interacts with his surroundings, as with the tree at his window ("Tree at My Window"); admits to a share in human foibles: "To scare myself with my own desert places" ("Desert Places"), and occasionally has dealings with a neighbor ("Mending Wall"). But he remains a somewhat detached and insulated observer. Does he have a grandmother? The somewhat odd question perhaps makes the point. One would search Frost's poems in vain to find out.

Kinoshita, however, is frequently "in" his poems to a degree Frost is not. A poem may, like the late "Yûzôsâsan," contain a number of fictional details, but it and others nonetheless reveal a good deal of the poet himself. A reader hears of "Mother's sprightly voice" ("House Where I Was Born" ii) saying, "I hear Paris has fallen" ("After Dinner Songs" i), senses the poignancy of the dead father "whose image increases in me by the year" ("Recollections of Father" i), or envisions mother's hair found "squeezed into" a riceball ("Memories").

This tendency to personalize and/or internalize appears somewhat differently in Kinoshita's moving lyric, "Early Spring" (ii). A comparison with Frost's equally moving "Spring Pools" shows both poets at their reflective best.

SPRING POOLS

These pools that though in forests, still reflect
The total sky almost without defect,
And like the flowers beside them, chill and shiver,
Will like the flowers beside them still be gone,
And yet not out by any brook or river,
But up by roots to bring dark foliage on.

The trees that have it in their pent–up buds
To darken nature and be summer woods—
Let them think twice before they use their powers
To blot out and drink up and sweep away
These flowery waters and these watery flowers
From snow that melted only yesterday.

With a masterful command of rhythm Frost here depicts, among other things, a natural process; his mini–lecture on Nature's recycling describes the course of water from its appearance as precipitation through its seepage into the ground and up through roots to "bring dark foliage on." The flowers' transient beauty, and the lovely last line, mark the poem as an *ubi sunt* variant. Notable, Frost's homey admonition for the trees: "Let them think twice" before they "blot out and drink up and sweep away," lands obliquely on the reader. It would serve admirably as theme for an ecology seminar.

Kinoshita's spring lyric shares and does not share with Frost's:

EARLY SPRING (ii)

Pussy willow shadows peer through
finger–high barley shoots.
Even the trails of marsh snails still short.

Water from the thaw, flowing fresh from the distant gorge,
slowly stirs the waterwheel.
A single light beam probes the interior
through a chink in the mill shed door...
like that eye addressed to my innermost self.

Grain ceaselessly quivers and glows with fragrance,
little by little stripping off the hulls...
a mirror of my mind. •

Finger–high barley shoots.
Soft cloud shadows.
The dim form of a skylark on the wind.

Water from the thaw, flowing fresh from the distant gorge,
restlessly stirs the waterwheel.

Like Frost, Kinoshita begins with signs of spring fertility: pussy willows,
tender shoots, marsh snails—evidence of process. The essential water ap-
pears in stanza two in a couplet which the poet repeats almost word for
word at the poem's conclusion. There is more than one process at work,
however. The water's source, a "distant gorge," hints at its endless motion.
It turns the waterwheel initiating another process—reducing the grain to a
form suitable for consumption, a process the poet says (in the third stanza)
is "a mirror of my mind."

Moreover, the waterwheel itself is a symbol of the larger process, the
Tao/Way of spontaneous creativity with its characteristic embodiment, wa-
ter. Emerson and Thoreau would have liked stanza two, I think—indeed, the
entire poem. Kinoshita's "single light beam" becomes an inward eye, both
cosmic and personal, which "addresses" him.

It "speaks" in terms of images: the stripping of hulls from grain to get at
the kernel, and the restless signs of external nature embodying the creative
process—barley shoots, cloud shadows, a skylark on wind. Death, dor-
mancy, winter's—and the mind's—quiescence are beginning to quicken.

The repetition of the couplet at the end, with its small "restless" change,
appropriately reinforces the poem's cyclical "message." We see that it is
about many things, including that old poet's favorite, the writing of poetry.

For both poets, that writing can be playful, though for Frost, less eroti-
cally so. A minor exception, seldom anthologized, Frost's six–line "On
Being Idolized" depicts the speaker standing barefoot on a sandy beach and
feeling the retreating water suck the sand from under his feet. Tottering, he
says, "And did I not take steps would be tipped over / Like the ideal of some
mistaken lover." Given to ambiguity and the sly pun, Frost does not sustain
or feature the erotic as does the speaker of "Journey's End," fondling his
breast–resembling citron.

Both poets relish the appearance/reality notion of things or people appear-
ing other than what they seem. In the above poem, Frost satirizes the
"fallen" image of the lover. In "Sand Bath—Yubara Spa" Kinoshita draws
on Japanese legend to gently spoof the vacationer's "serene" transformation

into nude nymphs, a parody of the erotic dancing of the legendary nymph–turned–human.

But as with the earlier comparisons, similar objects of inspiration can produce quite dissimilar results. The concluding poem to Frost's late *In the Clearing* (1962) may or may not be, as critic Dorothy Judd Hall suggests, the poet's "parting signature, a quitclaim to his metaphoric clearing." Delivered untitled, the poem became "In Winter in the Woods" in the collected works. The first and third of its three stanzas are as follows:

> In winter in the woods alone
> Against the trees I go.
> I mark a maple for my own
> And lay the maple low.
> ....
> I see for nature no defeat
> In one tree's overthrow
> Or for myself in my retreat
> For yet another blow.

Typically ambiguous, Frost's poem features the felling of a tree. Are his woods simply a natural and prolific maple forest, or one of those ominous dark woods he elsewhere faces? Is his speaker's solitary winter effort to expand the clearing his "blow" against encroaching darkness? A bookcase full of Frost criticism attests the fact that critics relish such speculation.

On the plain sense level, the narrator chops down a maple, then trudges back home at four o'clock. He says he sees "no defeat" in this, either for Nature because of the "tree's overthrow," or himself due to his "retreat / For yet another blow." The happy ambiguity of the final line suggests 1) another blow (i.e., "attack," "chop") at the maples, and 2) a needed rest (as in "time to take a blow"). For me, the last lines recall a childhood wisdom/rhyme: "He who turns and runs away, lives to fight another day," but I confess it is merely a personal bell ringing, one not particularly justified by the poem.

One can of course, as some critics do, read more into the poem. My point is that if the poem hints of Death, for example, it does so by oblique and symbolic means. By contrast, consider Kinoshita's tree laid low:

FELLED TREE

> Today I stood by the roadside and watched
> a tall tree sawed down.
> Aware of its maturity,

the tree seemed to take the saw calmly
with a sense of satisfaction and confidence.
Even in twigs and leaves quivering on the ground,
I noted a composure born of fulfillment.

Night now.
I imagine a massive black cloth covering those scars
and stars sparkling beautifully around them.
I imagine that birds plying night skies
feel a chilly emptiness on their wings
at the height, at the spot where the tree spread out.

You who soon will saw me down,
do you suppose I, too, might know that repose, that hush
when my life ends?
Do you suppose I'll be capable then of feeling
what I felt today as I watched by the roadside?

Structurally, Kinoshita's three stanzas depict the scene of a tree being sawed down, the speaker's vision of a night scene above the spot, and a questioning of some Cosmic Sawer as to whether the speaker will be able to match, when he himself is cut down, the calmness and repose he has earlier envisioned.

Like Frost, Kinoshita's speaker records a tree felled and reflects upon its meaning. Both personify, Frost in that "Nature" can evidently suffer "defeat," Kinoshita in that his tall tree appears "aware," "takes the saw calmly," and with "composure," even "satisfaction" and "confidence." There is a kind of victory here—"fulfillment"—as opposed to the absence of defeat in Frost's lyric.

Critics are still arguing about the extent to which Frost entered or did not enter the "dark woods." There is nothing oblique about Kinoshita's approach; he goes straight to the Axeman. Having made the connection between the tree's demise and his own, the speaker wants know if the reality can ever match the poetic vision.

There are other differences. Frost's persona is himself an axeman, an active participant contesting Nature by striking a blow. Kinoshita's is passive, an observer standing detached "by the roadside," a point underscored by his appearance in both the opening and closing lines of the poem. Frost's "acts" by chopping, trudging across the snow, and, in reflection, by drawing inferences. By contrast, Kinoshita's "acts" by creating ("I imagine a massive black cloth...") a death scene of beauty and by posing questions.

Frost's woodsman leaves his mark on external nature, downing the maple; he contemplates "yet another blow." In Kinoshita's poem external nature itself acts—the fallen tree calm even as it "quivers" in death, the night birds recording a "chilly emptiness" in recognition of their felt loss. There *is* ambiguity here but of a different kind from Frost's evasive lines. For Kinoshita it emerges rather as large questions such as the role of the poetic imagination as a transforming force.

For Kinoshita, that imagination was rich and various. Not surprisingly it manifested itself in forms and modes that have no real counterpart in Frost. Shoulder to shoulder with "final questions," critic Philip L. Gerber writes, Frost "invariably withdraws, veers off on a tangent, or changes the subject." This is debatable (cf., e.g., "The Draft Horse"), yet one does not find among his lyrics the direct approach of Kinoshita's "Song of Death" where the speaker sings, "Soon I'll die and, / turned completely to ash, / gain a freedom never known." Nor would one find the "I the sickle. / I the barley to be reaped" of "Arietta—Spring Griefs," or "pass over a Bunsen burner. / Evaporated" of "I Turn to Vapor."

This tendency to merge a poem's persona with the subject at hand is characteristic of Kinoshita. To judge by his affinity for birds he is a frequent flyer, as poems like "Wren's Song," "Winter Crow," "Pheasant," and "Mallard" indicate. Here he imaginatively "chirps," "primps," "flees," and, dripping blood from a wound, "listens." These represent experiments in poetic soaring, flights of fancy to apply an old metaphor, intended—for one thing—to stimulate a reader's imaginative participation.

Among the other incomparables, i.e., Kinoshita features uncharacteristic of Frost, one not surprisingly finds bits of Japanalia probably unfamiliar to most Western readers. The same of course could be said of Japanese readers of Frost, as a poem like "Kitty Hawk," for example, illustrates. The railroad crossing, while no stranger to Americans, appears with a startling—or, for Kinoshita, annoying—frequency in Japan, and the poet recorded the phenomenon in poems like "At a Grade Crossing" (i), "Landscape," and "Morning" (ii). In "At a Grade Crossing" (ii), the impatient speaker complains of this disruptive presence:

> This is where the clatter of the crossing gate
> stopped me in my tracks,
> the place that put an end to my pleasure
> on this joyously sunny spring day....

In another work, however, the sometime offender seems rather to partake in the celebration of the day's exquisite beauty:

LITERARY FRAGMENT (i)

When cloud shadows visit clumps of dahlias,
when a solitary sunflower opens its eye
and reaches high...

the crossing gate will still quiver
and echoes from the shrinking train
will copy the roar of early summer seas.

Today's setting sun.
The lovely sun sets.
Cabbages firmly hug their hearts.

Understandably, a special portion of the Japanese experience etched deeply into the poet's psyche. One of the "twisted memories" (cf. the title of this collection) concerns the atomic holocaust which Kinoshita commemorated in a long, six–part prose poem, "Under Shared Skies—Hiroshima Reportage," as well as in shorter works like "At Hiroshima's Memorial Peace Park" and "Memories of Fire—Mourning Hiroshima Victims."

Frost alluded to the event only in a short but scathingly satiric indictment of the policy makers, "U.S. 1946 King's X."

Having invented a new Holocaust,
And been the first with it to win a war,
How they make haste to cry with fingers crossed,
King's X—no fairs [*stet*] to use it anymore!

The allusion of children's practice at play underscores the irony of international gamesmanship.

Sorrow, not satire, characterizes "Under Shared Skies." Characteristically, Kinoshita is "in" his poem—climbing to view the city from Hijiyama, planting his foot on the human shadow burned into the sidewalk, feeling the death–squeeze of the atomic museum. The appropriate modes here are irony and lyric tenderness; the poet skillfully controls both in his moving tribute: the famous Dome remnant "looms over the Cenotaph vault, patterned after the ancient *haniwa*," it "appears to sit" in his palm; "warm evening sunlight from the hospital window tints the keloids" on the cheeks and arms of Atomic Maiden "H."

Direct but not morbid, Kinoshita conveys the starkness of the terror: the contents of the museum "freeze my cheeks"; victim "H" puts "another layer of rouge" over her scars. But signs of renewal are manifest too. Kinoshita's ever–present birds are busy at their nests; their droppings "sparkle here or there on crumbling walls"; an impatient child—"fresh seed fallen on the atomic desert"—pulls on Father's jacket.

In its structure, the poem begins at a serene hilltop distance: "Summer has come again. Another August 6," then moves from "Lookout Point" down into the city with its Dome, shadow–burns, and other memories of the blast. Next, it pauses for an ironic moment to ponder the beauty of dead poet Hara's lyric, moves to a climax with the tragic fate of the Atomic Maidens, then withdraws by ironic distancing in the "astonishing" comments of a Cathedral priest concerning repairs: "Maybe they'll never finish this job, however long they work."

With its directness, lyric beauty, thought–provoking irony, impressive range of subject, and sense of the poet's presence, "Under Shared Skies" reveals much of the artistry and essence of this modern Japanese poetic voice. Though the poems often differ from Frost's renditions of similar subjects, Kinoshita's creations warrant this pairing of kindred talents.

Arthur Kimball

Professor Emeritus of English
Kantô Gakuin University

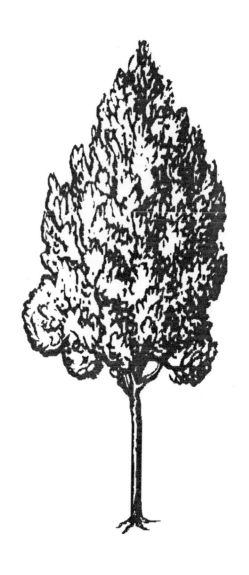

INTRODUCTION

– I –

E arly Kinoshita poetry consistently presents a persona who merely observes or reports. He is not intensely engaged in his observations. Though the language and viewpoint may be fresh, the report reveals little. It offers minimum insight into the writer, whose fate barely interests.

The opening prose poem in Yûji's award–winning first collection describes the leisure hours of white–collar urban bachelors:

> Sunday. —— We stroll about with joy in our pockets. Now and then we reach for it, put it back. Polished shoes, summer hats.... Oh, city! Always a newly–published book. (page 83)

Arresting images aside, these lines offer a remote, passionless and disengaged—very nearly a mannered—melancholy. The impersonal writing suggests potential yet borders on sterility. It's as though Yûji deals only with surfaces or engages in little more than mere finger exercises; he fails to get to the soul of the music. How can the reader care what happens to these bachelors? Twenty–three years later, however, Yûji does not waste his talent playing scales. Eager to exorcise alienation, he transforms surfaces into mirrors of his soul:

> My wife doesn't call to me.
> My children do not search for me.
> I'm cold—cold enough to shatter my ribs and burn them,
> to burrow hands deep in my shadow. (page 184)

These lines offer an anguished and engaged—a poignantly moving—melancholy. The deep torment of these words moves the sensitive reader to care. At least it is far more difficult to observe this persona with the same bemused disinterest that the urban bachelors elicit.

The artistic life of the poet Kinoshita Yûji (1914–1965) is a chronicle of how he matured between 1939 and 1962, the span separating these citations. Growth results from the poet's suffering inner self, his struggle to express the pain of shattered hopes to be a full–time poet in Tokyo. Japan's family system forced (Yûji might rather say condemned) him to spend his life as a pharmacist—and, worse, to spend it in rural Miyuki, then a small

33

hamlet on the eastern edge of Hiroshima Prefecture. There he tried to alle-
viate heartache in traditional ways. He ransacked memory to recall the hues
of his nostalgia. He sought the solace of unpeopled landscapes. He escaped
into Nature's serenity. When nothing eased his tensions, at least not for
long, he retreated into his troubled self. There he finally gained perspective
when he discovered, with many another modern, that tensions more likely
dissipate when confronted head–on. That also effectively engages readers
and so gives the poet greater leverage on feelings.

As he matures, Yûji produces more such verse. His writing cannot, of
course, ignore the way nature pervades his life. That is the primary given of
his environment. But he becomes less devoted to celebrating or concealing
himself than to fathoming a self fated to exist in rural landscapes. His ex-
treme diffidence made it a trial for him to write openly about private feel-
ings; it was always more natural and far easier to find an objective correla-
tive for them. Outright confession could never become his style. He had to
develop more subtle means to air his psychic agonies. Along the way, he
became more open without compromising his privacy. Nor did he modify
his belief that art must be distanced from experience. That is why, though
he becomes more "confessional," Yûji's best work never surrenders the
maker's conscious management of emotion.

The cliché holds: A poem's lasting impact exists beyond yet within its
lines. Yûji had to become more aware that the most affecting poetry moves
beyond verbal diversions, for art is never merely a matter of ordering fresh
images over the surface of a text—and he came to realize that. Had he not, I
suspect he might have remained quite satisfied to produce more descrip-
tions on the level of those urban bachelors.

From the outset, however, Yûji struggled with the protocols of his tradi-
tion. He too often succumbed to them: constantly enamored of the high–
sounding fragmentary insight, the scintillatingly packaged expression, the
isolated fresh figure. Surfaces are important, but they are not everything,
though writers—particularly on the Japanese countryside—are easily be-
guiled into imagining they are. A pastiche of fragments offers mere
ephemeral pleasure. Although there is beauty in that, only a focused heart
can generate the cohesive emotion that rises from buffed words the way a
genie emerges from a rubbed lamp. Such verse both teaches the reader
about life and shows the writer who he is. That is the verse Yûji had to, and
did, learn to write.

Unfortunately, critical generalizations about the earliest poetry over-
shadow every later development. When they think of Kinoshita Yûji,
Japanese invariably attach labels like "pastoralist," "nostalgic hometown

bard," or "regional poet." These reveal bondage to stereotype, not knowledge of the poet and his work. Commentators are wont to frame their generalizations on Yûji's first collection, an idiosyncrasy not limited to the Japanese or to journalists. Nor may it be possible for a Tokyo critic to avoid the discriminatory and patronizing stance that Yûji was, after all, a provincial pharmacist.

No one can deny the element of truth in such "tags." Yûji lived in the provinces. He spent his life as a rural apothecary. Over most of his career, traditional sensibilities affect much of his verse. Compatriots expected that. In composing verse, but particularly haiku, that, too, is what gained the respect of those close by. On the other hand, no one in rural Miyuki, however skilled, could write authentically about factory life, the demimonde, subways, or the trials of existence in the metropolis. Unfortunately, these verities do not make the critic less myopic or free him from comfortable stereotypes. Nor can they force him to evaluate a poet's entire career or to reject fictional platitudes.

It is unfortunate if inevitable that the very verse inviting the tag "nostalgic hometown poet" most appealed to Yûji's immediate audience. A growing regional reputation tugged his development toward that appeal, particularly after the 1958 appearance of *Fue o Fuku Hito* [*Flute Player*; literally, "one who plays the flute"]. This was the wrong direction for him to take. He surrendered too often to the increasing torrent of solicitations to write occasional pieces, lyrics for school and company songs, and verse for travel brochures. Because these requests attest to recognition of his talents, they must have been satisfying. However ego–stroking, accepting so many requests proved unwise for a part–time poet with limited energy. My lament is that this surely inhibited Yûji's maturation as a modern poet.

Other traditional expectations drew him off course. One is the Japanese love for visual imagery. Until the mid–1950s, indeed, Yûji's work relied heavily on observation, on the eye. The tyranny of the landscape prevented him from looking within. Another is the pull of nostalgia, partly a cultural expectation, partly a result of fragmented hopes. Yûji longed for those wistful days when it was possible to dream of the impossible. Cherishing the shards of shattered hopes, his instinct was to merge with Nature whenever the world threatened to hedge him in. Nature and past—one perceived through the physical eye, the other through the eye of memory—encumber him equally. Doubtless, they helped him recapture the primal experience of feeling assimilated and accepted by creation. Neither eased his frustration over being forced to earn "filthy lucre" as a pharmacist.

For all that, Yûji's diffidence helped him avoid bathos and self–pity.

Extreme reticence prevented self–indulgence but also checked self–revelation. Near the end of the 1950s, he at last tries to deal with, reveal, and thus hopefully unify his fragmented self. Ironically, the greater his regional éclat, the fuzzier his focus became and the more alienated he felt. He needed the applause yet realized how metropolitan critics might regard such work. He had to root himself in his art, whatever its appeal.

– II –

Yûji's interest in writing began in elementary school when he and his older brother Takuji worked together. At one time they collected and printed up a collection of fairy tales. From grades four through six, he fortunately had a sympathetic teacher who encouraged his retreat into imagination. The desire to become a writer never waned.

After he passed the entrance examination to the prefectural middle school in Fuchû, Yûji's life entered a new phase. He could meet many like himself with a commitment to writing and books. For five years he became a commuter traveling from Miyuki six days a week by train; the round trip took an hour. For a youth in a conservative, Confucian–oriented setting, that alone amounted to an emancipation of sorts. Only one car of the train that terminated in Fuchû served regular passengers. The others reveal the segregated educational scene after grade six in prewar Japan. One car was reserved for boys going to Fuchû Middle School, another for girls attending Fuchû Girls' School. In the later years of middle school, Yûji's literary preoccupations turned to poetry. To enrich his own verse, he began to read the French symbolists in the scintillating translations of Horiguchi Daigaku (1892–1981). He also devoured Japanese versions of Guillaume Apollinaire, Paul Verlaine, and the symbolist critic and apologist Rémy de Gourmont. By graduation his course was set. He would be a poet.

In 1932, Yûji left for Tokyo to study French literature at Waseda College. Till then, the countryside and its imagery dominated his awareness. Life in a rural hamlet, the seasonal transformations of nature, and a love for both nostalgia and conventional moods provided his writing with external structure. These also fleshed out his basic imagery and metaphors. Once in Tokyo, however, urban life, modern thought, and avant–garde poetry flooded his mind. The urban atmosphere and intense intellectual stimulation could not but challenge the bucolic imagery that dominated Yûji's awareness. Natural figures might work in verse unearthing rustic memories of boyhood, if but to make him homesick. To deal tellingly with experiences in the metropolis, however, a poet needed to mint fresh metaphors and create for himself an entirely new poetic. The trees and plants of Miyuki would not do. Unfortunately, three years in Tokyo were not enough to extract the country from Yûji.

Experiences at Waseda also forced familiarity with unfamiliar ideas and theories. Many that derived from Western scholars or literary critics were foreign to him. All along, he thought poetry a simple matter of giving words to feelings and insights. The "world of concepts," as he termed the atmosphere in Tokyo, unsparingly menaced this country youth. Ideas were such alien territory that he was reluctant even to apply for a visa. How he dreamed of familiar haunts in the countryside. There, on a mauve evening, as he later wrote while studying in Nagoya, he could wear his favorite flannel kimono and listen on the roadside "to reed flutes in the distance."

He could no more have anticipated the intellectual challenges of life in Tokyo than the pull that Miyuki's congenial sights, sounds, and smells constantly exerted on him. Years later, he revealed that he had been resigned to poverty but never imagined that writing might not bring in enough money to eat. This rustic young man had sentimentalized and glorified the life of a poet in the metropolis. He was barely living in the real world. Then disaster taught the meaning of reality. His older brother Takuji told Yûji early in 1935 that their stepfather was dying; the family needed someone to tend the store. That made it necessary to withdraw from Waseda and transfer to a college of pharmacy so he could run the Kinoshita Apothecary. Yûji's immediate response was stony silence. Then tears. How give words to a moment that shattered his dreams? Twenty–three years later, he published "*Misosazai no Uta* [Wren's Song]," a reaction to that experience:

> I'm returning to the countryside.
> I'm going back alone.
> ....
> Think of wind's roar that rousts you late at night
> as my song.
> Consider it my broken flute. (page 164)

In another work, he describes that roar as "wind's words rumbling across the wilds / in sunset's darkening wake" (page 184). This is, of course, the same "wind" that animated his flute—his poetry. Because that wind is also what gave life to his dream, he felt this 1935 event had "broken" him.

For centuries, the heir in a Japanese family, usually the first son, took his fate for granted. He would follow the profession of the House—he would do what his father did. This was normative in a rural society that revered family continuity. As the second son, Yûji had little reason to imagine this norm might ever apply to him. Fate, of course, had a different agenda. He

was not quite twenty one when his pharmacist stepfather Itsu died of tuber-
culosis. The family had designated him rather than his older brother the heir
to the apothecary. Not only had Takuji begun medical school in Tokyo,
Itsu's deathbed wish was that he continue his studies. Itsu also may have
considered that designating Yûji his heir would rescue him from the destitu-
tion guaranteed to poets. In that milieu, a family could not ignore deathbed
wishes; they bore the authority they had among Old Testament Hebrews.
Traditional values also required the individual to subordinate private
dreams to family duties. Yûji had no choice. He went to Nagoya.

Medicines, chemistry, and the laboratory nourished very little poetry. The
following lines suggest Yûji's dedication to studies at the Nagoya College
of Pharmacy:

> The microscope's cold touch,
> the mosquito's shriveled carcass (my trophy)
> on a page of *Organische Chemie.*
> Soft breezes steal in now and then
> to ruffle the balance
> the way they ruffle my mind. (page 86)

It's as though the cold instrument and the German textbook conspired to kill
the mosquito. There is no other natural image in these lines. "Stringy chem-
ical formulas" make the persona long for the grassy knoll whose aromas the
"soft breezes" wafted his way. On the knoll, he hoped to stretch out with a
favorite book of verse, likely by a French poet. In pharmacy school the lab
(and later, as a pharmacist, the apothecary) made Yûji feel claustrophobic.
Such places reminded him of his violated dreams. Thus their ambiance of
chill, death, and inertia, which he hoped to avoid.

Graduation in March 1938 qualified Yûji to practice pharmacy. Eman-
cipated from the antiseptic college laboratory, he returned home to land-
scapes he missed and loved writing about. His degree gave him professional
status in Miyuki. More important, it allowed him to don a white smock,
dispense prescriptions, and make a living. It also forced him to launch at
age twenty four a quarter century of sterile labor in pharmacy. He escaped
medicines by writing, reading, and enjoying camaraderie with fellow lovers
of literature. Poetry became his earliest buffer against the real world. It so
insulated him that his work appeared sometimes to toy with life. This
prompted a friend to comment that his verse did not stem from real–life sit-
uations. Yûji replied a bit defensively but metaphorically, "My poems issue
from the flask; they scoop up distilled water." Much of his work arose from
sufferings he had not yet discovered effective ways to communicate.

If filling prescriptions galled him, at least it supported his family in a way that no amount of poetry writing could. This was particularly true for a purist like Yûji. After his death, a childhood friend observed that Kinoshita could not have earned enough to set his table had he remained in Tokyo. Ever the idealist, Yûji felt he could never write for money, the way some poets produced limericks for recording companies. He was instead fated to make money filling prescriptions so he could write his own lyric poetry. Every spare moment extracted from the pestle he devoted to reading and writing. Let the business suffer! Whatever happened, however, he never gave up wondering what might have been, what his poetry and what he might have become, had he remained in the capital. But destiny had not favored him. Such sentiments gave him reason to stand on the edges of nostalgia and lament the chasm that separated him from his hopes.

This reluctant pharmacist sometimes lost track of the ingredients in a mixture. He was thinking of the past or at work on a gestating poem. That forced him to throw away the batch and begin anew. In one memorable incident, he could not remember the amount of a potentially lethal drug he had used; he worried himself pale over whether his customer might succumb. Fortunately, the concoction worked perfectly. When not wasting chemicals or mis–filling prescriptions, Yûji loved to take short, unannounced trips to the mountains or the sea. Or, after a night of working on poetry, he often slept till mid–morning. Once married, his wife assumed responsibility for opening on time; she took care of sales but was not licensed to make and dispense medicines. Time and again when customers came to get a prescription filled, the pharmacist was in bed or had gone she knew not where. Imagine getting prescriptions filled in such a pharmacy.

He well knew what sort of prescription filler he was; he did not fool himself. Years later he wrote to a friend,

> Well, for more than a decade now I've lived in the
> countryside...earning filthy lucre in the daytime,
> making poems at night.... Small wonder my head's
> turning numb.

Mixing chemicals he found abhorrent, the more so if the object was profit. To escape, he exercised his art, as Dylan Thomas wrote, "in the still night / When only the moon rages." Or in places far removed from the apothecary. He even tried to see his profession as an art. The pharmacist's sensitivity in getting a medication right, he claimed, compares to the poet's intuitive knowledge that a poem was "right." But he could neither "poetize" a profession he despised nor associate with those who practiced it. He consequently avoided other druggists, most of whom he saw as "money–grubbers," and gladly paid fines rather than attend required meetings to keep up with the field. He lived by pharmacy; he lived for poetry.

This lackadaisical and often irresponsible attitude produced few profits but some poetry. Yûji in 1939 self–published one–hundred copies of *Inaka no Shokutaku* [*Country Table*], a collection of twenty–three poems he had been working on for several years. The title, from the short poem by that name, describes his rural existence. With time burning all around him, he feels victimized by endless tedium:

> The buzz of honeybees
> stews me
> in a crock of griefs—
> yes, over a simmering flame. (page 90)

He submitted a copy to the *Bungei Hanron* verse magazine's annual poetry prize, offered since 1935 for the best book of verse published the preceding year. In April 1940, the judges deadlocked. Unable to choose a clear winner from the sixty–one entries, they awarded the prize to three poets. One of them was Yûji.

He published his second collection, *Umareta Ie* [*House Where I Was Born*] in September 1941. In spirit, most of the thirty poems in this book parallel those that had shared the Hanron Poetry Prize. Almost two–thirds evoke the nostalgia of youthful days, but some twenty percent deal with more mature experiences. The persona, for example, takes a trip to escape the dreariness of his job. An asylum he walks past reminds him of a schoolmate who had gone insane. The jabbering of a childhood friend, by then a seasoned barber, reminds him of his subdued rage. *House Where I Was Born* everywhere elicits memories of the past. It is as though Yûji hoped to sanctify his bucolic and dreary existence as "pill–roller" by baptizing it with warm childhood memories. He looked back, in any event, to days when hope for a future as a writer in Tokyo had substance.

Immersion in the past allows Yûji to escape, or at least tune out, the dreary buzz of those bees that so sorely reminded him of his griefs. Even writing of the future, he wishes to forget the present. Typically, rustic imagery shapes his wishes. In *"L'espoir* [Hope]" (1940), he addresses a phosphorescent fungus:

> Moon mushroom
> brought in yesterday from an old beech log!
> would that my half life ahead
> might glow like you,
> if only in gloomy kitchen corners.... (page 101)

He sees himself—keep in mind that the Chinese graphs for Kinoshita imply "Treeshade"—growing on a rotted tree. He perceives his existence similarly hidden, almost invisible in the dark woods. He, too, wants to be unaffected by his dank, sterile, shadowy environment. Filled like this fungus with inner light, he hopes he might be harvested and used. This wish for the future and hope of recognition serve also as a prayer for strength to overcome the present.

Simply observing and reporting, his "tyrant eye" continues its reign. And most works of this period still show more interest in sentiment for its own sake than in making the reader feel what he felt. Yûji, always more tempted to conceal than reveal, was not yet willing to create metaphors that might expose his hurt heart. His images unconsciously reflected traditional patterns: they gave immediate but ephemeral pleasure. As a modern artist, however, he may well have wondered how to keep the lucid but fragile surface sentiments of his verse from filtering so quickly out of the reader's mind. One admires from a distance verse that falls short of involving his emotions. Many prefer it that way, but could the poet be satisfied? If not, self–evaluation may have contributed to his standstill. In the summer of 1941, Yûji wrote a friend about his self–engagement and artistic impasse:

> Depressing weather day after day, or else it rains. No
> matter how much I sleep, I'm still weary—deeply
> depressed. My poetry writing has come to a stand-
> still, too.

During the early 1940s, his psychic struggles soaked up far more concern than the state of the world.

By Pearl Harbor, Japan had been militarily involved in China for four and a half years. One would never know it from Yûji's verse. Miyuki was too remote, and he was far too wrapped up in his own problems, to be bothered. Nor did the onset of warfare in the Pacific drastically affect his attitudes. Creative writers, who on 24 December 1941 formed a literature society, pledged support of national aims. Writing patriotic pieces at that moment was still voluntary. As the Pacific War expanded, however, writers had little choice; militarists frowned on frivolous expressions like lyric poetry. Yûji consequently took several stabs at "war poetry"; one experiment appeared in a 1942 anthology of patriotic verse. His sense of being isolated from the conflict ended the moment his brother had to leave for the front. Despite Takuji's six years as an army surgeon, however, Yûji did not support the Christmas Eve pledge to which many Japanese writers committed themselves. This choice affected his writing. Refusal to turn out patriotic pablum meant he had to cease publishing free verse. Fortunately, censorship did not extend to traditional forms, so he immersed himself in haiku.

This does not mean he no longer studied about and read modern verse. Japan's provinces, full of people committed to writing and ideas, provide rich literary stimulation for any who seek it. Poets, novelists, and writers of every genre—indeed, the entire rural intelligentsia—compensated for their remoteness from Tokyo and world events by gathering regularly to encourage each other and share views. War's gloomiest clouds could not dampen their camaraderie. Literary stimulation in Yûji's area included a visitor from the capital. Late in the war, regular B–29 bombing raids drove the established story writer and occasional poet Ibuse Masuji (1898–1993) from Tokyo. He returned to his parental home not far from the Kinoshita Apothecary and joined in this fellowship. There he discovered Yûji, whose pure language and unpretentious style impressed him. In Ibuse, Yûji gained a lifelong friend, an angling mentor, and an ardent supporter. Ibuse urged him to keep writing—whether in Tokyo or Miyuki made no difference.

During the last two years of the war, Yûji surrendered his carefree bachelor existence. He married in 1944 and fathered a daughter in 1945. Family responsibilities depleted his energies but did not drown his dream. Despite being more rooted to Miyuki, he refused to abandon his boyhood hope of writing in Tokyo. Small moment his dream was no longer attainable. Rationally, he knew that the apothecary, marriage, and a child made it impossible to leave Miyuki. In 1944 he wrote a friend that getting married

> resembles riding a train. A man and woman pocket
> their third–class tickets; once punched, there is no
> exchanging them till both reach their destination.

What does it mean that a man with a poet's depth of self–awareness and insight still longs to work in Tokyo—so he might indulge his adolescent wish to be a penurious poet? Why would anyone so stubbornly, and against all common sense, insist on dreaming the impossible dream?

Inability to publish lyric poetry during the war impeded Yûji's artistic growth. Nearly six years separate *House Where I Was Born* (September 1940) and his third collection, *Mukashi no Uta* [*Songs of Old*] (July 1946). Only eleven of the twenty–four poems in this postwar work are new. This shows how little time he spent during the war on any verse but haiku.

– III –

I involvement in the past continues—that's the implication of the title, *Songs of Old*. A man who imagines his youthful dreams have been betrayed, but who chooses not to recognize that fact, will find pleasure bathing in memories. Evoking a gentle nostalgia for those unruffled days before World War II also satisfied local readers. It was not the most effective way to calm a troubled psyche.

Fortunately, Yûji does not simply indulge his yearnings. Several works suggest the ferment of maturation. The last four poems of the book, for example, reveal growth in the way he deals with questions of life and death. More, these works treat their subjects with greater depth of feeling than we see in earlier works. These poems hence suggest a fresh departure. "Visit to a Grave" describes the persona honoring a young, unrecognized poet (page 146). He notes how present realities soak up good intentions. He, too, had hoped to remember the stilled voice whose grave he honors, but disturbingly he finds that immediate concerns squeeze dry his best intentions. "Hinomisaki Village" touches on death—Yûji's own (page 112). "At Hinomisaki Village" explores a new theme: the insignificance of human existence (page 112). "Youthful Days (i)" suggests how life in the mesmerizing countryside paralyzes political action (page 113).

All four works elicit more intense emotions than the sentiments of previous poems. At thirty, Yûji has begun to come to grips with the meaning of life and mortality. Perhaps his constant headaches and poor health contributed to the maturing process. Perhaps he also realized that while indulging nostalgia and sentiment might move his compatriots, it becomes a self–limiting enterprise for the modern poet. Two years after publishing *Songs of Old*, Yûji confessed he was well aware of his penchant for the sentimental. Tongue in cheek, he rationalized his sentimentality as a result of Fate: "The loneliness and melancholy of my life may derive from having been born in autumn." Whatever temptations kept him from his resolve, he knew he must become more adept at probing—not simply airing—his melancholic disposition. He must learn to get below and beyond surfaces, to plumb the soul itself.

He also managed to perfect his ability to deal tellingly with natural scenery. The French symbolist poet Francis Jammes (1868–1938) reinforced Yûji's bent to use subject matter from his environment. Whatever the overall objective, no artist can long rely on contexts foreign to his experience and hope to succeed. Jammes treated with fresh language and imagery the plain people, animals, and humble life of the countryside where he lived. Fated to remain in Miyuki, Yûji similarly hoped to write about his native region, Bingo (synonymous with Hiroshima Prefecture), "out of deep affection for the total environment [fudô]." He once wrote a friend,

> In Bingo, I write verse that nobody in Tokyo can possibly write.... Someone will come [from Tokyo one day] to seek my poetry.

He knew that jaded men of letters had journeyed from Paris to meet Jammes. The purity of his language and the clarity of his vision rejuvenated them. Could Yûji have imagined any Tokyo writer setting aside his sense of superiority to find inspiration in the provinces?

Flute Player (January 1958) takes Yûji well beyond the regional poetry Jammes championed. Works in this collection uncover new ways to help the poet survive a sense of failure and estrangement; they show that years of study had borne fruit. Many poems explore the poet's ideas of death and creativity (the title means "the poet"). All illustrate Apollinaire's prescription that the poem's surface be simple, the subsurface complex. Yûji's surfaces mirror the simple joys of his native region; his subsurfaces reflect the complex feelings foreshadowed by the last four poems in *Songs of Old*. His imagery at last becomes authenticated by deep emotion and the ability to penetrate surfaces. We now can view Yûji's art and his world in fresh terms. Confrontations with self, death, and creativity in this work have no precedent in his previous writings. His imaginative powers remain fertile, his imagery as fresh and as rooted in his environment as ever. But he no longer projects the negative impression of a sentimental man recalling his boyhood. He keeps sentiment at arm's length as he probes his psyche. Avoiding self–pity or tears, these works evoke private agonies, hopes for the future of his art, and a new identity as an artist.

In "*Michi* [My Way (i)]" (page 152), the opening poem of *Flute Player*, he makes his new identity clear. He stands at cliff's edge, implying that he faces both fresh challenges and discontinuity. His metaphor for this enlightened view is a sudden visual perception: the trail he takes through the grove abruptly ends, apparently by "leaping into sunset / like a drying rack." This suggestion of entering a new dimension, of achieving a new awareness, characterizes many works written after 1958. He had found the courage to confront his griefs and disappointments and to accept his fate. New confidence allows him to end *Flute Player* on a note of realistic if heavyhearted hope. Yûji aspires to a death that shows the same repose and dignity imagined in a tree cut down along the road:

> You who soon will saw me down,

do you suppose I, too, might know that repose, that hush
when my life ends?
Do you suppose I'll be capable then of feeling
what I felt today as I watched by the roadside? (page 168)

Many works published during the seven years between the appearance of
Flute Player and his death in 1965 reflect this new awareness. Straight-
forward surfaces mask a subsurface of complexity and dour melancholy.
Transparency of language often shrouds tortured feelings. At times, Yûji's
psychic pain even renders his moody thoughts opaque.

A letter he wrote near the end of 1960 describes changes in his views of
his art. First he quotes a favorite poem by Itô Sei (1905–1969). This work
describes a person who needs consolation but wants it saved for the future
when, perhaps, he might need it more. Yûji then reacts as follows:

In times of trial or anguish, I wrote poetry allowing
escape from feelings [that sought consolation].... A
pity that I have only now become aware of this habit.
I shouldn't try to escape agonies and afflictions.
Rather should I constantly fix my attention on them. I
ought to write in a way that will uncover from them a
new self and help me find a way to live in affliction.

His "new self" had already emerged in the poetry of *Flute Player*. Yûji
elected not to write poetry as mere escape. He would write as therapy or
catharsis, living less in the past than in savoring moment–by–moment his
various burdens.

Existential awareness begins to moderate, even if it does not subdue, the
romantic in him. He will no longer devote himself to exploring internal
landscapes or exploiting Bingo's scenery. His expanded awareness will
confront and struggle with the meaninglessness and anguish he thought his
existence caused him. Statements in a lecture delivered around 1960 point
to the revolutionary shift in attitudes that *Flute Player* demonstrates:

One should attach greater import to intellect than to
sentiment and to the images than to the music of the
poem.... One distinctive trait of modern poetry is the
way it treats, lightly and without exaggeration, man's
intense grief and the pathetic, solemn themes of life.

Lecture and letter suggest a pivotal epiphany. Existential concerns had at
last invaded Yûji's romanticism. His long–standing interest in sentiment

and landscape now become means, not ends. Expanded awareness would confront the meaninglessness and ache of his existence. He thought now of subordinating natural imagery and sentiments to a concern for "man's intense grief and the pathetic, solemn themes of life." Yûji had taken a momentous step toward maturation—as a man, to be sure, but also as a modern poet.

Through these last years, cheerful celebrations of seasonal rhythms—especially in the commissioned verse that his fame extracted from him—camouflage the graver tones infiltrating his serious poems. Nothing more inspired him yet more inhibited his growth than the celebrity his writing brought. Regional critics recognized his free verse, and he acquired a reputation as a haiku poet, editor, and mentor. He also became editorially involved with modern poetry journals. He was asked to speak on radio and write lyrics for school or company songs. Aspiring poets swamped him with requests for help with their work. He was talked into writing verse for an illustrated brochure celebrating the 1962 centennial of Japan National Railways. Recognition inspired him to move ahead toward his newly adopted goal of dealing with "man's intense grief and the pathetic, solemn themes of life." Unhappily, it also forced him to shoulder countless tasks that interfered with this objective and depleted his energies. Worse, writing the verse others requested of him prevented him from feeling he might achieve his goals.

At times, commissions found him flat and thus challenged inspiration. They also put more pressure on him than he could endure. He became more testy. His brusque attitude toward customers upset his wife, who marveled that people rarely took offense. Even poetry buddies often received little more than glassy–eyed silence when they greeted him on the street. People accepted his eccentricities. After all, this improvident businessman—whom his wife had to restrain from bankrupting the pharmacy by selling medicine at bargain prices—was a recognized regional poet. In the family, too, his behavior was often unconventional or inexplicable. His daughter Akiko describes how he dealt with her return from college:

> Whenever I went home for vacation, Father always
> came to the train station [in Fukuyama] to meet me.
> Despite not having seen each other for some time, he
> barely even glanced at me. He only said, "So you're
> back!" and took my bag. He dashed off so quickly
> that time and again we became separated by the press
> of people in the station and returned home our sepa-
> rate ways. I wondered why he'd come to meet me.

Then, when my vacation ended and it was time to leave for Tokyo, I'd have my shoes on at the entranceway and discover that he had disappeared, so I'd hurry to his study and say goodbye. He never responded with more than an *Oh* or a *Hmmph.*

If Akiko asked about a literary problem, "he never answered directly, but later I'd find a reference book in my room."

Presumably he did not think interacting with people was worth the effort. This was particularly so after 1960 when Yûji began telling friends, "I've only got another four or five years, you know." His deteriorating physical condition may have contributed to his irascibility. Nor was his psychological state perfectly sound. On balance he could not have been satisfied with the results of his "success." That's a mere guess, of course, for he confided his inner feelings to no one. Nor does anybody know when his agonies began or when he perceived the seriousness of his ailment. His older brother Takuji served as a general practitioner and ran a clinic but a few blocks away, yet Yûji never bothered to seek a consultation. He had become inured to suffering. For nearly forty years, this man preferred toothaches to seeing a dentist. Self–treatment did not control intestinal discomfort, so he finally submitted to examination; X–rays revealed blockage of the colon. When doctors operated on 17 May 1965, they discovered widespread cancerous growths. It was too late.

After the surgery, Yûji tried to carry on normally. He tired quickly, however, and could not even sit on the riverbank near his home to fish. Concentrating on poetry was out of the question. He nevertheless agreed to write a piece commemorating the twentieth anniversary of the 6 August 1945 atomic bombing of Hiroshima. The *Chûgoku Shinbun* [*Western Honshu News*], a leading regional newspaper, wanted the work by 30 June 1965. Early that day, Miyako reminded her husband of the deadline. He believed he had an additional day to finish the poem. Returning later, she found he had finished writing, so she dispatched the poem special delivery. After July 1, he could not keep food down and had to be fed intravenously. He died August 4 at 0130 the day before his last poem appeared in the newspaper.

This ten–line work, "*Nagai Fuzai* [Gone So Long]," radiates a mood of subdued sadness. Though the work lacks the thinnest ray of hope, it gives no hint of rage or self–pity. These are the final four lines:

Summer 1965.
I descend that staircase of twisted memories,

searching what was lost,
jangling the key ring in my mind. (page 207)

The poem appeared with a large photograph of the devastated dome that lay under the epicenter of the atomic blast. Exposed steel girders and the spiral staircase of the ruined Industry Promotion Hall testify to the bomb's power. Of course, the tragedy the dome symbolizes merely allows Yûji to explore private feelings. This work, another of the poet's touchstones to personal loss and loneliness, boasts a universality that exists, then, on several levels.

Standing alone at the top of the spiral staircase, the persona surveys the past locked in memory. Those stairs lead nowhere—except metaphorically to death. To the poet's eye, however, they descend into the dungeons of time. There he feels he must unlock the cells of memory; he must discover what he has lost. Going down those steps twisted by the atomic blast depicts withdrawal from art and from life. This act echoes an early observation he made that writing poems resembled going up a spiral staircase: the poet goes round and round attempting to describe the same reality from varied angles. These descriptions, he hoped, would communicate a three–dimensional appreciation of his insight. Now, however, Yûji descends those spiral stairs. Nothing remains but awareness of lost memories, broken dreams, and frustrations. In younger days, he compared time's passage to a bird's upward flight from tree to sky. Now, with no sky and no tomorrow, he can only move downward and inward. In his last moments, he perhaps hopes that his store of reminiscences might dull the thought of surrendered dreams. Perhaps this final act might help him see what he has gained as well as lost in life.

Perhaps Yûji hopes his descent might unlock every twisted memory and allow him to discover meaning in it. Facing the shadow of death at least offers the rare opportunity to plunge into reminiscences without being trapped by them. Memories and hopes, past and present merge in death; there, sufferings also cease and dreams end.

– IV –

R eaders may ask, why translate a man Japanese critics do not recognize as one of their nation's leading poets? If his work appeals, however, why not? It is easiest, after all, to make convincing translations of work one enjoys and respects. Beyond that, a simple discovery: poetry lovers among my acquaintances prefer Yûji's verse to that of Japan's recognized "major poets"—major, at least, in the eyes of the critics.

Critics and academics laud "major writers" and "great literature." This is understandable when "great" describes works that common folks cannot understand without extensive commentary by specialists. The celebration of T. S. Eliot's *The Wasteland* fits that description. A poem like this gives the academic much to teach and the critic much to explain. Whether this poem is truly great or only tantalizingly impenetrable, only time will tell. Meanwhile, without help the uninitiated cannot even understand, much less enjoy, it. *Voila!*—critics have a way to justify themselves and their expertise. Is it likely, then, that a specialist might laud competent works of art the average poetry lover can understand and appreciate on his own? Translations of a poet like Yûji raise that important issue. They also make us wonder: is there but a single poetry, the kind academics describe as "great," the kind that creates it own cottage industry of criticism trying to explain it? Or may there be another category of proficient verse that speaks to poetry lovers age after age—in whatever culture? Like Yûji's work, such verse might be well crafted. It could also move deeply without dealing profoundly with profound issues, or without qualifying for the critics' "great" category.

More seriously, a counter question and a corollary. Why accept the evaluation of Japanese critics? Aside from the often implicit whimsy that non–Japanese cannot fathom the nuances of indigenous works, what makes the judgment of these critics so infallible? As the Finnish composer Jean Sibelius once told a maligned young composer, who ever set up a statue to a critic? Japanese critics are, moreover, excessively tribal. And they lack objectivity. Only rarely do they clarify their criteria of evaluation. One wonders, therefore, what objective standards their taste reflects. Or is it purely subjective? Equally relevant is the corollary: How may the non–Japanese reader have confidence in indigenous evaluations of what qualifies as "first–rate" Japanese poetry (or a "major poet") without familiarity with what does not fit that category? In a word, how comprehend shadow without light, male without female, good without bad, major without minor?

Our culture and distance from Japan offer the unique opportunity to make independent judgments. From a fresh perspective we can ask several simple questions Japanese find awkward or displeasing to ask of themselves. Why do those whose kiss of recognition transforms frogs into poet princes hesitate to acknowledge Yûji's verse for what it is? Why no evaluation based on all he accomplished instead of his early work alone? Nor do provincial poets often earn the imprimatur of the high priests of the Muse in Tokyo; why is that? This is especially true when, as in Yûji's case, studied neglect of his mature work justifies the pastoralist stereotype. We can, of course, choose to believe that non–Japanese readers are incapable of appreciating the nuances of indigenous poetic language. That would end discussion and confer the desired infallibility on the Japanese critic. I am not disposed to do that. Surely, we must make every effort to comprehend their standards of criticism, but why be bound by them? Making the work of a poet like Yûji available through translation offers an opportunity to test those standards.

This is not to claim Yûji is a "great poet." He is, however, a very good one. He deserves at least that much recognition. If the translated Kinoshita Yûji comes across in English as a forgettable provincial poetaster, the discussion is over. We ought then ignore his work and invest our energies in understanding those poets the academics have certified. On the other hand, some who find Yûji's work engaging may believe it worth reading. Even perhaps worth preserving. In making our own decisions, at any rate, we shall both clarify our criteria and discover those that Japanese apply to their "major" poets. We can then verify their evaluations on a wider scale and decide whether we agree.

Yûji's work is also worth translating because it teaches something of the agonies writers must undergo when they adapt tradition to modern life. His career exemplifies the way a poet can become "modern" while honoring traditional sentiments. His oeuvre also suggests how to balance new and old without surrendering authenticity, compromising private vision, or rejecting the past and one's artistic roots. More, Yûji's role as a transitional poet shows how one writer has tried to wed rural nostalgia to an urban sense of estrangement. His production hence bridges a generation rooted to the soil (and the particularistic values of indigenous literature) and a generation rooted in the city (and the universal values of world literature). That's why his struggle may speak to writers in developing societies about how to confront radical change.

Explaining why I translate Yûji suggests also why I think he transcends the "pastoralist" or "nostalgic hometown poet" labels. I find him a modern lyric writer who, in the mold of Robert Frost, uses natural imagery to describe the human soul—its terrors and trials, its vagaries and visions. His best verse expresses a mind choked with disappointment and taut to the breaking point. To imagine that the nature poet should delight and not terrify overlooks the fact that Yûji seldom used his art as a simple camera lens pointed at landscapes in Bingo. His poetry serves rather as windows through which he learned to expose his feelings artistically to public view. The driving power behind Yûji's mature art originated, then, not in external but in internal landscapes. His buried life most characteristically finds expression through Nature in ways that reveal complex tensions between "traditional" emotional needs (nostalgia, melancholy, the serenity gained by immersion in observed scenes) and the sufferings common to modern man (vague anxiety, unease, estrangement from Nature, self, and others). The world of outer space—for him the rustic countryside—becomes an extension of the poet's inner space, his most private self. Tensions between traditional and modern, inner and outer, characterize all of Yûji's verse, although the later work most successfully renders these tensions in whole poems that please a taste for modern poetry.

His competence as a poet and ability to move people or give pleasure compel admiration. Moreover, Yûji stands—I repeat—as an important example of the links a poet can forge between his poetic past and contemporary experiments in free verse. He never dealt with his heritage by repudiating it. His increasing hostility to machine technology and civilization much rather urged him to repudiate such negative "advantages" of a growing urban industrial society as pollution. In this he was ahead of his time. What he saw happening to the landscapes around him contributed to his growing disenchantment with people and society. How seek rejuvenation in Nature if it no longer exists? This forced him to rearrange the past to survive the griefs and anxieties of the present. Simple language describes his anxiety and alienation. Though often too contemporary for the traditional palate or too traditional for some contemporary tastes, his language appeals to the average poetry lover. This "in–between" position matches his unique sensibility. It insulates him from the need to be stylishly "in," inauthentically to ape avant–garde Tokyo poets, or to represent himself as a Western poet in kimono. He happily escapes extremes, whether topical or faddish, and remains as difficult to date as any good lyric poet.

How does a writer deal with the weight of received tradition? Yûji managed by synthesis: He "modernized" traditional elements in his work and simultaneously "traditionalized" modern elements. He merged, mingled, and melded them. Traditional aspects often suggest the promise of growth or dynamic potential. For example, Yûji perceives the latency of the future in the stubby horns of a tethered calf. He sees the possibilities of shared love in a bird's nest. In grain being milled, he discovers the kinetic relationship between thought and action. His work maneuvers these rustic images noted in Miyuki's landscape into fruitful metaphorical statements of the human condition, thereby expanding their "meaning." On another level, these figures imply frustrated potential or the static boredom of the countryside—aspects of Yûji's "modern" sensibility that reveal how much his synthesis reflects his inner self. *"Teishaba Nite* [At a Train Stop]" (1949; page 122) illustrates the interplay of such imagery.

> The inbound had just pulled out.
> The pungent odor of a citron tree
> hovers over this forsaken train stop.
> A woman who also seems to have missed the train

rests on a bench and begins to knit.
Shriveled, unhatched moth eggs stick to the enormous clock face
labeled OUT OF ORDER.

The persona missed the train at this small rural station, perhaps the one
serving Miyuki. He knows he will have to wait some time for the next one.
Not even the tangy aromas of a ripening citron tree distract his customarily
caustic feelings toward trains and waiting for them—in fact, waiting for
anything. The positive activity of the only other person in the station con-
trasts with the persona's empty frustration. Then he notices shriveled moth
eggs on the oversized clock face—its "company issue" proportions more
appropriate to a larger, urban depot. As the persona and the knitting woman
missed the city–bound train, both natural and unnatural orders of time have
somehow failed. Time's stoppage allows the persona's unstopped irritation
to continue uncurbed.

A notable traditional aspect of Yûji's aesthetic is the view that poetry is
immanent in everything. Reading his work reminds of the universality and
wholesomeness of this view. Whenever the pressures of routinized exis-
tence threaten peace of mind, a long–standing remedy in Japanese culture
has been "return" to nature. While not unfamiliar to Westerners, such retreat
has never served in Japan as the romantic escape it often becomes in the
West. During the 1930s and 1940s, in fact, even the Japanese government
extolled the fundamental values of the soil. Leaders claimed that farms
comprised the basis of the nation [nôhonshugi]. Official policy assumed
that subordination to nature was supportive and cathartic, that because
nature teaches a man where his roots lie it shows him how to see himself
more clearly, and that the "natural realm" cleanses and restores the psyche.
No less an authority than Carl Jung believed that retreat into the country
could return a person to an even keel and allow him to continue as an ef-
fective and contributing member of society. Despite feeling as alienated as
any modern urban intellectual, Yûji also found that being absorbed in nature
helped ease his bitterness. Temporarily, at least, it made life bearable. What
modern, however sophisticated, might not benefit from that?

Tree poems express the positive benefits of this absorption. Although not
always as obvious as in the 1958 "Jumoku no Yô ni [Treelike]" (page 170),
the collapse of distance between poet and tree allows the latter to blot up the
poet's fears, anger, loneliness, and sense of being superfluous or estranged.
As stated, the family name Kinoshita creates a direct association with trees,
but Yûji's tree poems do not rely on that connection. They rather appeal to
the ancient and universal mythic identity of man and tree. After describing
how he resembles—or would like to resemble—a tree, Yûji concludes the
poem from the positive perspective of enlightenment.

> I have blue skies for visions,
> evening stars for thought,
> and rings reserved for hugging my inner self.
> I have no thing, so I have every thing.
> I am one, so I am all.

The last two lines echo the Buddhist rhetoric of enlightenment. Relationship with trees also reflects ancient Japanese beliefs that man never stands as an adversary to Nature. Natural objects rather represent ideal forms of human existence. Trees for this poet represent "beings" that transcend life's emotional turmoil and embody the hope of equilibrium in the face of disaster, even death.

Belief that poetry lies immanent in all of creation has a universal appeal. More than a psychologically wholesome view, it is at base humanistic. Because the whole earth inhabited him, daily life wherever he experienced it provided material for poetry. Every observable phenomenon potentially stands as a correlative of what he was or what he felt. So "resin / oozing like poems / from the cut ends of stacked logs" serves as effectively as "lumps of coal in storage bins" to express his self and inspire poetry (page 161). Might this prescription not provide enlightenment for the modern urbanite, whatever his culture? Could it help heal the scars of discrimination? Love and poetic inspiration, in fact, imitate the possibilities of enlightenment: they are present in each person but not always realized. No contradiction could consequently exist between the way Yûji sought his essential self and the truths of human existence under the leaves and in the grasses at Miyuki "as though searching for a violet," and the way an urban poet might seek them under the soot and in the cabarets, factories, or institutions of Tokyo.

Wherever the poet lives, his search requires using sharp images. Crisp imagery had power, Yûji believed, to stimulate imagination and through it to communicate human experience. The opportunity to be exposed to such images alone justifies translating his work. Like countless poets before him, Yûji leaves abstract ideas to thinkers or philosophers and concerns himself with the tangible and the phenomenal. He aims to deal with experience, its pains, its griefs. It matters less whether the figure originates in the city or in the country than whether it opens a window to feelings. That attests to poetry's universal human appeal. Yûji, after all, believed that the strength of an image derives from its dimensional solidity. A "bodied" image will resonate with experience and so affect any reader who takes the trouble to re–create the scene in his mind. The imagination for Yûji throbbed with latent power. It could readily elicit any feeling, any insight, the poet expressed in concrete language. Images, in a word, transcend language and culture. Their universality enables translation.

We need to hear that. We also need to know the limitations of lyric poetry. Familiarity with Yûji's work soon makes us aware of an unavoidable shortcoming. Lyrical verse written anywhere, anytime, suffers from a marked paucity of themes. For all its lucid, visual appeal, Yûji's work often gives the impression of narrowness or redundance. Writers who choose to focus on feelings limit themselves to a mere handful of emotions. This restricts the scope of their verse. To compensate, some like Yûji try to explore their emotions from various subtle angles. He commits to this method also because of a perfectionistic drive to express himself to satisfaction. It is also true that the indigenous bent to examine ephemeral moments of sentiment affected him.

Strategic attempts to expand his range would only produce inauthentic poetry. That is why Yûji's habit was never to move from one "stage" to another, as a self-conscious poet might. That may play well with Western critics, but it would compromise artistic integrity. For him, integrity meant close attention to the inner life and its physical environment. That's how he hoped to produce the perfect poetic expression of feeling. He is thus less concerned to expand than to exploit his themes. He does not honor variation for its own sake. That feelings remain more limited in scope than the realm of ideas does not concern him. In the Japanese view, the subjective and not the objective—love, not logic—characterizes the ideal person. Yûji's verse, indeed that of any good lyric poet, teaches that the most admirable human is the one who truly feels.

★   ★   ★

Y ûji's place in modern Japanese literature remains unsure. Critics, who still dismiss him as passé, substitute facts for journalistic clichés. The facts are these: In 1940, his first book shared the important Bungei Hanron Poetry Prize. In 1958, he published *Flute Player*, a milestone in his creative life. In 1966, his posthumous *Works* won the Yomiuri Literature Prize for poetry and haiku. In 1978, the magazine *Taiyô* [*Sun*] included samples of his work among thirty-four notable but deceased poets active since 1926.

Yûji probably wrote fewer than 400 poems between 1930 and 1965. This includes the eighty-four pieces in his unpublished teenage notebook, *Watashi no Bunshû*. Emily Dickinson wrote almost 400 in a single year. This total does not include nearly 600 haiku, lyrics requested for company or school songs (at least eighteen for elementary and a dozen for middle schools). Nor does it include a yet undetermined number submitted to or requested by local magazines and newspapers. The 326 works in *Twisted Memories*—360 if one excludes every titled part of a larger work—derive with few exceptions from three sources:

(1) *Watashi no Bunshû* [*A Collection of my Work*], a hand–written manuscript of poems dating from the early 1930s; I refer to this as *Youth Collection* (designated YC).

(2) *Teihon Kinoshita Yûji Shishû* [*Poetic Works of Kinoshita Yûji*, 1966]; many pieces are missing and the order is sometimes confusing.

(3) *Ganshu no Shijin: Kinoshita Yûji* [*Diffident Poet: Kinoshita Yûji*, 1975] (designated GS in the in dex), published on the tenth anniversary of the poet's death.

I render fifty from the first, all works in the second, and fifteen from the third. Over twenty poems derive from texts other than these sources. These include, "Wharf" (ii) from a 1932 edition of *Wakakusa*, a copy of which Dr. Kinoshita provided. The family discovered "Exacta Ticket" among Yûji's effects after his death. The magazine *PHP* [*Peace, Happiness, Prosperity*] published "Late Night Whistler" in 1960.

"Gone So Long" depicts Yûji about to descend into twisted memories— to become a Shade as he enters the oblivion of the world beyond life. There he will begin his last search for lost joys and shattered dreams. This singer of songs knows that he will soon die and "have a freedom never known" in life. Perhaps he will even be free from caring whether people remember his work. He is far too good a poet to be forgotten. Consider his lyric gifts, his attempts to merge tradition and modernity, his role as a transitional poet linking country and city, tradition and modernity. These enhance his significance to the history of modern, not merely Japanese, poetry.

ACKNOWLEDGMENTS

I buse Masuji first urged me many years ago to translate the poetry of his friend and countryman. I sincerely appreciate his encouragement and regret that he died before he could see its fruition. Only after I began working on Yûji did I discover that, during language school in Tokyo, one of my teachers—Nishio Toraya Sensei, now of the *Kokoritsu Kokugo Kenkyûjo*—had initially introduced me to the works of this poet.

Yûji's widow, Miyako, his late older brother, Dr. Kinoshita Takuji, and his daughter, Miyazaki Akiko, responded to questions, provided requested information, supplied copies of unpublished poems or documents, and offered constant support as well as much–cherished hospitality during my visits to Miyuki.

Professor Ben Befu, to whom I dedicate this volume, invested considerable time, energy, and expertise in critiquing early drafts of several hundred of these translations. His unparalleled solutions and suggestions corrected countless missteps.

The late Iida Kakuyoshi, his widow Aya, as well as Tamesada Nobuyuki and his late wife Yukiko, offered warm hospitality and backing when I first began working on Yûji. The late Professor Nishihara Shigeru of Onomichi and Mrs. Kurita Motoye of Ekiya not only provided vital data but shared reminiscences and insights into the poet and his work.

Professor Iida Gakuji and the late Professor Ôhara Miyao of Hiroshima answered countless questions about the meaning of the poems. They also laboriously compared many earlier drafts against the original.

For comments on early drafts of the poems or the Introduction, I thank the poet Thomas Fitzsimmons, Dr. Donald Brannan, the late Dr. Elva Kremenliev, and Professor Arthur Kimball, who also provided the essay comparing the work of Yûji and Robert Frost.

Professor Okimoto Jirô of Onomichi provided priceless help, especially in amending numerous errors in translating Yûji's youth poems. He also supplied a number of lost sources and responded with scholarly zeal to interminable pesky questions. I thank him also for writing the essay on Yûji's haiku.

The noted poet and critic Ôoka Makoto graciously allowed use of the 1982 Preface he wrote for *Treelike*.

Thanks, finally, to Mitsuko for endless typing, tedious checking, proof reading, and substantial help with appendixes and indexes.

Responsibility for the final product remains, of course, solely my own.

*   *   *

Some translations and certain statements in the Introduction I derive from Chapters One and Eight of *Kinoshita Yûji*, Twayne's World Authors Series #662 (Boston: G. K. Hall, 1982).

I am also grateful to Henry Holt and Company for allowing citation of the Robert Frost poems from the 1969 book, *The Poetry of Robert Frost*, edited by Edward Connery Lathem.

Earlier versions of several poems appeared in the following:

Chelsea — "Late Summer"

Contemporary Literature in Translation — "At the Temple," "Evening Scenes," "One Day of a Journey," and "Pheasant"

Literature East and West — "A Lad," "At an Inn," "Country Table" "Hinomisaki Village," and "Youthful Days" (i)

Treelike — Published by Katydid Books (Oakland University, 1982; second printing 1989); this work (which appears as a *taiyaku*, that is, with Japanese text on facing pages) contains earlier versions of some one hundred fifteen poems

Triquarterly — "At a Train Station" [now titled, "At a Train Stop"], "February," and "Treelike"

CONVENTIONS

N ames of Japanese nationals appear in indigenous order, family name first; thus, Kinoshita is the poet's family name. Japanese customarily refer to Kinoshita by his "pen" name, Yûji (the graphs differ from those of his given name, which has the same sounds). That is generally my practice as well.

A superscript asterisk (*) after a title indicates the existence of a note on that poem in the appended materials.

Italicized words or technical terms in the poems also appear in the notes (ABC order).

A bullet or raised period (•) after the last poetry line on a page indicates that a new stanza begins on the next page.

A pointing finger (☞) in the notes references a related note or poem.

A shadowed box (❑) in the notes indicates poems that have virtually the same or similar content.

✳   ✳   ✳

Poems stand generally in chronological order (arranged by known publication dates). Wherever possible, however, I try in each collection to reflect the way Yûji sequenced his works. His original ordering may be verified in the appendix COLLECTIONS (page 211).

The first known publication of a poem appears in the English index.

Editors ordered some of the verse in *Teihon Kinoshita Yûji Shishû* [*Poetic Works*] in what I find a confusing manner. Notice, for example, the quite radical alteration of poem order in *Flute Player* (1958). With the exception of the prose reportage on Hiroshima, "Under Shared Skies," works in this collection appear below in the sequence Yûji intended.

TREE SYMBOLISM

M ost graphics in this collection intend to prompt the recollection that the Chinese graphs for Kinoshita's name [literally, "below the tree"] denote "tree shade." Yûji's last poem depicts him standing in the shade and about to burrow deeply into the shadows—indeed, to become a Shade, a Shadow—by entering the eternal darkness of death.

More relevant to his earlier work is the complex folklore, mythology, and symbolism of the tree. These provide an informative backdrop for reading all Yûji's verse.

Trees represent the generative and regenerative power of life in the cosmos. This makes them one of the most basic symbols. The annual cycle of a deciduous tree imitates man's life; spring regrowth suggests inexhaustible life and reflects the human urge for rebirth and immortality. As pictures of life and death, trees imply "absolute reality." Hence the "tree of life" and "tree of death."

The Hebrew tradition adapted these concepts in *Genesis* as the "tree of the knowledge of good and evil." Adam and Eve found that such knowledge relates to life and death—not to mention acceptance or obedience, rejection or judgment, joy and grief. In short, the tree contains symbolic associations with many facets of human life.

Roots embedded in the ground and leaves reaching for the skies encouraged primitive thinkers to see trees as the axis of the world. These plants symbolize links among hell (roots), earth (trunk), and heaven (branches and leaves). Not surprisingly, folk consequently regarded a tree as the central element in cosmic life. For them, a tree represented the ideal existence.

Many ancients furthermore looked at a tree and saw man in microcosm. Or they regarded the tree the epitome of beauty, wisdom, justice, or even poetry. Although a cursed tree, Christian tradition has, through the cross figure, added associations with punishment, sacrifice, and redemption.

These aspects of tree symbolism can assign a poem's imagery greater depth than at first glance seemed possible. Being aware of that may in some cases open fresh windows of appreciation of this poet and his work.

POETRY

PART I — THROUGH 1939

Youthful days—prologue[*]

Is that rain's chalky faint patter
on the gardenias,
or the swish of an old nun's habit—
violin of washed–out blue...?

Dreams diminish to shades.
You married, became a mother.
My love sickness, my whistle, my sentimentality
... rusted.

Lizards swarm in rings.
My regrets, a white flower.
Beneath its petals,
lapsed youthful days lie mute.

Firefly

Could that firefly
have hatched from the hollow of the boy's hands?

Without a word,
he showed me
two or three emerald lights
glowing in the grotto of his palms....

Morning poem[*]

Nerves honed to needles,
the blue cat gazes from the *engawa*
into an azure sky. •

Morning and its verdure
quietly mirrored,
quietly quivering,
on lips scarlet with Dutch lipstick—
lips glistening with the hue of her blood....

WHARF (i)

Evening assembles discreetly on the quay.
Dusk's din—
lonely as the surf.

A ship's whistle fires stringy griefs into night skies.

How melancholy these port scenes.
The dreary passions of that night—too weighty for the eyes
of a sailor gazing into horizon.
Lamps in town kindle pent–up lusts.

Shoes of gloom groan over cracks in the pavement.
Melancholy again closes in on his steps, turns to waves...
oh, how it closes in
on this nomad's strides!

BACK GATE*

Convalescing,
Mother
combs her hair.

Heating bath water
burbles faintly
beyond the flowers.

Everyone, come!
Let's light up
our round little red lanterns.

Aromas
of roasting corn:
quiet...soft....

M OTHER——SICK

The stench of Mother's medicine
stifles her constant cough.

Is that cheerlessness
flaring up
from her disheveled hair...
from soiled *tatami*?

Hands of gloom
have suddenly gripped this room.
Well, little sister,
go close the shutters.

Let's think of Dad
who died so long ago.

Yes, beaming black eyes shroud traces of lovely dream!

P EAR FLOWER

Spring
clings hesitantly
to your face.

Dimly–forgotten love
gleams
on your white cheeks.

Little girl—surely you're the innocence
that night gloom or a hazy moon
might sire.

With gentle diffidence,
a fledgling wind comes again
to murmur at your crib.

A PRIL

Clad in verdure,
he smiles a green smile—
his grin the scent of fresh leaves. •

Though he has
verdant passions,
he hasn't yet known love.

Greenly translucent,
he lacks
a single thought.

His chest
endlessly resound
with xylophone airs.

M AY THOUGHTS

May's blue soles
and long blue sleeves
peer from sky.

Stretch out in the field
and look up.

Above,
someone with massive blue soles
stealthily
steals up on us.

Above, a blue
transparent woman—
serene, luminously clear.

V IEW OF THE SANITARIUM *

Spring sentiments turn desolate
in the consumptive girl's heart.

Breezes throttled white.

The eyes of a slithering snake glitter
under a decayed downspout.

The snake urgently senses foment.

In that pastily eradicated vista,
the girl peddling *cordata*
recklessly scatters
venomous smiles. •

No longer a single lover
for her now honeycombed
consumptive breast
to hold.

R AINY DAY

Eyes in the ceiling.

Those sharp eyes
strap me down,
depress me.

J UNE POEMS——FRAGMENTS*

Aralia Leaves
A passing shower mirrors on aralia leaves
the pallid neck of a melancholic girl,
her sickly pale face.

Rain
The stench of wet tobacco clings to stained fingers.
My thoughts similarly dank.

Morning after Rain
A handful of sunbeams streams over stained *tatami*.
On my stomach, I put an unlit cigarette to my lips
and relish the light.

Mornings
Each morning after rain has scrubbed the green,
I stroll straight into verdure on the hill.

P ORT——IMPRESSION OF "O" CITY*

Thick air
crowds longshoremen's brows.

The hostility edging thick eyebrows turns to curses
that shrill through sky.

At each lull in the din, sea's roar chokes the town.

HEATING THE BATH WATER (i)*

Sunlight scatters
over shriveled
corn.

Flaming bean stalks
mutely radiate
their scents.

The scratching of a hoe
greets me
from beyond the fence.

Crickets
chirrup
by the hay mound.

S LAUGHTER HOUSE——IMPRESSIONS OF "F" TOWN*

The bull plods with a weighty sulk;
my feelings sink similarly into gloom.

Have Spanish blood and the bull's doom
blanched here
on soil so sterile
it lacks a single lilac bush?

Watching, I felt the bull's black–banded indignation
boil up from grass tips,
from sooty soil.

Here,
even air,
even the landscape,
chokes.

JUNE SONG

June——I'll dress in pure white.
I'll stroll gazing into azure skies.

June——I'll speak to lovers.

I'll swim through lovers' eyes.

June——I'll play with doves.
I'll whistle like a bleached dove.

June——I'll go to the beach.
I'll peer in silence at sea's blue back.

JULY*

Today again on the balcony,
the man's sleek hands
toy with a green apple.

A woman sans eyebrows whistles away,
acknowledging,
as symbols of this white season,
gulls that mew on far–off shores.

WEEDING

An utterly clean
sky
over the corn.

Beyond the thicket,
someone
whistles.

Fingertips
sultry;
soil sultry, too.

Slivers of dew
on the eggplant.
White feet.

The throbbing hum
of insects
in the weeds.

T HOUGHTS WHILE SICK*

A feeble sunbeam
on the nun's pale neck.
A green lizard skittered noiselessly over the soil.

Chalky cortege after chalky cortege
passes under white jasmines.

From distant shores beyond my windowsill,
the blanched fingers of nostalgia reach again today
to my bedside.

Hollow surf roars
in the empty vase....
My ribs flutter from branch tips
like leaves from a withered tree.
Sealed in icy late–fall gales,
my soliloquy flutters lonesome to the soil.

M Y HOMETOWN (i)

Invisible rain mists through this oil.

In the frame,
places where colors now begin to fade
have for decades
nourished the melancholy on its side of the room.

E ARLY SUMMER*

We'll hear the candyman's flute
when full–leafed cherry trees break into song.

When parasols spin,
we'll see the far–off sea.

The bellies of young sweetfish will glitter
in the depths of tepid rivers.

Soon, oh, soon,
Mother will be well again.

T WILIGHT IN SPRING

That pale girl moaned
when she was killed.

Nobody
remembers her.

Silently, so silently,
elves gather evening up.

H EART'S FRIEND

Every recollection has faded, hasn't it?

Passion heartlessly abandoned us.

Glints of grief somehow
traffic meaninglessly between us,
as though to search out
fired–up feelings of love.

The heart has a staircase, doesn't it?

Unstopped feelings
diffidently climb the steps in my heart
and head into distance.

How command their halt?
My head still droops intently…
oh, this shepherd boy without a horn.

T WILIGHT——SONG OF "F" TOWN*

Whenever dusk creeps
sluggishly in,
the town cowers—
meek as a black cat.

The reluctantly dragged–out moon
leans like an old man
against the corner of a building. •

Girls in this town wear expressions
equivocal as chalky moonflowers,
and yet they sometimes
fling metallic smiles
at boys.

F IRST LOVE*

In the lamb's belly,
a broad green field.

I stretch out on grass, arms round the lamb's neck,
and read aloud Verlaine's verse.
Then that field in the beast's translucent belly comes into view.

As dusk spreads like an elegiac curtain
over the field,
the lamb's head mournfully droops.

I don't know how to console it.
Its eyes see nothing,
nor could my anemic lips
squeeze a whistle out.

S EPTEMBER——LITERARY FRAGMENTS

Air
If I stretch out a hand,
air seems as easy as water to scoop.

I swim in a home of clear glass.

Winds
The beat of my scrawny heart
becomes ever more exact
when autumn winds steal by.

Lonely Grove
Having become a tree rooted there,
I set loose my cares.
I free them into the distant blue.

Autumn Letter
A blue, mist–scented envelope fluttered in through my window.
I don't know who sent it.

I'll just send back a blank page
of early fall.

AUTUMN ETCHED IN ME *

Walking the hills alone.
Playing with the baby.
Trying to snatch the shadow of a dragonfly darting over our yard.
Lighting a candle and reading a book.
Trying to smile like the skies.
Hearing crickets, yet holding back my tears.
I think of my departed father.
I listen laconically to my aging mother crab.

MY LIFE (i)

I have a formidable pistol nobody knows about.
When night comes, I go out and load it.

I live to shoot this gun.

SKY——VAGRANT*

Though it's October already,
sky wears no hat…

mouth agape like a fool.

SLOPES

Hilly landscapes intrigue me.

Hills make me nostalgic.

I always feel that on the other side
I'll find a fascinating fairyland
to tantalize my brooding eyes.

SAND

Sand's shy. •

When I clutch a handful of him,
he stealthily hunches up and,
without a sound,
runs from my palm.

NOCTURNE*

Listen to the silent grief
of this autumn night—
the scattering of jasmine seeds.

Listen to the gloom
of this quiet autumn night—
the build–up of leaves
in heart's mortuary urn.

Listen to the faint nocturne
of this autumn night—
that so long–ago love
we shared.

KIN*

Does my great aunt still flit those shriveled hands through the reel,
through archaic aromas of raveled waste yarn?
...Those sounds rile up reminiscences.

I existed by mellowing my aunt's hands.
Time and again she wanted to strangle this little nuisance of a lad.
In those days,
sasanqua blossoms daily coughed up blood
in her ample, moss–covered yard.

My aunt detested me
and I cursed her heartlessness.
Meanwhile, she raised me, an orphan,
and I managed to grow up.
     She looked after me not out of love
     but because of the thickness of our blood.

Could such cursed and heartless blood
run through my veins, too?
I can't possibly love my aunt.

But now that I'm free of her and my native place,
whatever prompts these glints of nostalgia
in my eyes?

T UNNELS

Tunnels are fantastic!
When I saunter through one,
I hear streams spurting through the depths of my brain.

Tunnels are fantastic!
My dead father cries out from them,
"*Heeeere*! ... *Heeeere*!"
It's a soundless, somber cry.

R AILS

Rails—how wretched!
From afar, they appear to clutch each other's hands.
But draw near and you find
they glare at each other with a chill.

P ASSING AUTUMN*

The white hearse
passing under plane trees
bundles up blanched memories
as it fades creaking into distance.

Lingering in this muddied, ashen town,
oh, even now I raise my arms
in endless remorse
and continue my wordless dirge.

Dejected eyes look blankly after the silvery rain
that soaked me...
oh, mute autumn girl,
will you return again on this boundless chalky road?

F IVE MINIATURES

1. Forest
Fired by sky's blue flame,
he reeks

like aromatic incense.

2. Town
Look into the bottom of this urn,
stagnant with riled water.

3. Utility Poles
Autumn's boundless sensibilities
stabbing the sky.

4. Clouds
These cotton balls squeeze the fairy–tale chest that years and years ago
belonged to grandma and me.

5. Stream
I hesitantly touch a toe to water.
A glance at the surface tells me it's fordable.
Autumn streams like crystal.

L ATE AUTUMN (i)*

The wall enclosing me—
simply too white.
Melancholies mound one on another.

Listen, fly,
staggering over
smudged *tatami* seams,
have you, too, discerned the anguish of this season?

White sedge hat cocked,
autumn will pass beyond my window, head drooping.
Yes, it will wend far into distance.

C IGARETTES*

The man again today
chokes back feelings in this landscape
no brush could paint.

Faded scenes of home in his opened palm. •

From a sooty October room where thought has turned inert,
smoke wafts his nostalgia
high into the blue.

𝕃 ATE AUTUMN (ii)*

Someone rattles open the back door
and a voice says,
"I've come to use your bath."
A fallen leaf blows in.

It's getting colder and colder;
I'm chilled to the bone.
Let's sit by the sunken hearth
and talk.

Scattered persimmon leaves
rustle at our back door.
Grandfather will soon
want the *kotatsu.*

ⓄCTOBER WIND

Look! A dim shadow
stirs under the elm.

My, oh, my.
It's wind
panting—
such bony shoulders.

ⓄCTOBER ——LITERARY FRAGMENTS

A Clear Day
One morning on the dike
I wait for a balloon,
for a wonderfully expansive, red balloon.

Rendezvous
Waiting, I wondered if I should clutch and pocket
a handful of sky's blue.
Like a balloon, my heart somehow swells.

YARD AT NIGHT *

I bury
my green *akebia* fruit
and go to bed.

How many nights
must I sleep
before they're ripe?

Listen! A *niisan* cricket
chirrups
under a downspout.

Someone passes
our fence
yelping like a fox.

OCTOBER

On the apple at the tip of the girl's white fingers,
the sunny window of a Western house.

Days on end I sit by that window reading my book,
letting a sponge on the table
soak up all I feel.

My fingers turn page after page...
each blank.

PARK*

A scene where the noon cannon's distant boom
rends autumn sky.

The fountain spurts nostalgia high and pure white.

The blue of today's skies
copies the eyes of a lanky Italian
who saunters there.

F RAGRANT OLIVE*

Pungent olive aromas
stick persistently to my fingertips.

Before I know it,
I'm a lad basking in the sun on the storehouse wall
of my far–off home.

S KY*

How wonderful those autumn skies.
My stare soaks them up.

Look! Mother's come all the way from home
to see me.

BOREDOM*

Scenery suffocates in broad daylight.
Potato blossoms flower full in the girl's breast.
The pale nun's passion rusts.

Ah, I now crave the vitriol
to dissolve those chasms in my palms...these sallow hands.

MORNING ——RAIN LETS UP

Deluged by liquefied verdure,
my palms seem translucent.
A splendid morning.

Shall I shave this vulgar mustache
in that mirror of roadside water
buoying sky and woolly clouds?

S IGHS OF MY EIGHTEEN YEARS

Youthful days fly by
as I follow my art,
recognizing people and the world
as foes. •

As you might imagine,
deprivation kindles
warped views.

WHARF (ii)*

– 1 –

A warship rusts at the wharf.
Blue sailors wander over the sea
into horizon—
one by one by one.

– 2 –

So lonely…
wharf's wind–driven lights
sidle up to me.

– 3 –

A blind woman
drowns herself in silence.
Through the distance,
moon raises a white hand.

– 4 –

When I walked the wharf alone,
I soon found ancient blue Spanish stamps
pasted all across
my brow.

B. COUNTRY TABLE

and others

『田舎の食卓』その他

PORTRAIT OF THE CITY*

– 1 –

Sunday. —— We stroll about with joy in our pockets. Now and then we reach for it, put it back. Polished shoes, summer hats: we white–collar bachelors. Oh, city! always a newly–published book. Watch the pavement in the backwash of an orangeade wind. Plane trees along the boulevard cast shadows and print lovely poems to brisk applause.

– 2 –

Department store. —— Elevator! Drop us to hell or raise us to heaven— as you please. The roof garden. The distant range. Blue skies. An advertising balloon. Ah, we now feel more pathetic than these caged animals. City! —— captive in your vast palm.

ON A SUN–WASHED TRAIN

It's Sunday. I ride this sun–washed train
with the air of a youthful bank clerk
ensconced here for years.

Passengers read newsprint reeking of ink,
their faces like stale bread.
A wind puff lays a willow leaf on my lap.
When did the tree bud?
When did its flowers fall?
I've quite forgotten.

Passengers absorbed in newsprint
pretend not to notice each other.

They read newsprint reeking of ink.
As though spring had hooked us with its line,
an ad balloon streaks my window with a stringy shadow
stretching as endless as ennui.

JUNE *CHANSON**

Gentle breezes blaze cheeks leaving the barber's;
it's as though I walked near the sea.
Colorful as new dust jackets, girls spill onto the streets:
lovely dream films fluttering among fresh plane trees.
The airliner's roar
injects my brain
with such pleasant anesthesia!
Oh, swaying bus straps
cast nimble shadows
over passengers' white jackets—
like smiles,
smiles.

PASSING SHOWER*

Town darkens in an instant. Then a momentary hum...like ferns stirring.
Standing in bookshop doorways or at food counters in department stores, we
may recall the shutters on our south–side windows. Or those curtains it was
time to change. —— Brightness then returns again to Earth. Around me, an
ether–like cool. Sun's sparkle puts me at ease. At moments like this, I sense
the loveliness in death, in death's face. —— Looking into blue skies, I see a
rainbow. I see an airliner flying in an arc. Then I recall those Carniolan
honeybees we once kept back home. I wonder where they're buzzing now?

AFTERNOON LETTER *

Today —— how bright the sky. Walking through town I find life loath-
some—as painful as when I couldn't climb our fig tree. I go then to the de-
partment store and use the urinal. That beautiful color flowing over the
snow–white tiles calms me down, cheers me up.

Today a liquid *mélancholie* bubbles up again under that avenue of young
plane trees—skies effortlessly luminous. I go to a restaurant—alone—and
devour with the macaroni my so slender private griefs.

SUMMER'S END*

Under roadside trees at dusk,
a terribly chilly breeze nips at
the nape of my neck.
Casually, I look back.
Has spry autumn's white hand fingered me?

A far–off sunset tingles town's tiered roofs.
Ah, once more the curtain rings this summer down
with a stunning finale—
like a tragedy…a comedy.

I'll fling my threadbare straw hat
from this bridge.
Sayonara.
Sayonara.
I'll watch it stagger briefly till it vanishes
into dimming water.

𝔽 RESH AUTUMN LYRIC*

Wind touches a Gillette blade to my cheeks, my neck.
Air bares its sparkling white teeth.
My mind today—serene as someone middle–aged,
meek as water–sprinkled pavement.

An airliner skimming over sky's blue silk
beckons:
—— *How about a trip tomorrow?*

Those white flowers have bloomed again
from the stone embankment around the courthouse.
My coin purse as empty
as this head is filled with nostalgia.
Friend! Aren't you being especially sensitive today
    about those stains on your shirt—
stains that betray your pathetic past?

𝕊 LOTH*

Sunset marks time at the park entrance.

Sloth! I feel slightly relieved as I stand before your cage—
slightly relieved.

The hues of that distant glow seem, after all,
to blaze with the flames of a talent besting either of us.

F INGERS OF A NEW SEASON*

Reaching up—up,
the vine touches gentle fingers to a white window frame
in our chemistry classroom.

Wings glistening like duralumin...
autumn has come again, my friend.

The microscope's cold touch,
the mosquito's shriveled carcass (my trophy)
on a page of *Organische Chemie*.
Soft breezes steal in now and then
to ruffle the balance
the way they ruffle my mind.

Listen to fall's last fly buzzing
on a sunny rock—
now a bright hallucination imagined in the ear,
now the endless Brownian movement
of pathetic particles....

Come, shrewd friend, sit on the grass here.
The pomegranate has mellowed considerably
beyond your brain.

What catches in my throat today
like stringy chemical formulas?
When I stretch out on the grass, ah,
a shrike's cry jabs a sharp blade into me,
plucks something out, carries it off....

S ONGS OF EARLY SPRING*

– 1 –

Under a suburban sky
spread out like a parachute,
I stuff scraps of *mélancholie*
into my guitar.
Laboring up a mandolin–shaped hill,
I crunch through snow
deep as my remorse.

– 2 –

Spring has already visited
the world's most far–flung borders.
Clear weather day after day—
pussy willows glisten bright as down on a girl's arm;
clouds stroll beside me
with enormous, shadowy strides;
the tail of a bunting in a mulberry orchard
composes airs of early spring.

– 3 –

Imitating onetime hopes,
trees stand square into sun.
I duck under them
the way one passes through the gate to spring.
Laying back the tall grass
as though searching for a violet,
I search then for that other me.

– 4 –

Floating on the lake's copper sulfate glow:
a bird's carcass,
a devastated musical score.
Bullets from someone's pent–up winter
probably ripped them through.
Look! A chirruping bird comes to bathe.
It splashes up rainbow
after tiny bow.

S QUALL*

After a long stretch of clear skies,
a band of clouds sparkling like ampules
descended on our hamlet.
It rinsed my *pensée*.
It rinsed everything dry.
Under this lovely sun,
bird droppings crusted on the bronze statue
glisten like fresh medicine,
fresh medicine.

B ONJOUR*

I open the window
and summer billows like a parachute.
It traces a sparkling arc
over shrubs.

❀   ❀   ❀

Summer has come glaring like carbon paper.
I buy a light blue lamp shade.
Skies today remain as fresh as laundry powder.
Yes, even my insomnia will be reaped
with the wheat.

S UMMER SKETCHBOOK*

Wood sorrel leaves
sour as summer recess—
my middle school vacation
weighted
with endless homework.
Blue–blue sky.
White–white clouds.
Using this shepherd's purse seed,
I've been printing *katakana*
on a blank page in my sketchbook.

❀   ❀   ❀

I squat in the field
and chew mint leaves
flavored like a Gillette blade,
like their Latin, *Mentha piperita*.
Oh, memory sliced off
with my tongue!

M ORNING (i)

A clear sky bares its lovely neck.
Wind trembles corn tassels.
Fresh leaves ferment
like green ale.
Look! Sweeping directly overhead,

a seaplane soars off
then discards us on the floor
of this bright glass jar....

S LEEP*

The simmer of an August afternoon.
A young man sleeps
under a majestic chestnut tree,
his mouth agape
as though poisoned by an upas tree.

HOUSE WHERE I WAS BORN (i)*

Perfectly cloudless days stretch out
like a new circus tent.
Morning newsprint! —— You trudge about
delivering fresh topics of conversation to every home.
Tell me, what's happened to our world...to our
world (...but I've mourned so many kinsmen here)?
Each event then fades away
like the monotonous melodies of honeybees.
Day by day aprons dry quickly
in that grove of blooming silk trees.

VILLAGE ——FRAGMENTS*

My village a freshly–laundered *yukata*,
the aroma of cheap mint–colored soap—
cheerless and still.
But barley straws make such nice whistles;
let's make the straw sing!

❀   ❀   ❀

A clear–eyed goat
rests like me
at thicket's edge.
Rain sparse as his goatee
quivers on the water.

❀   ❀   ❀

A bull napping under a fig tree,
imitates me—
like ennui, his monstrous twisted horns
too much for him.
Yes, I suppose I, too, shall age here,
a horsefly buzzing forever near a shiny coil.

Sunset's final flush.
Earth cheerful, my village cheerful, too.
The eyes of livestock in the vegetable garden
misty as the eyes of young boys.
Let's go to the river and watch its water glow
like Ophelia's cheeks.

C OUNTRY TABLE*

Time the hue of hay
burns everywhere about me.
The buzz of honeybees
stews me
in a crock of griefs—
yes, over a simmering flame.

L AD

Soft as a snake's tongue,
rain from the south licks my cheeks.
I always carry a book with comely wrappers
to open like a private secret
when I'm alone.
As I stretch out on a patch of May grass,
huge hands suddenly blindfold me ....

S OIRÉE*

– 1 –
Evening edges into doorways
like a trapped beast—
brooding,
bringing straws of light. •

Look! A hay–hued moon is up.
Young men
nibbling corn cobs
like harmonicas
head for the fragrant *shiso* field.

– 2 –

Evening spreads a lovely net
that catches children still at play—
the scent of air as light and fresh as ether.
I sit on a rock under a tree, the rock a white egg
that summer had held and warmed till now.
This moment of cool gathers round me.
My eyes meek as a cow's.
My ears drawn to the flow of sap.
The distant marsh glowing like magnesium.

F AMILY*

– 1 –

Weather cheerful as crucifers. Jump rope shadows quiver on dried shirts
as pleasantly as though death were dancing a reel. The buzz of honeybees,
their unhurried bustle. Morning papers and milk bottles bloom like lonely
flowers by the stone gate——life's daily routines....

– 2 –

With nightfall came a rain soft as merino wool. As though to braid the
hours, a girl on a hard chair knits a sweater, her baby soon due. Simply
waiting brightens the mind. Her slightly disheveled hair mirrored on the
window. Scents of sun on grass pulse from its pane.

AUTUMN SONG *

Sky a cracked walnut.
I stretch out on grass
a parody of Proust's mustache.
As I tumble down with shadows,
warm sun lays its hand on my shoulder.
Ah, my springtime!
Above me
a kidney–shaped cloud
tows a kidney–like shadow.

Autumn's Edge ——Fragments*

Summer ended the way one shuts a ponderous tome.
Like the high–school student who just finished his assignments,
we probably do not recall
the row of clouds whose geometrical tracks
vanished beyond horizon....
All that's left of summer:
the shriveled carcasses of stunning insects
pinned to fresh wooden boxes that,
like our other trophies,
reek of preservative.

❧   ❧   ❧

A cocked air gun on my shoulder,
I lead my dog.
My dog leads his tail.
Lightbeams jampack the grove;
trees lament being pocketless.
Sky among branches—blue litmus.
As a young man in a striped shirt cuts down a tree,
I find myself hoping that a fresh light ray
freed by the gashes
might turn the tables and cut him down....

❧   ❧   ❧

Your news today upsets me, my friend,
the way those *salvia* seeds filed and forgotten
in a blue envelope distress.
Sky erects a lovely gallows.
Wind teases the last few tassels of corn.
A golden olive tree heavies the air with fragrance...
even a gentle slope
and a stretch of black clapboard fence.
Everything perfect now
for me to rattle on impetuously
about my beloved Chekhov.

❧   ❧   ❧

The dry gully glistens,
white as a songbird's breast.
Marigolds bloom along a riverbank

sinuous as my visions.
Though my livelihood
remains as sparse
as smartweed seeds,
I can still be carefree, my friend
(if you don't mind a carefree dotard).
As I stand dreamily on grass,
some ducks waddle by to goad me on.

E ARLY SPRING (i)*

Fly more joyfully, more boldly,
little wren,
timid wren
chirping along the ground.

Plum blossoms mirrored
in the eyes of a tethered calf,
in the latent horns I put my finger to—
faint warmths,
footsteps from afar.

Fly more joyfully, more boldly,
little wren—
over finger–high barley,
over the waterless millrace.

POETRY

PART II — 1940–1949

A. HOUSE WHERE I WAS BORN

and others

『生まれた家』その他

Day in the city*

– 1 –

Hail pelted my shoulders as,
grimy bills in hand,
I left the bank's stony gloom.
The busy street's bustle—
a hometown friend calling from behind.

I see dozing cattle
and a clump of swaying ferns.
I smell a parsley patch on a clear day.

– 2 –

Bright sun returns to soil.
Fleeting holiday! Choking on the pavement,
     my lonely holiday!
I write a letter home. The green of the stamp stings my eyes.
I have some coffee at a restaurant,
dirt–colored coffee,
take an elevator to the roof of the department store,
then gaze into distance at the crisp, clear ranges.

Spring*

Larks have built a little nest
in the hat I threw away last year.
Nothing could have pleased me more
than having my hat drown in a sea of wheat.
The lark chick leaves a dropping on my palm,
a greeting.
Ah, its parents cry
in the far–off tepid sky—
cry in my semicircular canals.

97

INN

I slipped off my dirty undershirt
the way I stripped away a sordid youth.
Then, changing to a clean one,
I savored the scent of *yomogi* on this sunny day.

Night brought motherly rains.
They'll loiter beneath my window to check
that I blow out my lamp and sleep.

EVENING

– 1 –

Gentle winds rock those trees by the church.
The quivers of choir voices and organ tunes
linger beneath their leaves.
Branch–framed skies look coolly luminous,
like eyes at prayer.

– 2 –

Spider–web fingers clutch
——the squall that just passed by,
——sunset's distant glow,
——the carcass of an insect
gaunt as Christ.

GOING HOME*

I'll be in many places,
rejected or embraced by arms
as tender now as they ever were.

I'll be
in a sour sorrel stem,
in the hollow sound it makes when snapped in two.

I'll be
under young persimmon leaves,
diffident as a lizard
on a sun–drenched rock.

I'll be
on grass along the stream,
in water glistening with fish
like joys that slithered from my grasp. •

I'll be
by the storehouse under our mulberry tree,
tattooing my mouth with mulberry juice
like an Ainu.

I'll be
on treetops where songbirds build their nests and,
eyes glowering with plunder,
on rooftops, too.

I'll be
fondly wearing my flannel kimono
on an evening mauve as a *shiso* leaf,
listening by the roadside to reed flutes in the distance.

Ah, I'll be
under those shadowy *yusuraume* by the well,
loathing that friend,
honing my knife.

L ATE SPRING FLUTE*

I play my flute.
When I rest my hand,
graceful tunes
fade from fingertips—
no way to stop them.

I play my flute.
If I tilt my head slightly,
those graceful
finger–stopped tunes
become mine.

S HOWER*

Rain falls as sun beats down...
like that European country scene in a picture book,
that old lady coming from a far–off house
the picture of a guinea hen.

Hamlet after bright hamlet.
Hamlet after dark hamlet.
Even barley's blond neatly groomed
with a comb of sparkling rain...
like a modest lass.

AT A COUNTRY BARBERSHOP

My boyhood friend reeks of soap.
Though young, life's routines already soak him
like the scent in soap.

That wooden bridge and the muddy waters in his face
(the small chin scar from a childhood fight)
flicker across the mirror.

Talking of the bloated corpse on the river yesterday,
he deftly shaves away the griefs of this fellow
who ran out of money and came back home.

The bridge flickers in my mind's eye
as it did so long ago,
its riled waters flowing still...
twenty years—like lonely rage.

NIGHT WIND

Someone blows a straw flute
that utters human sobs.
Night brings wind,
a supple, scant breeze
that quickly strips the mothball fumes
from my kimono.
I sense ripened wheat
rustling in the dark.
I sense June stretched out in wheat,
slowly rattling its last.

LATE SPRING (i)

The waterwheel finally stopped.
Time had weighed it down.
I lean against a tree trunk and wait for a shower,
for fresh water to turn the wheel again.

VILLAGE *

Two faces emerge
like gossip
from under a blooming chestnut tree.
As they near, I catch the scent of acne lotion.

L 'ESPOIR*

Flask–shaped
lily bulb
fattening in the field!
How I wish my thoughts
rivaled your weight.
Moon mushroom
brought in yesterday from an old beech log!
Would that my half life ahead
might glow like you,
if only in gloomy kitchen corners....

HOUSE WHERE I WAS BORN (ii) *

Sea crowds my eyes. A wave clears the seawall,
and once clear spends itself as others build.
Swaying sunflowers imitate straw hats;
pine pollen dots white bathing suits;
laughing voices; shining aspirins of sweat....
I sit on an old chair
before that house sinking expansively within me.
Smells of broiled fish ... sounds of tableware ...
things I once rejected now besiege me.
Mother's sprightly voice calls from the kitchen window.
A yellowed book slips from my hands.
As though in anemic rage, wind rapidly flips its pages
for me, for Mother, for all....

EN ROUTE*

Home! That two–*sen* copper forgotten in my bamboo bank!
I've come home. For no special reason.
I've come home. Because it's home.

Picking through the trees,
wind coils like a riled garter snake
round my neck, round my arms.

Home! That two–*sen* copper forgotten in my bamboo bank!
I've come home. For no special reason.
Oh, one of countless butterflies swarming on radish blooms.

R EVENGE

Children die dressed in their best,
chilling slowly like shaded rocks at sundown.
Just as the children put an end to that snake yesterday
under clear skies in the field,
summer has taken them
with those pretty poison sumac berries
——to the festival of Death.

AFTER DINNER SONGS (i) *

– 1 –

A fresh summer has come again
with the sparkle of a sickle reaping wheat.
I wear this scratchy
over–starched *yukata*.
Mother, I wear
my twenty–seven years
like this over–starched *yukata*!

– 2 –

I flush immediately after
a mere spot of saké.
By now I'm used to it
and to a needy existence, too.
I call to the shower in the foothills:
Hurry here
and growl under my window
your gentle growl!
I'll fling my griefs
at you
the way I flip away my loquat seeds.

– 3 –

I hear Paris has fallen.
Mother, you say it
as though it's alien!

I now stare at, now sniff
this armful of pure white lilies
just picked today.

I hear Paris had finally fallen.
Mother, you say it
as though it's alien.

S ONGS OF OLD——FRAGMENTS*

Night has come. Night—a magnificent summer day shrouded in blackness. And I shrouded in it, too—in something huge, something unfamiliar....

—— Night after night I go to bed, a book of Rilke's poems by my pillow. Under my tiny lamp, I notice the grass–stained prints that meandered here or there over the book's white pages. That explains how free I was to sit on the grass as I did on sunny cloud–free days. And how I could snare happiness—like catching some bug with a cast of my cap.

I promenade through the grove at dawn. —— But only after the dryads finish their festivals. Rows of tall chairs, backs reaching for sky. Here and there flowers scattered like bread crumbs. Resin hardening like lonely thoughts. Even now the pond sparkles—a Gillette blade slicing away those dreams still stacked on my forehead....

I loved the ether–like world fashioned of blue sky and treetops. I loved that beautifully pleated world that wind and water painted. At times I've wished I were there. —— If I could be...ah, Mother! I'd likely come straight home instead. Once home, I might sit at that desk with all those penknife nicks. And, Mother, I might ask whether you'd planted your flower seeds.... Then we'd talk about things like the dog we once had.

HIGH NOON IN SUMMER

Weariness sawed them down.
They sleep
like fallen logs,
a cicada chorus cleansing their sweat.

As they sleep,
a gadfly alights on their saw
and fervently polishes its blade....

VIPER

I can't believe we once swam here.
How chilly the water looks today.
Children! Take care near that pond,
for like a viper
lurking still in clumps of grass,
summer might suddenly strike your legs.

B LANKS IN SUMMER NOTEBOOKS*

A cicada hums compulsively on a high treetop.
Vacation already over. *Sayonara*, my friends.
We, too, will be pinned,
each to his own school,
like bugs to wooden cases....

L ONELY BOOKWORM

Twilight. Dusk comes also to my collection of verse. Even cicadas have ended their chirruping—the way a baby stops crying. Something cold, something cloudy settles swiftly into the valleys of my mind. —— A hard wooden chair bolsters me. I lean on a hard wooden desk. Words stand and light my lamp, then leave my pages far behind.... In their wake, only sounds of clinking dishes, whiffs of boiling fish.

S UMMER DAY

Evening rolls up shadows
    strung like hammocks between the trees.
Cicadas drum me awake
from a nap shallow as a hum.
I rise,
cast my shadow over the glittering, waterless gully,
yawn at the bushes beyond.

L OGGING

I hear an axe, the echoes of an axe. Reporting the tree's tale of grief: the quivering of splendidly sandwiched air layers. Resin oozes from wounds in its ranked arms, glistens like tears in sunlight sifting through branches....

❀   ❀   ❀

The deeply–biting axe wedges momentarily. The trunk grips the axe tight to mask its naked scar.

❀   ❀   ❀

Dozing one summer afternoon
in the shade of that tree,
I read a book and indulged foolish reveries.
I bathe today like rustling waters

in the shade of another tree—one awaiting the woodman.
Let axe blows ring out.
Fell the tree quickly…and with it
my long, my listless summer day.

M *ÉMOIRE**

The brevity of summer days—
the warmth of a fresh–laid egg on china.
A cricket chirruped autumn
near a straw hat reeking still of sweat.
Our trophies wilted far faster
than wildflowers shrivel in gathering boxes.
I chomped my dried fava beans the way I chomp solitude,
making snappy sounds.
A fingernail moon.
Buckwheat blossoms copy bread crumbs.
One cloudless afternoon I carved that name on an oak.
My love, I've fretted more about you
than about the English that keeps slipping through me,
than those Latin words I never learned.

S UPPER

Coming as though scheduled,
the bird chirps from a twilight branch.
No one knows what to call it.

Only the evening paper, as blanched as its dreary information,
holds dusk's dimming.
Artificial flowers open in the glass—
life's lean routines!

Summer, too, will soon pass….
Silently we stare at private sorrows
the size of chips on a teacup.

Evening showers have been visiting
off and on for some time now,
as though expressing something they forgot to say.

They sparkle the mane of Time's steed.

DAY OF A JOURNEY *

I feel tempted to drop anchor straightaway and make myself a carefree hostage here.

Let me weigh that anchor now. I stuff my shirts and things into a suitcase. I stuff my books. I stuff myself.

Well, time to leave. I call, *Sayonara!* though no one's there.

Wind polishes my shoes. A girl washes her hair beside a limpid brook.

Cows and sheep drowse near the thicket. *Sayonara!* I'm going home. I tip my hat—though no one's there. Aromas from a fragrant olive tenaciously track me. Soon I arrive at the tiny train stop. The aged wicket man leisurely punches my red, tongue–like ticket. He opens a hole the size of my sorrow at leaving. I board a relic coach. Oh, I'll not come to a place like this again.

IN A LITTLE PORT TOWN*

The circus left—abandoning to litter and autumn breezes an empty lot that looked like a rotting tooth.

At every lull in waves' refrain, however, I still hear plaintive echoes from the ragged little band. The bare feet of the girl crossing the high wire appear often in my dreams—where she frequently falls....

Those days I was reading *Fanny* and *Marius*. That's why I couldn't bear the sound of steam whistles. —— Jetty, jetty somewhat too narrow for my feet! Twilight has been coming in over you, clomping its wooden shoes, imitating an old salt's gait. —— Oh, how I struggled each night trying to cast sleep's anchor into the seabed's titanic night...!

AUTUMN AFTERNOON

Coming home from a job interview
and weighing the day's rewards,
I pass a silent and hushed
asylum
and remember a friend gone mad,
the one who sang sweet love songs till the day he died.
It's autumn,
the sky a deep, clean blue.
Only the wrapping on my new book flashy and beautiful.
My soiled shoes and shirt truly disturb me.
A burst pomegranate, picture of the brain.
Suddenly I shoulder the intolerable weight
of a fearful midday emptiness.

AFTER DINNER SONGS (ii) *

Wearing my new lined kimono,
I think ——— Truly, I care only for me.

I love no one. I....
Nobody—Mother, not even you!

Oh, flock of wild geese
raucously crossing the twilight sky...
the phosphorescence of that lonely fish
glowing on my plate!

Fogged as faintly as my cares,
the little glass coffee maker sings
of my self–concern.

The grass fire licking at the foothills
favors the tongue of an enormous snake.

FIELD

Clouds come. Clouds go.
Lumbering like cattle,
cloud shadows come and go....
By now, nothing troubles me.
Cloud shadows! Come here by me.
I'll give you my place,
this grass patch of toasty sunshine.

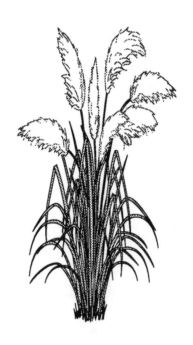

EULALIA

B. SONGS OF OLD · LATE SPRING

and others

『昔の歌』『晩春』その他

DAILY SOLITUDE

I've come to toss stones
    into this early spring bamboo grove:
Perchow!   *Perchow*!   *Perchow*!
I'm back today to throw stones
    into the grove's cheery replies:
Perchow!   *Perchow*!   *Perchow*!

GROVE (i)

Spring's first rain
passed through moments ago—
bathing larch buds,
straining its skinny neck, absorbed in thought,
imitating me....

SCHOOL*

– 1 –
Children, what do you jabber about?
Ivy silhouettes reach for the window.
Recess now.

A honey locust casts a dense shade net
to hold in children's dreams.
A fresh wooden fence glistens all around.

– 2 –
One child very much resembles me.
He sits in a far corner,
looking blankly to one side
while doodling
a newly–learned *hiragana*

on a desk deep in pine pollen.
Yes, at this moment a black kite imitates him
in a sky clear as dreams.

WHEAT HARVEST *

– 1 –

I've just returned
to a village where wheat sways ripe.
Everyone at work in the fields.
The glitter of fresh *aogashi* leaves along the road
and the so very distant waving of the wheat—
ah, a touch of seasickness lingers somewhere still....

– 2 –

I drink cold tea on an *engawa*
red with *yusuraume* berries.

Huddling till now under the pomegranates,
tiny cloud shadows quit our yard.

They flit off toward the fields, over the wheat,
to tell everyone I'm back.

SEASHORE TOWN

All sorts of ships lined up
like skewered bugs.
That's the town where we stayed one summer.

One boat listlessly tooting,
one dragging a bright wake
as it leaves for open sea....

Whatever do you suppose happened to that house
where we all dreamed similar dreams
in similarly divided rooms?

Evening after evening, summer–end cicadas
hummed on the hill behind that house.
What boys now listen to those hums
as they pause while dressing to leave?

One boat listlessly tooting,
one dragging a bright wake

as it leaves for open sea....

That's the town where we stayed one summer.

T ARDY

I heard lovely choruses from the school
wreathed in fresh leaves.

Oh, late again!
A small white butterfly
flit round and round my dismay.

I still vividly recall
how I've continually felt
as forlorn as I felt then.

B ED OF FRESH GRASS

Treasuring my thimble of leisure, I again feel driven
to visit the knoll where yesterday I drowsed.
Skies stretch softly cloud–free,
imitating the sheepskin cover on my book.
Sky spreads over the soiled cover
with fragile grace.

Here's the dent where I sat yesterday.
I wonder who's been here since?
Wildflowers flattened to the ground
in shows of feeble grief.

Even now I hear their laughter.
Scraps of discarded food...
perhaps a family as poor as mine.

Late in spring on that greening knoll...
like peeking at a blithe secret—
amusing yet sad.

V ISIT TO A GRAVE *

Late summer's setting sun glitters on treetops,
on pebbles in the dry ravine. •

I rest now, take off my hat,
lay my shadow beside me like a cane.

I rest—a butterfly savoring memories.

Water in my bucket mirrors a cloud puff
I think of as your face.

Ah, cicadas hum in the distance,
hum directly overhead.

Among them,
one who may stop singing as young as you.

That tender voice suspended in space,
then lost forever...never recognized.

I, too, may find myself forgetting—or perhaps
simply beguiled by other more strident voices.

HINOMISAKI VILLAGE *

I pass through sighing pines,
then an expanse of mulberry trees.
Beyond their leaves, a sleepy town.

How bright the air, how bright the water
at this tip of Izumo.

Haunted by the fierce pounding of waves
on the afternoon of my short day's trip,
I find myself thinking of Death.
When will I walk this ocher plot again?
As I wander aimlessly from home,
what happens to memories of my thirsts for the far off?

I note June sun high above,
the lighthouse trailing its long shadow,
ants mindlessly thronging blue–black mulberries.

AT HINOMISAKI VILLAGE *

– 1 –

I come here
to pace the long lighthouse shadow

lying on summer grass.

I come here
joyous as a child
to pick mulberries near the hill...

...alone and quite heedless
that a one–day trip soon ends.

– 2 –

I come here
to think.

There exist
only sea's roar, wind in the pines
(ceaseless since ancient times),
and my flimsy life....

Only my life—much slighter
than a feathered seed in wind.

𝕐OUTHFUL DAYS (i)*

They sat under clear skies on a grassy hilltop.
One said, "In a century, good times will surely come."
That made another laugh.
The third said nothing.
All three were young and filled with endless protests.

That hilltop hasn't changed.
Grayed eulalia sways as in days long past.

He who trusted in the distant future died young.
The one with violent thoughts ended up in jail.
The third had a family and lives in poverty.
When he roams that hilltop under autumn's clear skies,
he sometimes recalls the words,
"In a century...."

Then for no reason
he sees visions of fern fronds
flickering aimlessly in sun's liquid light.

AT TABLE*

I strip a month from the calendar
the way I strip a plaster from my shoulder.
February already.
January gone
in a breath.
I hear
a greenfinch singing
just steps away on withered grass.
We sit
speechless,
like *nikogori* on a plate.

EARLY SPRING (ii)

Pussy willow shadows peer through
finger–high barley shoots.
Even the trails of marsh snails still short.

Water from the thaw, flowing fresh from the distant gorge,
slowly stirs the waterwheel.
A single light beam probes the interior
through a chink in the mill shed door…
like that eye addressed to my innermost self.

Grain ceaselessly quivers and glows with fragrance,
little by little stripping off the hulls…
a mirror of my mind.

Finger–high barley shoots.
Soft cloud shadows.
The dim form of a skylark on the wind.

Water from the thaw, flowing fresh from the distant gorge,
restlessly stirs the waterwheel.

PLAYGROUND*

Here, the children's playground—
a year–round baseball field.
Soft winter sunshine
warms the lot. •

Dragging long shadows,
the tattered backstop mimics those drying nets
we once saw on a school campout at the beach.

Green hills, the water tower,
and a white apartment house
float into the pitcher's windup.

Children! Children! Children—you, too,
are pretty new balls
someone has pitched into the world:
rolling...bouncing...spinning!

Passing like a storm,
a commuter train fouls the umpire's call.
Empty bottles stacked on that bike trailer,
belonging to the saké dealer who serves as ump,
glisten brightly.

By now, as many spectators
as players.
The picture story man,
one foot on a bike pedal,
a distant onlooker.
This the baseball field,
a cheerfully pleasant playground.
Even mitt–shaped clouds
watch intently from their skies.

Children! Children! Children—you have time yet
to learn that life's bitterness
is like the grit filling your shoes
after losing a game.
Children! Children! Children—you have time
till the day you find yourselves
the way you hunt for the ball—
choking your clothes with burrs!

B EAUTIFUL MAN*

The late Takamura Kôtarô wrote,
Beauty is power.
Beautiful man,
your limbs
supple as trees in May! •

Eyes and ears attuned
to the most distant,
your Atlas–like feet
tread any soil.

Beautiful man!
Under resilient skin,
your bursts of energy
hum like a dynamo.

You forever
confront the future
wreathed in leis of hard–earned sweat.

God–made man,
brimming with beautiful power!
Now is time for you
to fashion
in that whole blessed frame of yours
your own fresh deity.

S UMMER MOUNTAIN*

That nostalgic mountain soared
over early–blooming *gentians* and *bellflowers*
arranged full in a large vase.
A deep, burning sky stretched out
in the blossoms' colors.
Water in the gorge
stung my hands like oxydol.
Mountain! You call me, you lure me,
like those high, those distant echoes I heard then.
Ah, now I crawl
round that vase
like an *ant*.

ON THE HEIGHTS

Sooted hills haul in nets
     cast by light rays.
Opening its doors, the bus again swallows
     what it disgorged in the morning.
So long! Bye–bye! —— Vacation!

Ah, a drunk full moon
    on the hip of a hill.

AUTUMN DAY (i)

Autumn now.
Green fall fruit,
still not fully mature,
tests its weight
on branch tips.

Autumn now.
On fall straw in a corner of the chicken coop,
a single porcelain egg
holds a small, pale shadow
against the sunset's distant glow.

JOURNEY'S END*

As I was saying good–bye, a girl from the inn
gave me a ripe citron she'd picked in the yard.

I fondled the fruit
on the long way to the train stop.

How deep the pleats in those hills
soon to be buried in snow.

Fondling my citron
as I leaned against the fence at the stop,
I waited an eternity for the inbound train.

RECOLLECTIONS OF FATHER (i)*

I saw Mother weep.
In late fall as sunset's glow filtered into a kitchen corner,
I saw her shedding tears for Father.

I remember nothing of him. He died young…
a star vanishing beyond the verge of night skies
as I slept.

But I think about him,
an isolated and peevish man;
a father who ignored his family;

a father whose image increases in me by the year.

When he died, I saw Mother sobbing.
I vaguely remember only that—in late fall
as sunset's glow filtered into a kitchen corner—
I saw her shedding tears for him.

S NIPPETS FROM AN AUTUMN SKETCHBOOK*

Summer Camellias
What scattered these camellias?
Autumn's first rain
or its first wind
awake at last this dawn?

Wildflowers
That path to the orchard.
The tightly–folded ocean flickering.
Butterflies that stormy winds
strip from wildflowers.

Autumn Silkworms
Even shadows from children's lamps sleep fast.
Silkworms will enter murky cocoons tonight
when stars fall in streams.

Acorns
Acorns are falling.
I finally finish Turgenev at the baby's bedside.
Acorns never stop falling.
My sleeping child! You've fallen like an acorn
    from a distant branch.

L ATE AUTUMN (iii)*

Dusk winds rock heavy–lidded trees. Sky colors wane weakly among emptily intertwined branches.... Gone are light ripples from the midday sun that shone so tirelessly bright. Gone, too, those dream–like light rays the trees had cheerfully scattered over ground. And also the white hands of autumn that helped ripen and now have plucked the fruit.... Bringing rain, wind keeps rocking, rocking the trees.

I sit at my desk. A chilly wall behind me. —— Somewhere, sounds of water. I hear the reluctant sounds of something dropping into deep places. I think then—a chilly wall behind me—of our brief autumn. Of the many nuts that never matured.

ℝ ECOLLECTIONS OF FATHER (ii)*

I remember nothing of Father's face,
nor even a flake of his voice.

When he left this world...
that day a gale.

Our full–blooming magnolia swayed all day.
Skylarks sang as though to say adieu.

Watching grass spears stir,
I lean now against a window,
listen to wind rustling through the sparse grove,
think of Father.

I remember nothing of his face, you know,
nor even a flake of his voice.

Since that day, I've entrusted to others
eyes that noted someone near to me,
ears that heeded someone near ....

𝕎INTER DAY (ii)

Tree hearts waken
and re–blossom in soft sunbeams.
I stand by blooms that hardly seem to bloom
at a spot where I was hauling my shadow over the soil.
Those flowers seem now to glow....

𝔸RIETTA ——SPRING GRIEFS

I the sickle.
I the barley to be reaped.

I the wise sickle that gleams
as though tomorrow might never come.
I the grains of grief
reaped day after day.

R IPE BARLEY

How gracefully wind's fingers
plait the barley's ripened beards.

T O THE FAR–OFF CAPITAL*

The affection in my new serge kimono!
Wrapped in Mother's love,
the comfort of an evening in my village....

What so poignantly warms me
as I walk by brambles blooming faintly white
renews my resolve to return
to the far–off capital.

F ATHER AND CHILD

I hurried back from town,
whimpering offspring in tow—
a poor father unable to grant his child's wish.
She gave up and fell asleep.
Dried tears track her cheeks.
It feels like rain.

M EMORIES OF SNOW*

Snow falls.
Snow falls from those exquisite branch tips
even as the wagtail
shakes snow pellets
into the splendor of soft sunbeams.

Snow falls as it did when Mother strapped me to her back.
Ah, the tenderness in "Mommy" as I called to her—
terrified by my first glimpse
of snow.

A NTS

Ants on mulberries.
Ants blacker than mulberries.
Ants clinging fast
lest they slip.

Sea's roar.
Again ... the roar of the sea.

L ATE SUMMER*

A squash tendril creeps up to the platform
of this tiny train stop.

A ladybug peers from the folds
in a closed bud.

The commuter train arrives.
No one gets on.
No one gets off.

The young ticker taker nonchalantly punches
a millet leaf growing by the fence.

NOTES ON EARLY AUTUMN *

Those winds blowing through cracks in the kitchen wall—
breaths of autumn.
Oh, my mind startles as easily
as fresh bean curd on a white plate.

Going to the grove behind our house,
I gaze awhile at sunset.
Roars from the rapids.
The wail of autumn wind.

I pocket a wrinkled leaf
for my child—
a lovely sunset in the leaf.

Already several early promises of rice.
Even sword beans sprouting
    from seeds spilled by the road
dangle their green pods
mid a line of pale red berries.

F LOWERS

Path to the orchard.
The tightly–folded ocean twinkles.
Stormy winds
strip many butterflies from blooms.

Autumn Grass

The child lay fast asleep.
Jumbo ants on bread crumbs,
traces of autumn on tableware, on handkerchiefs.
And nearby, the sea.
Surf sounds seem to breathe with the sleeping child.

Autumn Day (ii)

Let tea leaves expand
in the hot water I pour on them.
Let the deep green so long held in swell full
—with reticence.

Night School Student *

The pointer's shadow
stretches and shrinks
across the wall maps.

At pauses in the teacher's talk,
insect voices fill the room.

The bliss of study
but, oh, what grief.

A katydid greener than the color of Siberia
alights on my text,
flourishes its feelers.

At a Train Stop *

The inbound had just pulled out.
The pungent odor of a citron tree
hovers over this forsaken train stop.
A woman who also seems to have missed the train
rests on a bench and begins to knit.
Shriveled, unhatched moth eggs stick to the enormous clock face
labeled OUT OF ORDER.

WINTER (i) *

Those days I wore a long black cape.

At night I purposely dimmed my lamp
and immersed myself in Dostoyevski.
How powerfully his dreary tales gripped!

A thin–blooded sunset
stained the galley window of the *Café Automne*.
A girl was washing dishes alone.
I liked her
though I didn't even know her name.

My teeth bothered me then.
Day after depressing day bothered me like toothaches.
Wearing my long black cape,
I walked across campus through dry winds.
In my cavities Mother sits, on the verge of tears.

POET OF THE *RUBAIYAT**

The carcass of a mosquito and a four–leaf clover fell out when,
for the first time in years, I opened my *Rubaiyat*.
This book preserves ancient autumn nights,
    hills under springtime sun...
recollections that now come back to me.

Omar Khayyam, poet of the *Rubaiyat*.
I, too, streamed like a creek to this land.
Like wind through the wilds,
    I'm but a single person passing through.

Omar Khayyam, poet of fine wine, roses, and the new moon!
Buried among roses,
you sleep under a Persian blue sky
on the outskirts of Nishapur, the old capital.
In this small East Asian island country,
I write of unquenchable solitude, deprivation, despair.

HOUSE

Rain–scattered *yusuraume*
lie around the entrance.

That's where you live
bringing up your children and waiting for their father
who may never return.

L ITERARY FRAGMENT (i) *

When cloud shadows visit clumps of dahlias,
when a solitary sunflower opens its eye
and reaches high...

the crossing gate will still quiver
and echoes from the shrinking train
will copy the roar of early summer seas.

Today's setting sun.
The lovely sun sets.
Cabbages firmly hug their hearts.

D AILY CHORE

Each morning I gather the eggs.
The usual train–smoke shadows come
to peek into the chicken coop.
Eggs still warm on the straw,
the mute hens gawk at me.
Momentarily I feel the thief.

G ROVE (ii) *

The path through the grove melts away.
Even the rapids dissolve into distance.
I sit under a tree
on a rock chilled by those summer cicada chirrups
soaked up during the heat.

H EIGHTS *

Not even the pleats in those mountains
conceal the butterfly's white.
Cha blossoms,
tsuwabuki blooms,
a lustily–singing jay,
and...the sea.

ⓄLD HOUSE *

With two or three others,
I lived a time in that house.
Those days poverty was pride,
misery a joy.

I still vividly recall
the second–floor window facing south,
the lone geranium pot,
a time–worn oil painting on the wall.

People I've never seen live there now.
Bright light spills onto the street.
Voices and music fill my ears.

They're all mine.
They were mine...once.
I left them behind in that house—
I'm sure.

ⓁATE SPRING (ii)*

In dirt moist from a midnight rain,
I plant a walnut—
a *Juglans Sieboldiana* my teacher gave me.
(Whatever makes that hard seed burst in the soil?)

I drink goat's milk
under a cherry tree already in bloom.
There's a nick on the rim of my cup
and a picture of a Spanish galleon
(sails billowing in the breeze).

No one else here.
Merely passing near is enough
to shake *yukiyanagi* petals loose.

I consider getting a cat.
A blue one'd be fine,
but even a white one will do.
I ask my daughter, just back from the charity concert,
"Was the light on in that window?" •

Unable to sleep,
I turn my light back on.
A butterfly that strayed into my room
rambles the rim of my cup.

T O TOKYO——FOR ÔMI TAKUJI*

Hoping to make some money for a trip to Tokyo,
I braid rope.

Nothing special to do in Tokyo.
I just think it's time to mourn my youth
lost in the university district where I lived long ago
(by now, Takuji, we have more past than future).
Yet whenever I get enough together, the train fare doubles.
I just can't work the braider fast enough to keep up with fares.
I've treadled enough to walk to Tokyo by now.
I've braided enough rope to reach Hokkaido.

Hands in pockets, my child comes back to where I work,
a room overlooking withered fields.
She says there was a thick layer of ice
    on the pond this morning.
Spreading her frosty red berries on the *engawa*,
she tells me she'll make some Christmas candy.

F ARMING POEMS
Heavy Frost
Buckwheat stems under the sickle—
as pink
as bird legs...
or the numb hands of the child
who tagged along
and watches from the path.

Harvesting Rice
I eat my lunch leaning against the sheaves.
I reap the rice. I eat rice for lunch.
How pathetic!
This year's rice on the ground,
last year's in my lunch.

Out Front
This splendid weather
bleaches out the green in drying racks.
Everything drying dries perfectly,
putting distant hills to sleep.
A feather and a crimson berry
lie on unhusked winter rice.

POETRY

PART III — 1950–1958

A. JUVENILE POEMS

and others

『児童詩集』その他

CHRISTMAS EVE

Sounds of wind—
chorusing voices that vanish into space
join now to carol
at the doorways of every home.

Each sparkling star—
a tinkle from a frozen bell,
a teardrop of prayers and love
from people I do not know.

Christmas!
My God

has given me again this year
only chills that ice the mind.

EXACTA TICKET*

In the end I brought it with qualms
for 1 and 6 to win and place.
What paid was 6 and 1.
If only I'd made a slight switch
in my one • six hunch.
Oh, just a slight switch for my poetry
——for me.

SPRING BELL*

Children! Toll the bell,
toll it gingerly.

At noon on this fleeting spring day,
a peach grove peeks through the bamboo thicket. •

Children! Toll the bell,
gingerly.

Send the sounds sleeping in it
off into the distance.
Let them range far, far into distance.

Children!
Toll the bell.

At noon on this fleeting spring day,
hills pulse in youthful prime.

VALLEY *

The waterwheel turns leisurely
to keep nearby plum blossoms from scattering.

Girls pass each other along the valley trail,
their new straw baskets filled with pussy willows.

A mountain bunting's ceaseless song
spurs trees to bud.

I wonder who chatted here?
Trampled butterburs.
Mounds of cigarette butts.

NEW LEAVES ON CHERRY TREES (i) *

Afternoon at a sea–side park.
Every cherry tree fully clothed in green.
Having shed yesterday's fragile blooms,
the trees now sink deep in proud repose.

SONG OF THE REED (i)*

A reed warbler behind the cotton ginnery
chirrups during lulls in the clatter of the gin.
A daytime moon
soaks its shadow in the water.

South winds—blow on!
A ladybug alit on me,
so for some time now my back's been itchy.

South winds—blow on!
Feet so chilled,
head hot enough to burn.

RIVER*

Sun began sinking toward me.
It seems somehow to have dropped into town.
Stone embankments to the right, to the left,
     chomp me like white fangs.
Light flushed from windows
has already made my face filthy....
(How far, I wonder, to the sea?)

Sayonara.
Sayonara.
A nameless flower
blooming on the hip of the embankment
gently sheds its pollen over me.

NEW LEAVES ON CHERRY TREES (ii) *

Skies float among intermingled branches,
midst leaves trembling with excitement—
why is this such an uncommonly lovely sight?
It's because the trees preserve the vision
of their blooming,
because they pulse with peace and pride
after the curtain falls on their stunning show.

WINTER NIGHT

Still night has come,
time to lean on loneliness
the way I lean, chin in hand,
on my nicked–up desk.
Even north winds wailing steadily since dawn
have left now for places
where I suppose fierce rage and regrets as well
can find repose....
This thought strangely soothes my mind.

HARBOR TOWN *

Rain has poured since dawn
on canna blossoms—summer's embers.
The ship I just left
whistles wearily.

LITERARY FRAGMENT (ii)*

When cloud shadows visited
clumped dahlias,
when the lone sunflower reaching high
opened its eye...

the crossing gate was still quivering...
echoes of the off–dashing train
like the roar of an early summer sea.

Sun begins to sink.
The lovely sun sinks.
Onions squeeze their cores.

JUNE SKETCHES*

The rains come. Rains come. They come scurrying at evening—and always from those woods where the cuckoo sings its plaintive tunes. Rain upends butterbur leaves, glistens beards of ripened barley, tramples the scent of gardenias in our yard.

DELUGE*

Rain, rain, endless rain. Though it washes homes and fields away, the torrent at last tapers off. But what of the immeasurable torrent engulfing local news —— Killers, families wiped out by murder and suicide ...?

LIGHTNING (i)*

Lightning flashes in the distant sky. A night when water drains hurriedly from paddies. A reed–thin bolt pastes a country landscape on my window. A massive zelkova reaches solitary from the paddy.

WHITE FANGS

An alluring autumn noon conceals its fangs. When a crossing gate unexpectedly checkmates me in town, or when I walk along a fence in a hushed residential area and see green fruit testing its weight on a branch tip...those fangs suddenly sink into my shoulders with fearful force!

Oh, the chill, the chill!

DAY AFTER DAY *

Autumn. Morning. Tugging fragrant olive scents, people head for the train station, for their bus stops. No, the aromas trail them like puppies.

Autumn. Morning. Stifling belches from their *miso* soup, people head for the train station, for their bus stops. No, they stifle daily griefs meeker than eggplant in *miso*.

TIME

Scents of autumn on this year's straw.
Glints of fall on each trampled, unhulled rice grain.
Ah, flapping its wings like Time, a bird flies up
from tree to tree, from tree to sky.

WINTER (ii) *

I'd come through this wintering field to see the train. Dragged by my son. We hurried but missed it. The three P.M. freight had passed not a moment before.

Putting an ear to the tracks, the lad listens to the train's receding echo. Lighting my cigarette, I reach for the tail of the train's stretched whistle, still hovering close.

QUEUE

Life bores and depresses, regardless of what you do. For example, I'm queued up waiting for the bus. It's a long, long queue. I can't stir from my place in line. Won't someone take me away from here? Won't someone take me off?

I WANT ...

to be as mute as coal,
to burn as fierce as coal.

WINTER GROVE

An echo resounds like a gunshot.
Barren branches merge like gun sights.
You in the distance,
take aim from where you are. —— Shoot!
You in the distance:
a single shot will fell me.
Stopping your round deep within,
I'll breathe my last.

SONGS AND WINGS

Water told the cloud, "I once was cloud.
I had ample wings like yours."

The cloud told water, "I was water once.
I had a crystal voice like yours."

BLACK UMBRELLA

Grass invites shadows. Cloud shapes drive me off. They come directly overhead. Where shall I go? I've got to go somewhere. I feel now as though someone opens an immense black umbrella over me.

WINTER DAY (ii)

After my stroll through the fields,
I boisterously brush off the dry grass clinging to me.
(A crow primping itself.)

The mirror on the station platform
glistens like that pond.
(Ah, the pond glistens back serenely now
     from its straw–dry field.)

RED MOON*

A woman selling mackerel came by.
I took one and gossiped awhile on our *engawa*,
holding the fish wrapped in a butterbur leaf.
The mackerel vendor remembered Father,

who often read from a picture book to little me—
that old Western tale about a lamplighter
walking through town to set the gas lamps.
Father read till times like this when pages dimmed.
My long day faded to dusk.
The lamplighter in my village is the evening breeze
that makes its rounds lighting houses with an invisible wand.
I went to the well and washed the fish smell from my hands.
Over the vista of ripened barley has risen a grand moon
redder than the mackerel's eyes.

ℂ ALLER (i)*

Apparently she stopped by after I'd just stepped out. I figured she walked over through the snow. Wet boot prints tracked our entry. Reddish mud in the prints told me it was certainly she. Trickles from her umbrella at the spot where I figured she'd been looking at the potted plant. Why couldn't she wait a bit longer? —— Why leave without a word? —— Why always behave that way? Melted snow even on aralia leaves.

ⒶT THE PARK*

Sounds from the tennis courts
shuttle leisurely
between a lost time and now.

I close the book I'd been reading
and gaze into the branch–framed sky.

I carve your name
on the pale bark of a magnolia
so I'll forget it, so I won't recall.

One day my life, too, will end up
like this paperback,
leaving memories small as grass seeds
scattered through summer.

Spring locusts hum.
Bird droppings on the bronze statue
glitter like cuneiform.

AT A GRADE CROSSING (i) *

There's no reason to take this road.
Had I felt like going a bit out of my way,
a number of other paths would do.
In the end, that would have been quicker.
So much is clear to me now.
If only I'd realized it sooner,
I might not be so upset.
Perched on the horizontal gate,
a mantis the hue of withered grass
brandishes its sickles.

MEADOWLARK NEST *

I found a lark's nest.
Nobody
knows about it yet.

It's there by the mill shed
in that barley field
where you can see the clinic's red roof.

Five teeny eggs
side by side.
I've told no one about them yet.

MOUNTAIN PATH *

I began to sweat,
so I stopped to rest.

Sitting on this rock
chills me.

I see the sea.
I see the sea.

It make it disappear behind the eulalia plume
I hold.

NIGHT ON THE COUNTRYSIDE *

Night on the countryside
pitch black.
It seems the hue of soy sauce.
Only storehouse walls

are bright.

The walls float dimly white,
like *tôfu*
in soy sauce.

T RAIN SMOKE

Smoke from the locomotive
flutters like a white scarf—
over barley fields,
through leafless limbs,
into dried–out grass.
It flutters,
then promptly disappears.
It flutters,
then promptly disappears...
this morning in spring.

A FTERNOON AT THE CHALET *

No one answers.
I bet they all went up the mountain.
Someone left
a sprig of red azaleas
on the *engawa*.
The kitchen wall clock
strikes three:
Bong ... bong ... bong.
I hear the leisurely sound of its spring
winding down.

R AINBOW AND SNAIL*

The rainbow fades;
only its scarlet band remains.
A snail clings
to a silverberry leaf.

I recall them clearly.

That's when I was scolded
and went out into the field
behind our house.

INTERURBAN IN SPRING*

White straps hanging
in the spring–time interurban
swing and sway.
Fields of green wheat,
fields of scarlet vetch,
fields of yellow rape
parade past the window.
When the train goes round a bend,
when the coach pitches,
everything inside
swings together, sways together,
nearly sending me out the window—
swinging…swaying.

KATYDID *

A green katydid
lands
on my book
this cool
autumn night.
He leisurely
stirs his feelers.
The katydid landed
on the tip
of the Eiffel Tower
in my opened picture book.

BAMBOO THICKET

Grass withered.
Trees withered.
Halfway up
the dead hush
of this brushwood hill
lies a bamboo thicket.
Only there
do gentle breezes blow.

The hill resembles my little brother's head
where the clippers
had left a spot

(how long ago was that?)
around his boil.

ALL IN A ROW

All in a row,
all in a row,
little squares
on the harmonica—
fetching tunes
in every one.

All in a row,
all in a row,
square windows
on the flat—
people busy at something
in every one.

M EMORIES

Picking wild grapes,
I strayed from friends.

Mounds of white cloud
fenced sky out of the gorge.
I heard the freshet's faint gurgle.

Eating my rice balls alone,
I found a hair of Mother's
squeezed into one.

T OWN IN THE DISTANCE*

Visible
under walnut leaves,
that town in the distance.

Each time I come to fetch
bundled brushwood,
I gaze at that town. •

I can go only twice a year:
Obon—New Year's.
That town....

I pick up a stone.
I fling it
with all my might.

Heating the Bath Water (ii)

A baby pheasant peeps
on the hill behind our house.

Why doesn't it start,
this fire for our bath water?

The chick still peeps
its charming peep.

Why doesn't it start,
this fire for our bath water?

Smoke smarts my eyes.
They answer with a tear.

Quiet Evening *

I have no idea what happened
to the princess the knaves carried off,
or to the prince who galloped off to find her.

Father left
in the middle of the tale.
I wonder if the two managed to meet again?

In the distance,
flames in fields being burnt over
flicker faintly...
dusk serene.

ⓄNE DAY IN THE KITCHEN

"I'm home," I called.
Silence.

Mother likely went somewhere.
And I was given this cherry blossom sprig for her!

I hear grumbles
from a dark corner.

I check.
Clams in a basket grumbling,
grumbling to themselves.

ⒽIDE AND SEEK

I hide behind sheaves of straw
made from this year's rice.
Smells of autumn sun.

There's the tagger.
Sounds of his *zôri*
come toward me,
pass by.

Close behind,
a wren comes along
flit–flit–flitting its tail.

ⒶPPLES*

My big brother often told me that apples are best
munched skin and all!
Whenever he said it, he munched one,
skin and all.

Late on a chilly autumn night,
I peel the skin from my apple,
cutting it as thin as I can.
Mother lights the incense on our home altar.
My brother died
fighting in the tropics
long, long ago.

C ITY SHOWER (i)*

Late autumn rain,
a passing squall.
I keep dry under the canopy of a clothing store.
Sun soon peeks out again.
Wet sidewalks mirror the hulking department store,
mirror bare trees lining the boulevard,
mirror people,
horses,
carts...
everything.

P ATH THROUGH THE FIELDS

My aunt
pulled down a corner of her shawl
and wrapped it round my neck.

That long chilly path
through the fields.

Stacked sheaves huddle together,
warming each other
like living things.

That long chilly path
through the fields.

L ITTLE HARBOR TOWN*

Little harbor town
that Mother and I passed through
on the train....

Somebody's
half–eaten ice cream
melting on a window ledge.

As the train waited at the stop,
I heard wailing waves,
a chirruping cicada.

That much I clearly recall.
I passed through thinking
I'd not likely come a second time
to this quiet little harbor town.

C HRISTMAS NIGHT*

A freight train
scatters sparks
over the tracks.

Icy winds
this Christmas night.

Sparks from the locomotive
break up and disappear
into tiny,
star–like bits.

I watched them
through icy winds
this Christmas night.

T O A FRIEND IN THE CAPITAL*

I grew the rice myself
and pounded it into *mochi*,
so I'm sending you a little.
I tied the package tight,
cramming half a year of my life into it.
I made the rope, too.
Have a nice New Year;
send me some interesting news.
Don't think about how I wince
when the rope chafes my chapped hands.

H ORIZONTAL BAR

Look!
When I jump
to grasp
the horizontal bar,
I grip
the snowy summit
of that distant peak
as well.

M Y FATHER*

Mornings
I boarded a rush–hour train
and stood before people reading newsprint.
Behind the papers,
mustaches and glasses.

When he sat down to breakfast,
my father also
opened up his paper.
Mornings were always like that.

B. FLUTE PLAYER

and others

『笛を吹くひと』その他

IN TOWN

Shadows from tall buildings
fence each other.
The clover
grumbles.

OVER SHADED ROCKS

Stones mince flowing water.
Stones dissolve into running water
then perch on benches of shimmering air.

INDOOR MUSIC

The door shut,
water sings in the glass.
A distant street scene
in a lemon slice.

UNDER SHARED SKIES——HIROSHIMA REPORTAGE*

I. FROM HIJIYAMA

Summer again. Another August 6. Hiroshima's skies stretch out, as they
did that day. Soaring clouds shadow memories. A three–minute drive and
we're on Hijiyama. From Lookout Point I watch a monstrous flame pillar
that white clouds paint—flames of illusion. I scan the city fanning out to-
ward the Inland Sea. These flames of life have in fact raged for a decade.

The Atomic Bomb Dome appears to sit in my palm. The gutted, rust–
colored City Hall, unchanged since the bombing. Visible, too, Peace
Memorial Park and several sparkling, serpentine rivers.

147

Cicadas humming in Hijiyama's oppressively green verdure kindle fierce memories. Behind me, capped with an arching Quonset–like roof, the Atomic Bomb Casualty Commission Laboratory Building. From its windows, the endless chatter of typewriters. Is that the clatter of a rotary press as well? ... Sounds akin to pattering rain. I can't banish these festering lesions. Beckoning streets queue up over memories, over scars.

II.   ATOMIC BOMB DOME
Wreathed in barbed wire, the Dome stretches its morning shadow over ripples on the river. I see the soles of those who on that day scurried up those spiral stairs...into heaven.... That staircase silhouette now twists into summer grass.

Empty windows—eternally gaping eyes. Flocks of sparrows build nests nearby. We wondered: Shouldn't those be doves making nests? But sparrows better fit these ruins. Chirping together, they fly up, flit down. Straw scraps dangle from their nests. Droppings sparkle here or there on crumbling walls.

The shadow of death on the stone walk in front of the Sumitomo Bank— gone now. A small iron railing rings its site. A single decade obliterated that form. Rather, people carried the shadow off bit by bit. Whenever at the heat of day they scuffed down the scorched walk, each stepped on that form.

Eyes cast down, I, too, plant my foot there. Sometime, somewhere, we may again have to print such a silhouette on stone.

III.   BEFORE THE CENOTAPH
A monstrous bus stopped, disgorged its tourists in front of the A–Bomb Cenotaph in Peace Memorial Park. In the distance, the Dome looms over the Cenotaph vault, patterned after an ancient *haniwa*. From here, the Dome's empty windows seem to smile sorely over the phrase: *The error shall not be repeated.* The Dome recedes then fades from view as we leave the Cenotaph and head for the museum, its contours suggesting a bird cage.

The displays freeze my cheeks, chilling me more deeply than the Dome. The clock's red–rusted hands point still to that fatal moment. Something crumbles, dissolves into sweat and heat, then coils round me, bonds like glue. The tourists move on. Someone prays before the Cenotaph. The man has a pull cart and a small child with him. Collapsed in a heap, he's there a long while. Empty juice cans jammed on his cart drip yellow liquid over the green clover.
>   *Daddy, let's go home.*
>   *Come on, Daddy, let's go.*

The child pulls on Father's jacket from behind. This boy—a fresh seed fallen on the atomic desert with no shred of that memory in him—badgers his father to take him home.

IV.   VISION OF A FLOWER

Children's straw hats and insect nets appear and disappear among grasses in the castle ruins. Where once one heard barked commands and clinking bayonets, now only weeds grow rife. Hara Tamiki's poetry stele stands among them. Crowded by grass scents, we sit near the stele. It's impossible now to decipher the inscription unless one knows the text:

> Memories chiseled on the stone of that far–off morn...
> shadows on sandy loam.
> In the heart of our crumbled land,
> one glimpse of a solitary bloom.

Someone even made off with the stele's brass plate inscribed with Satô Haruo's calligraphy.

Why can't Hara—this committed poet who loved peace more than any-one—find repose...even in his grave? When what long ago should have disappeared survives, why is it that what ought not have disappeared becomes so readily trampled on? Hot water spouting from a half–shut tap arcs tiny bows. We think of the many things someone should more securely shut.

V.   ATOMIC MAIDENS

Atomic Maiden "H" says that whenever heat builds up in concrete struc-tures, she feels stifled and her cheeks tingle. Warm evening sunlight from the hospital window reddens the keloids on her cheeks and arms. She makes it a point then to put on another layer of rouge.

Only white lace gloves can hide the scar furrows on her arms. August's burning light brings to mind those hundreds of thousands of faces and arms that lace curtains screen in row houses.

> I've just written my Dog Day cards. Most to a hand-
> ful of convalescing friends at work. They have about
> half the blood that normal people have. All along,
> they've survived by swallowing raw blood at night.

"H" continues: "I try to live for a day that will come—no, that must come. That's my prayer." Canna flowers on the hospital grounds bloom as scarlet as the fires of memory that have smoldered through the last decade. The people "H" invariably appealed to, written on ballots dripping blood, never responded.

Nearby, the Memorial Cathedral for World Peace; its bells peal evening. I pray not just to God above, nor yet about the rouge or the lace gloves...but for the blessed day that may blot up all these memories, all these scars.

VI. CATHEDRAL SCAFFOLDING

The peals linger pleasantly, soothing those massive lesions that Hijiyama reopened. Dusk's slanting sun creates stencils of ghostly light and shade on the cathedral's brick wall. Inside, they recently held a memorial service for Atomic Maiden "N," who died in America during treatment. Near the shimmering stained glass, one still hears the pipe organ and chanted prayers....
"H" recites her poem to "N":

> Maiden of Destiny,
> you returned to your native village
> where black rain still falls...
> the you in that tiny white box.

Push that button in the shared skies of the sun we also share...and you set up one person here, dog another for a decade through Purgatory, take yet another to an invisible world.

A scaffolding stood near the oleanders by the Cathedral entrance. A priest occupying a bench on the grounds muttered words that continue to haunt me:

> They've been repairing that section for ages by now.
> They're still at it, as you see. Nobody knows how
> many years it'll take. Maybe they'll never finish this
> job, however long they work.

AUTUMN DAY (iii) *

He's been living alone
since his wife left him.
He straps the baby to his back
and hangs a shopping basket on his arm,
carrot tops and radish leaves exposed.
Only friends know about the paperbacks—
the Rimbaud and Baudelaire—buried at the bottom.
He always
displays his books inconspicuously,
though if he could he'd hang the baby on an arm
and strap the verse to his back.

One arm bandaged
(certainly he was drunk again last night),
he apparently dozed off
while sitting on the balcony
of his third–floor apartment.
Back against the wobbly railing,

he seemed about to tumble down.

Below his third–floor perch—bare asphalt,
so if he fell he wouldn't survive.
Then I suspect that he and his poetry
(not to mention yours and mine)
could sprawl out—a sorry sight—and sleep in peace.

He turned his head dreamily my way.
I doubt he noticed me standing by the road.
Suddenly the baby cried.
Getting up turtle like,
he vanished unsteadily into his flat.

S OUTHWIND (i)*

Blood stains the grass.
The hen
being plucked
flies endlessly up
in her plumage.

E VENING FOREST

I see fire,
   I see fire,
      I see fire—
black as basalt.

S PARKLING INCESSANTLY

Sparkling incessantly,
the waterwheel turns
only for those primed for gushing water.
Interminably agitated and brimming with fragrance,
the mill hulls grain
only for those primed to inspire themselves....
Inside and outside separated,
sparkle and scent brimming side by side—
like links between mind and act.
Through crevices in the mill wall,
straw–hued sunlight peers now like a giant eye
at that lovely harmony, that lovely yield.

S UMMER SONG*

Herman Hesse wrote poetry
about what no one can hoard for long:
The verdant green of young trees.
A cuckoo cry in the woods.
Full moon on the hillside.

But in the end we never forfeit them, either.
Like veins in a leaf,
they burrow deep into rods of light
where they wait and age.

Stern summer!
Who will gather me in,
who will plant and nurture me
like barley, like rice?

Who ceaselessly brushes aside white clouds for the sun,
for that vast eye that never sleeps?

M Y WAY (i)*

My way through the grove vanishes,
leaping into sunset
like a drying rack.

C OUNTRY

Rain let up.
Horses shut their eyes.
Thorns of light pulled
one by one
from widely–scattered straw.

S OUTHWIND (ii)*

Bent neck,
closed eyes,
blood trickling on the grass—
the hen
being plucked
keeps flying up
with her plumage.

I TURN TO VAPOR

I turn instantly to vapor
with but a single pass
over the Bunsen burner.
Evaporated,
I'm no longer
in the furiously bubbling
flask.
Oh, that eternally hot hand
holding the heated glass!

YOU ON THE FLUTE *

You on the flute!
When you blow my flute,
I'll leave.
When you play enraptured,
I'll be gone,
flying hurriedly
from your fingertips,
from your moist mouthpiece.
On this lovely midnoon
I'll retreat
into blooming flowers,
into flowing waters…
leaving you behind,
ever farther behind.
You on the flute!
When you blow my flute,
when you change *Sein* to *Sollen*,
that's when I'll be gone.
You on the flute…
Hear!

WINTER FOUNTAIN

A fountain is loveliest
without water,
for into that chilled space
I then can sketch
what doesn't meet the eye. •

I sketch the fountain's high,
dazzling spurt,
the plunge that savagely impales.

INDOOR GAMES

– 1 –

The door opens
with a bang.
  (I close my me.)

The door shuts
with a bang.
  (I open my me.)

– 2 –

I turn the light on.
  (Someone, that much darker.)

I turn the light off.
  (Someone, that much lighter.)

– 3 –

I put on my coat.
  (You check yours.)

I take off my coat.
  (You reclaim yours.)

– 4 –

I read a book.
  (Someone behind me.)

I lay it down.
  (Gone.)

LIGHTNING (ii)

From night's murky core
lightning reaches out and seizes

—houses and trees.
—sleeping factory windows.

—a clump of rushes.
—feeble glints of water in the cove.

Then it quickly abandons them
to the pitch dark
where they lie.

From night's murky depths,
lightning reaches out and seizes
that lone path through the field
…and me on it.

Instantly my heart cries out:
Don't leave me here.
Take me off—
abandon me
elsewhere!

DISTANT VIEWS

– 1 –

Far in the distance
almost beyond sight,
trailing off
into sky, into water,
a dot at the tip of the cape:
Me!
At a point
beyond that point,
not rock,
not water,
not sky,
neither lingering
nor leaving—
it's me,
me.

– 2 –

A cliff.
Sky and sea sprawl out around the cape.
Midnoon waves
wash the bluff
with monotonous tenacity.
Then

a monster bus drives up
to disgorge its tourists.
Actually,
you're the gorgeous distant view
to which I'm invariably driven...
I the disgorged
bile.

ℂ HANSON D'AMOUR*

– 1 –

Suddenly my lamp darkens
because you light your brighter lamp
by mine.
My darkness darkens as night wears on.

– 2 –

Wretchedly spellbound,
I stand under your lamp.
As I look up at you,
a shadow suddenly reaches out
and your light flickers.
I, too, am snuffed out then—
nothing left of me
in night's wind.

– 3 –

I'm a cold black object,
a pair of pruning shears
laid aside after clipping flowers.
Yet I wait
greedily
for supple stems
to touch my blades.

– 4 –

One star lit,
its white weaker than clover.
I'm shivering on the grass.
It seems I've been here some time.
I'll go home shortly
and grope for
the light in my room.
Once on, I suppose I'll know
that I'm still here—

stretched out on this chilling grass.
Once circled by warm light,
I'll know for sure.
Well, I'm going home for a second,
just a bit.

Ⅿ EMORIES OF FIRE——MOURNING HIROSHIMA VICTIMS*

However far they stretch their gentle fingers
from the fence around that building,
vines cannot grasp the cloud.
Though floating near their fingertips,
it's very, very far away.

However softly the last locust buzzes
on that branch tip,
its hum quickly turns violent with frenzy.
Whatever had fallen silent wakens as one.

Whenever I stop at a street corner
or at a grade crossing in the country,
I tread my shadow.

However distant the sun,
however that form burnt then into the walk may fade,
I'll tread the shadows of those still here
with more force, more friendship, more fervor.

Ⅎ HE DEPARTED*

A partly–closed shutter
clatters in night wind.
Pulling up,
I listen to the racket and think,
this is how it was when you stepped out.

How many days since then?
Only that dilapidated shutter
clattering endlessly
seems still to wait for you.

I watch
you come home,

your cape flapping like wings.
I watch you mount the hedge fence
and enter your room from the roof
as night winds tug the shutter,
each gust opening it, closing it.

Pulling up,
I watch from under the feeble street light.

QUOTIDIAN SEAT

I knot my tie.
I knot up each day
with the most attractive cloth I can find.
Then I board the train
to hang from a leather strap.
You're sitting there,
always
directly in front of me.
Oh, how it chills—
that thick newspaper wall
spread against me,
that ever stretched–out crossing gate.

BLACK FLIES*

Crammed into cattle cars,
the cows rub heads,
eyes vaguely open.

Black flies
journey
on the cattle.

The cows
low gloomily
at the fate awaiting them.

The black flies
have come a long way—
gorged with blood,
jostled by the train,
shooed by the slow and constant swish of tails.

Where do you suppose such tenacious,

such merciless traveling companions will end up
when finally
the cows
become cuts of beef
hanging on hooks...
when, in due course,
the hooks dangle empty
in space?

B ANK

At that spot,
people enter,
people leave.
They enter
and leave—
leave
and enter.

What is it?
What do you suppose it is—
that gigantic beast
whose black craw opens
onto seething summer streets?

Those it unconcernedly chomps into,
drinks up,
spits out,
voids
without ingesting or digesting them,
one after
the other
after the other...
who are they?
What do you suppose they are
—those near the great beast,
those like windshield cleaner,
those on the other side
of that viscous,
transparent stuff ...
those who cordially
gather,
who join together,
incessantly astir?

S CENES*

– 1 –

Town's low eaves warp
and stretch
like discarded scarves.

Flicking its whistle's invisible tail,
the afternoon freight passes.
On that edge of town,
straw–dry fields,
just straw–dry fields.
Only the crossing gate
sparkles fresh,
stirs fresh—
now releasing the unseen,
now restraining it.

– 2 –

The canal zigzags,
not a cloud mirrored on its riled face.
Far behind it, a lovely street scene;
ahead, an expanse of reeds.
At that spot, pedestrians straighten their caps.
Rustling reeds erase their presence
like chalk on a blackboard.
Sun's blood–red afterglow begins turning
the reeds to rust.

– 3 –

Bright rusted chains
reach from water into space.
Such peace, such stillness
in what lies submerged.
Rustling reeds.
A warbler at song.

Look! Only what soars beyond the surface
can observe itself
twisting on the water
ember hot.
Rustling reeds.
A warbler at song.

– 4 –

An uncoupled boxcar
clanks to a stop.
It no longer moves.
It stands still, like it or not.
Cut free, now motionless—
merely an inorganic chunk of matter
under summer's glare.
Look! Sun–cast shadows
stretching longer, ever longer,
saturate
the boxcar's ferrous flanks.

Some cars enter the yard
loaded with cattle and timber.
Like it or not, they move…somewhere.
Coupled, they move by invisible force.
—Cattle with wearily huddled heads,
your tongues will soon be taken
      like grubby third–class tickets.
—Somebody uses his parasol tip to jab at resin
oozing like poems
from the cut ends of stacked logs.

Lumps of coal in storage bins
glisten blackly hot,
ignorant of how to fire themselves.
Not even sun's most radiant heat can light them.
Those hard little bits
dream only of fire.
In dreams,
several slip through the slats
into lush grass clumps.

Everything that moves,
that had been coupled,
that huddled together,
has by now left.
Not a one remains.
Not one returns.
A sizable cloud shadow settles
on the blazing platform.

MORNING (ii)

The lady gatekeeper reads a book.
A squash runner imitates the crossing gate.
The sea immediately beyond.
A darting lizard glances up at me.

SPRING VALLEY*

I meet a bridal party
on the narrow valley path.
An evening deep with mist.

Where could they be headed?
One by one the haloes of their paper lanterns
vanish along the stream.
An evening deep with mist.

Evening deep with mist.
The hand holding my lantern
still a bit chilled.

Beguiled, I gaze after the party.
Butterbur stalks fatten at my feet.

AT THE TEMPLE*

The pillars quite black,
floorboards also glistening black,
even roaches polished black.

At twilight, the bamboo grove
nearly touches the scullery window.

I sit as cool as the *tôfu*
soaking in a bucket.
A cuckoo sighs.
I hear peeling bamboo shoots.

AUTUMN DAY (iv)

A goat by a slat fence basks in the sun.
(Doesn't he look like a zebra?)
One or two butterflies chase their shadows.
Hunt for them.

MY HOMETOWN (ii)*

Everyone apparently went to the festival.
The entire village seems deserted.
Bracken soaks
in a bucket on our *engawa*.
Sounds of flute and drum float in on the breeze.
Leisurely trailing the train,
smoke from the two P.M. inbound scatters shadows.
A startled hen takes wing....
Ah, my native village.
I would always feel as renewed and lonely
as leaves garnishing my box–lunch *sushi*.
(I've come home today to savor that feeling.)
Suddenly the kitchen clock chimes.
I hear its spring unwinding, too...
one tear
like a drip from a leaky tap.

ON A WINTER FIELD

Sitting on withered grass,
I pick up a stone to strike the hobnail.
I strike what would leave me,
strike it hard.

YOUTHFUL DAYS (ii)

I sit on browned turf.
Behind me,
winter sun lays warm hands on my shoulders,
hands charged with love and grief.

I recall: —— The hands of people kind to me,
enormous hands ever stretching gently from behind.

I recall: —— Hands I unfailingly brushed away...balking,
at times gnashing my teeth.

Why? Why act that way?
No particular reason.

I stand, turn up my overcoat collar,
dash pell–mell down the withered slope.

WREN'S SONG *

I'm returning to the countryside.
I'm going back alone.
City's evening skies—I gaze at them awhile
through bramble druplets on the hill
as I chirp hurriedly over withered fields.
But I'm going home.
Awaiting me there:
drying–rack castles, straw–mound forts,
my tiny, tiny world.
Think of wind's roar that rousts you late at night
as my song.
Consider it my broken flute.

FEBRUARY*

My boy came home from playing in the fields.
He said the sun went down and he felt chilled.
He smelled like burnt–over fields,
like charred eulalia fronds, briars, and dry grass.

And now
I lean on my late–night desk,
calmly lighting private fires
to my mind,
to the dry grasses in my mind.

GLOOMY PAINTING

At an exhibition in a country town, I saw a picture you'd painted long
ago: a scene from a rundown section of Tokyo where I, too, once lived. An
ashen sky and rows of squalid roofs. —— I saw that beautiful rainbow
arcing even now in the distance, and those ambitious dreams ensconced be-
neath it. I wondered whether the painting's gloomy colors didn't serve to
calm it down, and whether it wasn't set in a crude frame to keep it from
soaring off. I, too, exist (both my yellow skin and my fleshless ribs) for
what goes sparkling off from my innermost self.

I gazed glumly at your painting…till a young woman started locking the
gallery doors.

Winter Rainbow

A rainbow appeared
as I crossed the bridge over the tracks.
Though just beginning to fade, it was breathtaking.
I thought of calling it to someone's attention
when a smoke puff from a locomotive scattered it
in an instant.
(I often have memories like that.)
I glanced back from the wicket.
Of course, the bow was gone.

Mallard

How long has it been? The fellow who shot me from behind the rushes has left by now. Lying near the roots of a tree deep in those woods on the bank of the marsh, I watch night's crystal sky through branch gaps. Blood dripping from my wound makes faint sounds on crinkled leaves...so very far away. I listen to the marsh freezing, dried grass and water chestnuts floating on it. I watch thousands of stars sparkle like wounds in the sky. Indeed, my bullet hole seems to sparkle, too.

Mountain Inn*

Time glitters eternally
like a waterwheel sated with water.
Time stands eternally still
like a waterwheel famished for water.
Sitting on a rickety cane chair at the inn,
I read Hudson on natural history,
then two Katherine Mansfield short stories.
Toward evening,
rain drenches the woods, drenches the lake.
That sweetfish now but a head on my plate
     continues staring with its black eyes—serenely—
into something dark, something cold.
I sleep, my gooseflesh limning the lake under rain.

Adolescence *

White clouds flocked together like sheep. They moved bit by bit in the wind. I tossed them some extra bread. I spread grass for them around this hill, see?

Young, I spoke only of lofty things—knotting eulalia fronds like this.

Even now sheep flock there. They move bit by bit in the wind. Dammit! I shake my cane at them.

L UNA PARK*

Grass grows lush.
The road
sinks deep
into luxuriance.

Clouds
embrace
oval warmths
in the water.

The fountain
rises tirelessly,
stretching its long shadow
over benches.

A warbler
sings itself awake;
a snail with a leaf umbrella
sleeps even through the green storm.

Ah, here
our youthful days
always succumbed with ease,
like iridescent beetles.

Yes, when we
leave here
we'll trample all things,
snapping them
like throwaway
chopsticks.

E ACH CHILLY GUST*

Every reed rusts.
Not even the blood–red hue of sunset's glow
can spark them.

Each gust of chilly wind
pales evening's flush.
Both the surface of the cove and the reeds darken
bit by bit.
Rusting and hanging their heads,
rustling reeds
ponder the blood–red hues
lost to each chilly gust.

𝕋 EN YEARS*

Air raid sirens blackened everything.
Nothing bright in night skies but the Milky Way
or the distant glow of the city in flames.
Gnashing my teeth on the riverbank,
I often saw stripped–off smartweed spikes
on the water.
I need only drop memory's ebony cloth
to relive what I felt then.
Sitting square shouldered in the dark,
our haiku teacher talked for some time
of Tu Fu,
describing this loyal poet's war–time miseries:
"Starving three years on rugged mountain trails."
"Gibbons weeping for me at high noon."
Saying goodbye, I groped out of the yard.
A small pomegranate wet with evening dew
touched my shoulder.
I relished in my palm
the forgotten weight of that season.
The Milky Way dwindled dream like.
Our teacher disappeared like the smartweed spikes.
Soon the pomegranate will fruit again.

𝔽 ELLED TREE

Today I stood by the roadside and watched
a tall tree sawed down.
Aware of its maturity,
the tree seemed to take the saw calmly
with a sense of satisfaction and confidence.
Even in twigs and leaves quivering on the ground,
I noted a composure born of fulfillment.

Night now.
I imagine a massive black cloth covering those scars
and stars sparkling beautifully around them.
I imagine that birds plying night skies
feel a chilly emptiness on their wings
at the height, at the spot where the tree spread out.

You who soon will saw me down,
do you suppose I, too, might know that repose, that hush
when my life ends?
Do you suppose I'll be capable then of feeling
what I felt today as I watched by the roadside?

I LOVE TO PICTURE

I love to picture:
the trickle of water deep in the hills;
sun and clouds in sky;
rampart vegetation;
boulders that drip light
and noiseless sounds.
And yet.
whenever I pass through such a place,
I slither like a fetid snake,
moving swift as a struck match.

HOTEL IN THE FOOTHILLS *

Oh, how sound they sleep,
having disposed of Camus and Sartre
as though mashing strawberries!

Rain let up.
Has it turned to wind?
Is that the rapids' roar?
The chaffing of barley ears?
Day hasn't dawned,
the lamp oil not spent,
those beetles not yet back to life.
Like parsley on the edge of a messy plate,
I bulge slightly from their sleep...
I bulge a bit from the night.

T REES

A slight breeze scuffled through fallen leaves.
Mixed with them, red ember–like objects.
The trees stood leaning into each other,
densely, distantly intermingling leaf–stripped arms.
Morning ... then dusk.
Glittering hot and huge, sun arched beyond the branches.
Stars (like eyes that exist only to be frozen within
       but to shed no tear)
twinkled as they lit up
among those densely intermingled arms.

C REAKY CHAIRS*

Creaking their chairs awhile,
all faces peer into sky.

Anchored to the shade of a large building
hangs a rainbow,
only its red band left.

I sat in this chair by the window
yesterday.
Where will I sit tomorrow...

...(testing what never melts,
what remains as perfectly clear
as the cherry in a gin fizz)...?

Tomorrow vexes me
like a packed elevator.
Tomorrow checks me
like an office door.

I imagine the rainbow will soon fade,
though we must fade
even sooner...

... fade from the chairs we briefly occupied,
fade each into his own slot...
slots more plentiful than manholes,
deeper than holes in socks.

T REELIKE

Treelike, I have a natural and a balanced bearing.
I have deep roots for anchors, for standing firm.
I have tough bark to temper heat or chill.
I have branches for touching and being touched,
green leaves for trembling with laughter.
I have a thick trunk for laying a soft mat of shade
          over afternoon lovers
and for storing the mat at dusk. I have unchanging height
          for watching the lovers leave,
balmy air, flowers—a sparkling lake
for mellowing young stallion winds that dash at me mornings.
I have blue skies for visions,
evening stars for thought,
and rings reserved for hugging my inner self.
I have no thing, so I have every thing.
I am one, so I am all.

L ANDSCAPE

I turn a corner
and town ends.

A grade crossing,
its gate down.

A brittle clump
of dried reeds.

There along the stream,
a factory with windows.

A face in one
looks my way.

A screeching freight train
slices my view.

The train snakes by
faceless,
glass–less.

Every morning, every afternoon,

a freight train screams through here.

Taking a single
stringy breath,

it heads for the tunnel,
mouth agape.

ℙ RELUDE TO AUTUMN*

Morning after morning,
fallen fruit reeks from the soil.

In afternoon's soft sunlight,
greening fruit proves its weight
on branch tips.

Sunset's stunning glow tints the smartweed.
Breezes sweep rapids' roar over the paddies.

Silkworms munching mulberries...
sounds crisp on nighttime *shôji*.
These worms will soon enter
the gloom of their cocoons.

POETRY

PART IV — 1959–1965

WINTER CROW*

Loquat flowers bloom
like powdered snow.
As lamps start to sparkle windows,
my heart and I pulse with warmths.
But, alas, I cannot share those wreaths of light.
Are peace and joy in man's realm
viewed only from afar?
Once I finish primping on this paddy ridge,
I'll leisurely stretch my wings, and then—
as though to spear the quarter
into which I point my beak—
fly off.

TO TSUNODA KAN'EI*

You walk up and I walk down
that long, long flight of stone steps
    on the hill at Senkô Temple in Onomichi.
Well ... Good–bye. ... See you tomorrow.

We pass each other
along that cheerful path lined with cherry trees
    on the hill at Senkô Temple in Onomichi.
Busy? ... Yes. ... 'Bye. ... Seeyoutomorrow.

One dark night on the hill at Senkô Temple in Onomichi,
    you walk up the stone steps
into starlight.
I walk down, into my flashlight's beam.
Sayonara. ... Sayonara.
... never to see you again.

INDOORS

The window shut tight,
no one in the room.
On the neatly–ordered desk,
an opened book, the inkwell sand dry.
Apparently the moment for a beginning,
or perhaps the wake of an ending.
Everything absolutely hushed—
only the eyes in that faded portrait on the wall
glitter sharply.
As though intimidated by them,
the ladybug peering in through a crack by the window frame
turns away, parts her back,
flies into burning light.

ONCE THERE WAS

Once there was a bird's nest
on that now barren branch tip behind the church.
Near sparkling young leaves,
a piece of straw dangling from the nest
tried to keep time with pipe organ and choir.
I always looked up fondly at that nest,
picturing little creatures bringing love in,
smaller ones eagerly awaiting it.
Once there was a time to love and be loved
near where stars dot whip–like twigs.
It's comforting to recall such scenes now
when I've turned against others and myself,
when I feel the freeze, the loneliness,
of being banished from every nest.

BEFORE KUMAHIRA TAKEJI'S POETRY STELE*

A life of poetry and wine —— How savory!

A life of poetry and wine —— How sad!

Takeji,
we would—or,
as one who belatedly strolls the same path,
I would—
stand on tiptoe

in May's burnished light and bright breezes
to peer into those,
into your dark and lovely deeps.

WHO'S THERE? *

Who's there?
Who? Who is it?
Wisteria bunches
quiver in wind.
A slight breeze with gleaming hands.

Who's there?
Who? Who is it?
A cloud that peers
through sparkling windows.
A cloud shadow tiptoes by.

Who's there?
Who? Who is it?
Visions
noise through night's abyss...
the rumble of rapids spurning sleep.

T O SOMEONE*

I see your house from here.
You seem to be lighting a fire.
Through gaps
in your wooden fence,
I notice flames in your range.

Twilight—snow the hue of loquat blooms
dazzles the eye.
Are your husband and children
sitting on the *tatami*
beyond those flames?

Like wind whipping wintered fields,
I hope to fan that fire you lit.
I hope to make it blaze.

S ONGS OF THE FOOTHILLS*

1. Morning

(Ants laid their eggs
in boots I wear to climb the hills.
The eggs dried so hard that when I walk
it feels like nuts are pinching my feet.)

On the roadside
the remains of a bonfire
quivers like a crimson *akigumi*
hanging on among wrinkled leaves
black as charred wood.
I always like to pause at such places
and warm outstretched hands in the chill
of what has not yet died out
nor even begun ....

2. Noon

(A *hônoki* leaf
flutters like a yellow butterfly
through the cypress grove.)

Water leaving terraced paddies
glistens white;
I hear it
even through dense woods.
The lad on the decoys
blows his lure.
Crouching like him by a stump,
I relish waiting intently
for the weak cries of the catch
reeled in inch by inch.
Weary of waiting,
I fervently hoped
a cloud slice might rather
touch down from sky....

3. Night

(Having read some five pages
    of Arsen'ev's *Journey to Ussuri*.)

A bright moon–lit night.
Only draining paddy water edgy.
It falls,

combines,
gathers,
melts into night.
Pop–clickety,
clickety–pop...
unmelted nuts
pelt my *engawa*.
Each time one drops,
I waken—startled
like a hen.

C ALLER (ii)

Someone standing in the heart of a withered field
calls his dog—
calls a pet he loves,
one who hasn't yet come back.

Twilight of a bitterly cold day.
I wonder if he nestles deep into his overcoat collar
as he yells
so stridently.
Could he be calling
me?

D AWN OVER THE SETO INLAND SEA *

Sea and isles,
isles and sea,
floating like the stage of the new century.
A vast energy now
invites us,
impels us over them.

The Nereids' alluring overture
already begun
in the blood–tinted light
near where clouds and water mesh.

There we'll sing airs
we couldn't sing yesterday.
We'll sing a song
after the song already sung.

We'll join voices lustily, on cue,
in lyrics that yesterday we failed to sing as one.

Sea and isles,
isles and sea,
come into view
behind night's drapes.
The throb of billowing hearts
sustains us,
lifts us over waves.

Not only do we work the curtain,
we're the chief performers—
both the marveled players
and the patrons cheering them on.

S ONG OF LOVE AND DEATH

Let's say Good–bye now.
I was as fond of you
as of that single black glove
lost under roadside trees.

Under sunset's glow,
your piano tunes
brim over and pierce...
brim over and pierce
murky ditch water
behind the church.

S ONG OF DEATH

Soon I'll die and,
turned completely to ash,
gain a freedom never known.

I'll see
with the hue of the flame that kindles me.

I'll speak
with the sound of the blast that kindles me,
and cradle •

with fresh love
the Earth that so long cradled me.

S INGING*

Singing children,
heads held high,
I'll sway my leaves and limbs for you,
like that tree by the window.

Singing children,
eyes bulging,
I'll underline the vital parts for you,
hurrying calmly along
like those fingers and feet at the piano.

Singing children,
comely, comely creatures!
I'll dash off before you finish your last brief air—
quick as that gadfly
hiding among flowers in the vase.

L ATE NIGHT WHISTLER*

Shortly after the last train,
at an hour people rarely walk these bounds
        of our country town,
someone regularly passes my house.
He whistles a passage from *La Traviata*,
or some Tchaikovsky melody—
pieces that even I am faintly familiar with.
I don't know if he's young or middle aged or
        who or where he's from.
Probably someone whose job keeps him late.
I may miss the rumble of the last train,
but his whistling usually catches my ear.
I find I hear him even if he isn't there.
When I sit alone at my desk late into the night,
I constantly remind myself
that invisible gossamer bonds relate people,
even total strangers.
I wonder if the whistler has similar thoughts
when he notices the light in my room? •

Late one December night
the familiar whistle broke off
and a bicycle bell startled me.
"Say, there's a bike here. Yours?"
The children had forgotten
to bring in the bicycle.
I hurried outside but (where had he gone?)
his whistling had already faded away.
Orion slanted sharply toward the south
in a splendidly crisp late December sky.
Mimicking the whistler,
I whirred the bell on our cold and dewy bike.

T EARLESS

Tearless,
I write poems damp with tears.
Loveless and dreamless,
I write verse drenched with love and dreams.
Never having been fulfilled,
I write of mudflats deserted by the sea.
Deprived of shining seeds and soft soil,
I write of flowers fainting from fragrance.
Poetry—glorious being...
heartless as the pen point
lost to my inkwell!

S ONG OF THE STREAM*

I turned there
like the twist of a doorknob
and ended up in town.
Sun started to sink.
Like folded handkerchiefs,
like chewed–up playing cards,
light spilled over me from windows on either side.
Exhausted, I'm unable to utter a sound.
And already so polluted!
—— Who is it? Who's singing there?
—— Factory's wastes. They're flowing from that pipe, see?

How far yet to the sea?
Sayonara. ... Sayonara.
What kind of flower is that?

Blooming from the hip of the stone embankment,
it shakes its pollen off.

DIARY EXCERPTS*

Date   Windy from morning. Wary of fire in the neighborhood.
Date   Given a lilac seedling; plant it.
Date   Once the wind died down, onion–headed stars light up.
Date   Night. Drizzle. The year's first frog.
Date   Nice weather. Bright petals spill over broad butterbur leaves.
Date   Clear skies. Visit young friend "N" and his wife, who's out.
        Has me wait till he puts the kids to bed.

MY LIFE (ii)*

Trees and flowers whisper crisply in the light.
A cloud pulls up to lay its shadow
over the gleaming fountain, over a round grass patch.

I passed through here asleep,
an infant in a buggy with the hood down.

My parents, my wife, my children, my friends:
those filled with all love and peace....

I open my eyes now to a world being shut
as though I were the last star to shine.
Cherishing what bird songs remain,
I speak my words in deep shade—
a lone tree loath to merge with dusk.

MY LIFE (iii)*

The village where I was born,
my childhood....

A single white road unwinds like a roundworm.
Houses, the wood, the grove
draw in their silhouettes
under a glittering afternoon sun.

Ah, the lovely longings of those days.
The awe of, the thirst for realities beyond the eye. •

Whence this weariness? this pain?
What passes by me now,
trembling more remote, more pinched
       than the candyman's flute,
imperceptible as a spinster's eyeteeth,
glittering like the rings on a young peddler's finger...?

M Y WAY (ii)*

The path I've trekked in grief,
my lonely Way:
the path I've walked alone,
tramping my shadow.

No one here, no one speaks.
Children chase bugs in summer fields,
everyone scattered.
Sun glistens in exquisite silence,
high noon like midnight.

Nobody calls me,
nobody knows where I am.

I've come
from no place in particular,
sauntered
toward no place in particular...
come despite myself.

I call to no one,
search for no one.
I call only to my solitary self,
search only for my solitary self.

My wife doesn't call to me.
My children do not search for me.
I'm cold—cold enough to shatter my ribs and burn them,
to burrow hands deep in my shade.

If someone calls to me,
if someone asks for me,
could I answer with a glint from that weed–held stone
loath to lose itself in dusk...
with wind's words rumbling across the wilds
in sunset's darkening wake?

At a Grade Crossing (ii) *

This is where the clatter of the crossing gate
stopped me in my tracks,
the place that put an end to my pleasure
on this joyously sunny spring day—
barely green…rape fields golden…
the train ushering in surf's distant roar….
What now would pierce me,
dashing at me, shining along the rails?
What stares me down,
mute as those black eyes on *soramame* petals,
crowding the tracks like ghosts…?

T o the Soil *

Listen, city people!
White clouds cover me
like the cream you pour
to color the coffee
set before you.

Close your eyes and recall
—the brook that I so cherish
running through wintered grass;
—just–sprouting barley shoots;
—shadows of children and thatched roofs;
—barren tree roots,
all those rhizomes
buttressing unseen tomorrows.

Each morning, haze from the compost pile
runs its tongue over me.
Morning and afternoon trains pass by,
their long shadows caressing me.

As though enamored of them,
I sidle up to hay mounds.
What you neglected to pick up,
what you've utterly overlooked,
I continue to clasp like gleaned grain.

Listen, you who cultivate the soil!
I've a firm grip on your hoes and spades.

Your tractors grin
near the deep gashes they've gouged.

Whenever you sit between the paddies and open your papers,
you all peer at articles
still reeking of the gunpowder
on your hands, your work clothes.

Oh, the new year:
1962!
Let's deck evening's gorgeous glow with dawn's blaze.
Let's graciously receive the welcome rain.
Let's let this year's first lark sing
beyond waves of green hills, beyond white clouds.

Call me
intensely, serenely.
My name is Soil.
My other names, "Love" and "Peace,"
enfold an infinite amplitude
that must embrace us all.

M Y POEMS

My poems
trickle from a midnight tap.
My poems arise from lonely corners
when lamps and cups and dishes have bedded down.
My poems begin
like tears, like words of love,
rising from places you do not know,
places you've forgotten to shut.
Oh, this long, black, chilly night!
My poems arise
in response to what freezes me
on long, black, chilly nights.

S TREAM

Barley yellows.
Feminine features float in a window
of the distant workshop. •

In a Western picture book,
hers would be the face of a housewife baking pie.

But the head I see from here
wears black hair and the look of ash...
like a lamp wick
lit through the night.

The little thread–like stream
rimming the workshop's colorless walls
flows direct—
like the ribbon on a trampled candy box.

HARBOR FESTIVAL ——SENKÔ TEMPLE, ONOMICHI*

They all went off
to see the parade of portable shrines.

Not a pair remains of the footgear
ranked in our entranceway like fishing craft.

My cold makes breezes blowing up from the sea
feel chillier than they are.

Each time a train rumbles through town,
the medicine I've been sipping gets as choppy as the sea.

Like the parsley sprig
poking from my box lunch,
I now feel dreadfully alone, dreadfully renewed.

TREE AT DAWN——A FANTASY

No eye watches—now.
Not a sound—now.
As stars still flicker in distance,
leaves and twigs raise a clamor,
but the trunk stands profoundly vital and serene.
Beads of dew slip softly, swiftly
down its side.
They peer like little glittering eyes
into year rings
deep within tough bark.

M ORNING (iii)

Smoke from the locomotive
lazes over barley fields
then disappears.
White, mask–like
smoke shadows
startle chickens in farmyards.
The private railroad stretches northward,
connecting one toy station with another.
Thinking I'm unlikely to see them again,
I lean vacantly against the window jamb
and gaze at the hamlets in this greening gorge.

AFTERNOON *

No response.
No one home.
A bunch of bracken
soaks up to its neck in a basin
at the edge of the *engawa*.
From the hill behind the house an echo
as though someone calls.
An impressive cloud shadow
strides over barley fields
to visit
those jonquils by the well.

S UBURBAN MORNING

Rains let up.
A rainbow.
We fold our umbrellas like bird wings
and stand at the bus stop,
prepared to face the new day.
We wait for the hours to grate each other
like cabbages in a shopping bag.

HORSETAILS *

Horsetails…horsetails
array their heads
at the bottom of the basket
like those giant matches
for lighting the bath water stove.

Chilly winds in tow, lights on,
an interurban passes by.
I feel forsaken.

S ONG OF THE REED (ii)*

Town's commotion fills my ears
like the buzz of restless bees.
I stand here,
my green horn–like buds
mirrored on ripples.

What to ponder? What to think about?
The day that so bitterly chilled me?
The future that forever shivers me?
Soaking feet still freeze,
only my head slowly warms.

Towing away the hubbub, pulling shadows
and glinting like snow holding out on far–off peaks,
gulls glide now through light ripples,
through the ripples of sound,
their wings have left in sky.

ODE*

Eulalias on the knoll,
leaves along the path,
footfalls, a retreating shadow...
autumn slips silently away.
It unleashes wind whips through the fields,
pins a cloud slice
to red fruit on treetops,
bends the fire tower's shadow over terraced fields.
From tree to tree,
from tree to sky
it makes birds glisten their wing beats,
gets what quickly withers
to polish the silver medal of evening's moon,
and forces water chestnuts to converse with stars
       that one by one light up
on the lake that fingers fox–brown fields...
thus autumn slips silently away

with huge strides...
eager to look back.

T RIP THROUGH THE INLAND SEA*

I'll always remember and often recall:
isles that appear and disappear,
    shadow–striped terraced fields,
fire towers tugging remarkably high
    and lengthy shadows.

I'll always remember and often recall:
the far–off mute horizon that lures me, that humors me,
waves' white lace fringe scalloping the shore.

I'll always remember and often recall:
endless roads in strange towns, sea's blue,
    late–summer oleanders,
the faces of men and women, old people
    and children who passed by.

Oh, I'll tenaciously remember and definitely recall:
this lovely day I lived to visit,
everything I saw and thought about when I was here.

C AMPSITE——ON HIRUZEN PLATEAU*

Scattered tents
like butterflies resting their wings.

Mt. Daisen tries now
to brush the clouds from its head.

Bellflowers,
wild pinks,
a Tagliavini aria surging from the lodge.

HIRUZEN PLATEAU——AT A CAMPSITE*

Not even the mountain's deep folds
hide the butterfly's white.

Shimmers from summer's passing

seep even from strung–up tobacco leaves.
A late bush warbler sings.
Summer bracken look up from the thicket
at tiny chestnut burrs.

Sayonara.
Sayonara.
The butterfly soars ever higher.

OSPREY ——ON OUMISHIMA*

Osprey, you taught us how to make *sushi*!
Storms at sea and in society are, after all, rough and bitter.
Only when memories, dreams, and ideals
start souring in life's nest
do they curdle into admirable savor.
Looking down at me now from your nest on the crag,
oh, osprey—sage and solitary bird!

USHIMADO ——OLIVE GROVES*

To the right, Yashima.
To the left, Awaji.
Verdant Shodô Island directly ahead.
Holding little green fruit,
olive trees smolder in silver.

Olives—synonyms for "peace."
But the person who explained this to me, a traveler,
had lost a hand and a leg in the war.

Must we teach both "love" and "peace"
with such stealth?
Olive trees now
tenderly and tranquilly bob their tiny,
sea–colored fruit.

AT OUMISHIMA *

> *My ears are conch shells*
> *yearning for echoes of the sea.*
> ——Jean Cocteau

Saké in the turbo tankard
sings

and rolls—
not in the ears
but in my hand …

… after the alluring, the astonishing show
that crags and rough seas staged.

S AND BATH——AT YUBARA SPA*

Dawn's mercury lamps aglow,
fairy–like nudes
float up through steamy mists.
Loss of her magic robe at Miho–no–Matsubara
once humbled a nymph into humanhood.
But now guests doff the spa's checkered *yukata*
and turn serenely into nymphs.

YUKI SPA *

Rows of tall cedar
stand deep, stand hushed,
but water's flow and people's hearts—radiant.

Serenading frogs still chorus.
Fireflies under the bridge
glow on, glow off,
in rhythm with the footfalls
of those who come and go.

L AKESIDE——AT TÔGÔ SPA*

Rain lets up at dusk …
sunset's far–off glow magnificent;
shoreline reeds rustle.

Smelt side–by–side on the plate,
their coal–black eyes glassing into distance.

Wrapped in the veil of travel,
my heart now
expansive as a savory pear.

S HÛHÔ CAVE • AKIYOSHI PLATEAU*

I hear the flow of water,
    I hear stalagmites and stalactites forming…
sounds that drive me to question my being.
Caging such thoughts,
the elevator penetrates the caves in a minute.
This a karst plateau.
An undulating green slope
hugs flower after marble flower.
Wild plants seem to crowd the blooms
rather awkwardly.
Yes, in the distance—sunset's opulent glow droops
like the udders of a cow.

AT SANDAN GORGE (i)*

I leave the waterfall.
I leave the roar of the falls.
Soon I no longer see the falls.
I no longer hear their roar.
A far–off mountain stream
mid the tree trunks in this virgin stand;
parched rocks glisten bright.
The last cicada leisurely winds down its spring.
Late summer's radiating sky and clouds
penetrate the leaves and twigs of a chestnut tree.
Ah, my dear, here I am—
a dangling cocoon
that winds now weakly flog.

ON THE IZUMO ROAD *

Wild rose petals mound on the broad leaves of a butterbur.
A summer bush warbler serenades.
Even Mt. Daisen's unmelted snow dims bit by bit.
A moon red as a mackerel's eye is up.

KIND TAGGER*

Hide and seek...hide and seek.
I waited, holding my breath.
Red sasanqua petals scattered
under the shed's straw eaves.

Hide and seek ... hide and seek.
The tagger runs past me.
His sandals fade
into that sunny spot by the nandina.

Hide and seek ... hide and seek.
The tagger never tagged me.
Kind tagger—make me "It,"
that me of those distant days!

B. POEMS PUBLISHED BETWEEN

1963 and 1965

昭和三十八年から 昭和四十年の間に発表された詩

ⓄNE DAY, ONE MOMENT*

A lark sings; it's noon.
Not even the rustle of restless reeds
can wipe that distant cloud away.

> My shoe string snapped as I knelt
> trying carefully to retie it.
> Life's fitfulness, its setbacks,
> that inevitable cold sweat I dab away....

Whirligigs on the water.

A lark sings; it's noon.
Not even the rustle of restless reeds
can wipe away that distant cloud.

ℙHEASANT*

I flee
into this bamboo grass,
this thicket,
a step ahead of what hunts me—
calmly ... quickly.

I have the sky to wing into
before his claws reach me.
Aware of the blue spreading above,
I flee—calmly ... quickly.

I flee
into this bamboo grass,
this thicket,
and take wing—

feeling in the instant
I'm borne up by blue skies
all my weight.

AT KATSUYAMA STATION *

Waiting for the inbound,
my cigarette
smolders on
half my day.

Sky very clear and hot.
Not a single cloud shadow
visits the platform.

A young woman walks down
the distant highway
driving a glossy black cow.

AT SANDAN GORGE (ii) *

Sounds of rain?
Rapids' roar?
The tremble of trees?

Night edges into dawn.
Lamp oil, too, soon gone.
Even my beetle friends, face up on the mats,
have begun to stir.

The red and green blouse
of the coed in the next room
reflects on our *shôji* during the instant
she passes by.

INVITATION TO A TRIP*

This year again that weed sprouted white flowers
from the hip of the stone embankment girding the courthouse.
May air displays its lovely white teeth.
Wind draws a fresh Gillette blade
       over my fresh–shaven cheeks. •

Gliding over blue silk skies,
an airliner seductively inquires:
How about a trip tomorrow?

Friend! Don't those stains on your white shirt
harass you wretchedly today—
like the woeful occupation that hems you?

S EA TRIP*

Just back to a village
bountiful with ripened barley.

Everyone out in the fields.
The flicker of new leaves on camphor trees lining the road;
the sway of far, far away barley beards...

ah, like a touch of seasickness
that somehow lingers on.

NEW YEAR'S DAY

We autograph our first step into the new year
tramping over snow, frost, and ice,
cramming 8760 hours into this single second:
      gunpowder tamped in my mind,
      my finger on the trigger.
Yes, tramping over snow, frost, and ice,
we are the pursuers, we the pursued—
the hunters ... the game.

B INGO CITIES • POEMS ... DREAMS*

Fukuyama and Mihara
stretch wings of industry east and west,
generating smoke, flames, and sparks,
metals, textiles, fats and oils—
not to mention cordial and heartfelt human relationships
that breathe new life into inorganic matter.

We'll set up a recreation center
between Onomichi and Matsunaga
with equipment and facilities for all working people.
The view from Senkôji Hill

and the serene expanse of Matsunaga Bay
will make the week seem
      as though it has only five or even three days.

Urban centers like Fuchū and Miyoshi to the north
serve as our dormitories.
Even at night, toll roads bleed white,
conveying us to playgrounds on our days off.
Old folks stroll about towing peaceful afternoon shadows
along the banks of the Ashidagawa, the Yamanogawa,
      the Nutagawa, the Gōnokawa...
their deep green trees stocked with birds in song.

Let's plant extensive orchards on islands
      floating to the south of the cities.
Our dream:
in spring—trees flowering white and noble as pear blossoms;
in summer—trees that satisfy like bunches of grapes,
glittering together like apricots or tangerines.

Let's create an institute of the arts
      on Mukōjima or Innojima,
with a course that ranges from kindergarten
      through graduate studies;
let's nurture the Latin–style beauty of balance
      in our people's hearts,
plus the elegance, the sagacity, the sincerity, the geniality
characteristic of our Inland Sea area.
Let's create something that tastefully cultivates
      people's hearts and abilities—
the way laver or even an oyster develops—
      unconcerned about
cold–hearted machines and institutions.

The sea now our stomping ground.
The sea now our free–time fishing hole.
Always there for children—parks and playgrounds
      bursting with blooms.
Instead of profits from the horse track and bike races,
make each citizen a shareholder.
Organize a professional baseball team, "The Bingo Dreams."

Put traffic between Fukuyama and Mihara underground
so all can walk about on their own two feet.
Name each street for the trees that line it:
Willow, Gingko, Chestnut, Plane, and the like.

Then we'll be free to take our chairs into the road
where we might drain afternoon teacups
listening to the Metro like a touch of anesthesia
resonating underfoot.

What shall we do with the smoke, the smog,
the sewerage, our trash?
We'll dispose of them
so they don't blacken our windows.
Let's continue to utilize the vast cleansing capacity
of unseen goodwill.

YÛZÔSÂSAN *

The *Yûzôsâsan* family
lives next to me.
The oldest son is Yûzô, the youngest daughter Sachiko.
Combining the two names,
　　　they call themselves *Yûzôsâsan*,
or the *Yûzôsâsan* family.
This is the practice in my district.
For example, in the *Mongôisa* family
the oldest is Montarô, the next Gôsuke, the youngest Isaburô.
Differences between the suffix *–san* or *–sa*
seem a result of euphony,
degree of affection, lineage, pedigree, and such.
In any event, Yûzô of *Yûzôsâsan*
had always been a bit odd.
One day he climbed up on his thatched roof
　　　carrying a hen that got sick and died;
he cut off its head with a Higo pocket knife.
Straddling the rooftop, he then began plucking it.
Blood dripped from the point of the thatched roof;
then Yûzô started dancing around
　　　like the chicken feather's pallid shadows.
A grizzly spectacle.
Around that time ashes from
the distant eruption of Sakurajima settled in our yard,
　　　on our *engawa*, in our fields...
sometime around World War I.
Holding hands, *Yûzôsâsan*'s Sâsan and I
plopped down on the ground and looked up at the sky.
I wonder what we were thinking
and whose name we called out.

It's October 1962 now.
As I near my second childhood,
    a similar day might again come.
What would I do then?
Whose name would I call out?
Those I can talk to about this no longer exist.
Yûzôsâsan's Sâsan,
having stuck a *yusuraume* pip into her ear,
    developed acute tympanitis
and soon died.

ⓄN A SUNNY DAY——THEME: THE WAY*

It's such a pleasantly clear autumn day,
I decide to get off the bus a stop early
and walk home.

First, I light up a cigarette
in the lee of a utility pole.
Having already lost my bearings,
I find myself walking in the direction
from which I came…surrounded by wavy green knolls,
identical crossroads before and behind,
I can no longer tell east from west.

Seeing a little bridge, I cross it.
Seeing rushes in bloom and reeds stirring,
I stand next to them awhile—
pond water darkly roiled,
no dragonfly soaking up its shadow.

Seeing a beautiful lady enter some lane,
I fall in behind her and,
bus pass in hand,
act as though I'm looking for a house.
But the lane's a dead end,
no lovely lady anywhere—
only a fragrant olive exuding its special pungence.

Endless clouds shut out the sky….
By now I feel as solitary
as that boy who wandered from friends
while hunting quartz and wild grapes.

AUTUMN IN JAPAN *

Shiso leaves; the green of mustard plants;
a picture painted cool on a plate.

Skies endlessly blue;
flocking dragon flies that soar like ripples;
bush clover ... eulalia ... sea's distant roar.

Moon high above the scent of mums;
cricket chirrups saturating rocks...

because of these,
I love the autumn in Japan.

CITY SHOWER (ii)*

A shower.
Passing rain.
I keep dry
under a haberdashery canopy.
Sun promptly starts to shine again.
The wet sidewalk reflects
the hulking department store,
even barren trees lining the avenue.
People, horses, cars—
all reflected, all in motion.

AUGUST SONG ——WATER'S THOUGHTS

I entangle no one
in my twisting, roiling ringlets.
I merely wash all things clean
with words that bubble and dance,
that melt and flow
from *Present* to *Future*,
from *Phenomenon* to *Thought*.
Ah, bending summer's glorious radiance
deep into my self,
my mind now
distant,
calm.

I CAN MAKE IT*

I can make it.
I'll survive
like flames on the morning range
that lick tough Chinese cabbage stalks.

I can make it.
I'll survive
like the *nikogori* on my midnight plate,
utterly severed from flesh and bone.

I can make it.
I'll survive
by somehow clinging doggedly
like that partially mangled and shabby
withered vine.

I can make it.
I'll survive,
survive alone—
having realized that life's a rock
over which I trip
in withered turf.

IN ITS SECOND BLOOMING

A flower in its second blooming blossoms faintly white.
Sun saunters through distance;
a vine withers round a rock...
but that flower blooms now like someone forgotten.

Oh, renew my life like this!
Someone ought to watch this bloom,
someone ought to linger here.
Light mellows softly, radiates softly
into the bounties of distant days.

HILLS IN EARLY SPRING*

I love early–spring hills.
Trunks and barren branches
hold life fires stored through winter.

Because of the anticipation and the awe
of that day when they'll begin to burn brightly,
they stand deep and breathlessly still.
I cherish the shapes, I cherish the spirits of those trees.
I wander the breast of early spring hills
like a white–faced bunting.
At times I sit down with cloud shadows
and talk to trees.

E VENING FOX*

At my desk late into the night,
I sit silent as my *nikogori*
and listen to a fox.

I think
—of our potted nandina, only its berries red;
—of drafts ensconced beneath my desk;
—of those pebbles
in the snowball
you tossed to me.

That evening fox.
What deplorable speed!
One bark near ... the very next one
two hundred meters beyond.

I, too, dash over a country lane now,
its crossing gate up.
I run with the famished fox...
like moonlight—at full tilt.

G LITTERING PEOPLE——FRAGMENTS OF A SPORTS POEM*

RUNNER!

You seek an altogether fresh domain
on your lined lane, your oval.
You gaze at a realm within
that no one else can know.
I saw it.
I could see
the tape enfold you.
We bend together and rustle in the breeze

you stirred…
like a deep woods.

LONG JUMPER!
You stomp the board
hard enough to stamp out vice.
Airborne with a footplant,
your hands grasp realities
that exist for you alone.
The weightlessness of white clouds,
the solidity of sky's blue,
suspend you fleetingly
in the spacious ether.
With a gasp
we become the countless grains of heated sand
that cushion your landing….

SHOT PUTTER!
You do not grasp the horizon,
but like every "love"
create it.
Decisively you thrust your arm
and square your chest
beyond that prodigiously projected arc.

SWIMMERS!
You captivate us
like fish in an aquarium,
but more nimbly, more slickly.
As our cheers resound from your spray,
each bead of water
captures face after face after face,
mouths agape….

YOU IN MASS CALISTHENICS!
Your white petals
create white flowers.
When the time comes,
you vanish from sight
like fleeing doves.
But look! Even now
the pollen you've scattered
sticks fragrantly
to each of us.

CLIMBER! (i)
You know how
strength and courage,
love and loneliness,
weigh on your shoulders.
You know sun's dazzle,
fog's depths,
the shortness of mind's rope.
You know
the vast range of consequence
in your toeholds,
in the pitons you drive.

CLIMBER! (ii)
You are now the one and the many.
You constantly yearn for what exists
beyond where cliff swallows scurry off—
distant silver peaks,
a pure white spread
that might stainlessly mantle
our domain.

ALL YOU
glittering people——
your focused energies create
stunning forms:
a living, active
contemporary art!
Standing before us with tear necklaces
threaded from the purest inspiration
in the world,
all you glittering, glittering people!

M ORNING GLOW, EVENING GLOW

Morning glow and evening glow
burn with blood's hue,
never abandoning water on the canal.
Listen! This heated thought
only gyrates through my slight five–foot frame.
It only reels....

AT HIROSHIMA'S MEMORIAL PEACE PARK *

Hiroshima's skies stretch blue,
yet on that day, that hour,
    ever more removed from us....
Only my hopes are fresh—
    hopes as slight as bird shadows
cast this moment on the grass.

S EASIDE TOWN——ON THE KURÉ LINE*

The moment the train stops,
waves' roar returns.
Wind in the pines
and cicadas on the hill behind the station
imperceptible now.

Half my life
melts pitifully,
trickling away drop by drop
like the partly–eaten ice cream
left on a window ledge in the coach...

sunset mirrored
in every drop.

Crawling leisurely
along the platform's lip,
a lone crab
brandishes with all its might
claws redder than sunset,
redder than oleanders.

AT AN INN IN SHINJI *

Ranked over the mats,
we slept like a plateful of smelt.
I awoke in the dead of night,
a fish in disarray.

People talking already
on the road behind our inn.
Glaring off the lake,
daybreak sticks like a stamp
to my sleepy face.

GONE SO LONG *

Once, people with burning hearts lived here
and breezes brightened window panes.
Once, windows framed peaceful scenes
and clouds linked as in a reel danced through the blue.
Oh, they've been gone so long.
The people—gone so very long.
Summer 1965.
I descend that staircase of twisted memories
searching what was lost,
jangling the key ring in my mind.

SUPPLEMENTARY MATERIALS

COLLECTIONS

The Poetic Works of Kinoshita Yûji
Bokuyôsha, 1966
Teihon: Kinoshita Yûji Shishû
『定本 木下夕爾詩集』牧羊社

Brackets indicate works previously issued. (P) denotes a work in prose. I add small Roman letters (i) and (ii) to works with identical English titles.

The ❖ marks works I dubiously label Yûji's collections. Half of No. 5 contains Fujifuchi's poems. No. 6 is a hand–made manuscript never offered for sale; it nevertheless boasts several lovely lyrics and illustrates how Yûji formatted his collections.

Less than half of the pamphlet No. 9, published a decade after Yûji's death, includes his poems. I render more than a dozen that to my knowledge appear in no other collection.

1. COUNTRY TABLE
Inaka no Shokutaku (Shibungaku Kenkyûkai, 10.1939; 23 poems)
『田舎の食卓』詩文學研究会

Part One: Memorial Trees Along the Road [*Machi no Kinenki*]
「街の記念樹」

Portrait of the City, On a Sun–Washed Train, June Chanson, Passing Shower (P), Afternoon Letter (P), Summer's End, Fresh Autumn Lyric, Sloth, Fingers of a New Season, Songs of Early Spring

Part Two: Country Table [*Inaka no Shokutaku*]
「田舎の食卓」

Squall, Bonjour, Summer Sketchbook, Morning (i), Sleep, House Where I Was Born (i), Village—Fragments, Country Table, Lad, *Soirée*, Family (P), Autumn Song, Autumn's Edge—Fragments

2. HOUSE WHERE I WAS BORN
Umareta Ie (Shibungaku Kenkyûkai, 9.1940; 30 poems)
『生まれた家』詩文學研究会

Day in the City, Spring, Inn, Evening, Going Home, Late Spring Flute, Shower, At a Country Barbershop, Night Wind, Late Spring (i), Village, *L'Espoir*, House Where I Was Born (ii), En Route, Revenge, After Dinner Songs (i), Songs of Old—Fragments (P), High Noon in Summer, Viper, Blanks in Summer Notebooks, Lonely Bookworm (P), Summer Day, Logging, *Mémoire*, Supper, Day of a Journey (P), In a Little Port Town (P), Autumn Afternoon, After Dinner Songs (ii), Field

211

3.   SONGS OF OLD
Mukashi no Uta (Chimata Shobô, 7.1946; 24 poems, 11 new)
『昔の歌』 ちまた書房

[Field], [Spring], [Lad], [Passing Shower], [Late Spring Flute], [Late Summer—part of "*Soirée*"], Daily Solitude, Grove (i), School, [Village], Wheat Harvest, Seashore Town, Tardy, [Summer Day—retitle of "High Noon in Summer"], [Sleep], [Blanks in Summer Notebooks], [Logging], [Songs of Old], Bed of Fresh Grass, [In a Little Port Town], Visit to a Grave, Hinomisaki Village, At Hinomisaki Village, Youthful Days (i)

4.   LATE SUMMER
Banka (Ukishiro Shobô, 6.1949; 9 poems, 7 new)
『晩夏』 浮城書房

Ants, [Late Summer], Notes on Early Autumn, [Flowers—from "Scenes from an Autumn Sketchbook"], Autumn Grass, Autumn Day (ii), Night School Student, At a Train Stop, Winter (i)

❖ 5. LATE SPRING
Banshun (Jojôshisha, 7.1949; 12 poems, 7 new)
『晩春』 藤山叙情詩社   藤渕欣哉
Half of this book contains the poems of Fujifuchi Kinya

[Ants], House, Literary Fragment (i), Daily Chore, [Shower—retitle of "Passing Shower"], Grove (ii), [Autumn Grass], [Autumn Day], Heights, [At a Train Stop], Old House, Late Spring (ii)

❖ 6. POEMS FOR CHILDREN
Kodomo no Tame no Shishô
(Fuchû Chû Gakkô, 6.1955; 10 poems, 9 new)
『子供のための詩抄』 府中高等学校

Apples, Christmas Night, Horizontal Bar, Katydid, Path through the Fields, Afternoon at the Chalet, My Father, [Little Harbor Town], Spring Bell, [Late Summer]

7.   JUVENILE POEMS
Jidôshishû (Kigutsu Hakkôsho, 11.1955; 21 poems, 15 new)
『児童詩集』 木靴発行所

Meadowlark Nest, Mountain Path, Night on the Countryside, [Afternoon at the Chalet], Train Smoke, Rainbow and Snail, Interurban in Spring, [Katydid], Bamboo Thicket, All in a Row, Memories, Town in the Distance, Heating the Bath Water (ii), Quiet Evening, One Day in the Kitchen, Hide and Seek, [Apples], City Shower (i), [Path through the Fields], [Little Harbor Town], [Christmas Night]

8.   FLUTE PLAYER

Fue o Fuku Hito (Matoba Shobô, 1.1958; 38 poems, 34 new)

『笛を吹くひと』的場書房

Part One: Winter Fountain [*Fuyu no Funsui*]

「冬の噴水」

My Way (ii), Country, Southwind (ii), I Turn to Vapor, You on the Flute, Winter Fountain, Indoor Games, Lightning (ii), Distant Views, *Chanson D'Amour*, Memories of Fire—Mourning Hiroshima Victims, The Departed, Quotidian Seat, Black Flies, Bank, Scenes [1, 2, 3, 4]

Part Two: Under Shared Skies [*Onaji Sora no Shita ni*]

「同じ空の下に」

Prose reportage on Hiroshima

Part Three: Night School Student [*Yagakusei*]

「夜学生」

Morning (ii), [Late Summer] Spring Gorge, [Wildflowers], [Night School Student], [At a Train Stop], At the Temple, Autumn Day (iv), My Home Town (ii)

Part Four: Felled Tree [*Taoreru Ki*]

「倒れる樹」

On a Winter Field, Youthful Days (ii), Wren's Song, February, Gloomy Painting (P), Winter Rainbow, Mallard (P), Mountain Inn, Adolescence (P), Luna Park, Each Chilly Gust, Ten Years, Felled Tree

❖ 9. DIFFIDENT POET • KINOSHITA YÛJI

Ganshu no Shijin—Kinoshita Yûji (Fukuyama Bunka Renmei, 9.1975)

『含羞の詩人』福山文化連盟

I list only the fifteen works I include in *Twisted Memories*.

Recollections of Father (i), Snippets from an Autumn Sketchbook, Journey's End, Recollections of Father (ii), Late Autumn (iii) (P), Winter Day (i), Arietta—Spring Griefs, Ripe Barley, New Leaves on Cherry Trees (i), To the Far–Off Capital, Father and Child, Valley, Song of the Reeds (i), River, Poet of the Rubaiyat

CHRONOLOGY

M ost information below derives from the chronologies in *Teihon Kinoshita Yûji Shishû* [*Poetic Works*] (Tokyo: Bokuyôsha, 1966), *Ganshu no Shijin: Kinoshita Yûji* [*Diffident Poet: Kinoshita Yûji*] (Fukuyama Bunka Renmei, 1975), and Sakuta Kyô, *Na no Hanairo no Fûkei—Kinoshita Yûji no Shi to Haiku* [*Rape-Blossom Hued Landscape— Kinoshita Yûji's Free Verse and Haiku*] (Tokyo: Bokuyôsha, 1981).

I am extremely grateful to Professor Okimoto Jirô of Onomichi for his invaluable input.

DATE	EVENT
1914.10.27	Born in Miyuki, Kami–Iwanari Village, Fukayasu–gun, Hiroshima Prefecture (now Kami–Iwanari, Miyuki-chô, Fukuyama City), the second son of Tsuneichi (who worked at the village hall and also ran a rice milling business) and Aya; given name Yûji (優二)
1920.07.22	A milling machine accident in his store kills Tsuneichi
1921.04	Yûji enters Iwanari Primary School
1922.08.03	Mother marries Tsuneichi's younger brother Itsu, a pharmacist
1927.04	Enters prefectural middle school in Fuchû (*chûgakkô*, a five–year course; now Fuchû High School); commutes by train some thirty minutes one way
1932.03	Graduates from Fuchû Middle School
.04	Enters First Waseda Higher Institute (*Waseda Daiichi* [day-time] *Kôtô Gakuin*) in Tokyo; plans to major in French literature; lives with older brother Takuji, then studying at the Nippon University Medical School; the boys cook for themselves in their rented room. Yûji regularly submits manuscripts to the poetry journal *Wakakusa* [*Young Grass*], famed for publishing the work of unknown poets
1935.04	Stepfather Itsu afflicted with pulmonary tuberculosis; because he desires the older stepson Takuji to continue his medical studies, Yûji becomes responsibile for running the family pharmacy; forced to drop out of Waseda, he transfers to the Nagoya College of Pharmacy
1935.09.15	Stepfather Itsu dies of TB

DATE	EVENT
1937.06	In Nagoya, Yûji joins a poetry study group founded by the poet Kajiura Masayuki (1903–1966), then residing in the city; joins with Kajiura and others in founding the journal, *Shi Bungaku Kenkyû* [*Studies in Poetry and Literature*], which later sponsors Yûji's first two collections
1938.03	Graduates from the Nagoya College of Pharmacy
.04	Obtains license in pharmacy and takes over operation of the Kinoshita Apothecary
1939.10	Self–publishes through *Shi Bungaku Kenkyûkai* his first collection of free verse (100 copies), *Inaka no Shokutaku* [*Country Table*], 23 poems in 67 pages; Kajiura Masayuki writes the Preface
1940.04	*Country Table* shares Sixth Bungei Hanron poetry prize with two other collections: *Taisô Shishû* [*Gymnastic Poems*] by Murano Shirô (1901–1975) and *Sensô* [*War*] by Yamamoto Kazuo (born 1907), both considerably older than Yûji; Horiguchi Daigaku (1892–1981)—the prolific poet, famed translator of French poetry, and a *Wakakusa* editor—served on the *Bungei Hanron* prize selection committee and strongly supported Yûji's book
.09	*Shi Bungaku Kenkyûkai* issues second collection, *Umareta Ie* [*House Where I Was Born*], 30 poems in 60 pages
1944.01	Marries Umeda Miyako (born 1919.08.09)
1945.07	To escape the bombings in Tokyo, Ibuse Masuji (1899–1993) returns to his place of birth, Kamo Village, not far from Miyuki; through meetings of writers in the area, becomes acquainted with Yûji, who takes fishing lessons from Ibuse
.10.29	Daughter Akiko born
1946.01	Anjû Atsushi, Ômachi Tadashi, and others establish the haiku journal *Shuntô* [*Spring Light*]; Kubota Mantarô (1889–1963), established playwright and noted amateur haiku poet, becomes editorial adviser
.07	Chimata Shobô issues Yûji's third collection, *Mukashi no Uta* [*Songs of Old*], 22 poems in 62 pages
1949.01.14	Son Junji born
.03	With seven local poets, starts the coterie journal *Kigutsu* [*Wooden Shoes*]; until he died in August 1965, Yûji serves as chief editor (through 46 issues); fellows include Yûji's brother Takuji and close friend Tsunoda Kan'ei
.06	Ukishiro Shobô issues Yûji's fourth book, *Banka* [*Late Summer*], a limited collection of 75 copies with 9 poems in 22 pages printed on hand–made rice paper [*washi*]

DATE   EVENT

1950.04	Participates with others in establishing the third reincarnation of the journal *Chikyû* [*Globe*]
.07	Jojôshisha issues Yûji's fifth collection, *Banshun* [*Late Spring*], with 12 poems through page 21; Fujifuchi Kinya's poetry occupies the remaining 26 pages
1952	Formation in nearby Ekiya (now part of Fukuyama City) of the *Muikakai* [Sixth Day (of the month) Club]
1955.07	Fuchû Chûgakkô [middle school] prints up a sixth collection, *Kodomo no tame no Shishô* [*Selected Poems for Children*], a ten-work, ten-page mimeographed manuscript not offered for sale
.08	On the tenth anniversary of the atomic bombing of Hiroshima, Japan National Radio (NHK) broadcasts his poem "Hiroshima" set to music; he also publishes "*Hi no Kioku* [Memories of Fire]" in the Asahi Newspaper
.11	Through *Kigutsu* issues his seventh collection, *Jidô Shishû* [*Juvenile Poems*], 21 works
1956	The composer Kokura Akira sets to music eight works from *Juvenile Poems*
.07	Publishes first haiku collection, *Nanpûshô* [*Southwind Sketches*]; joins formation of a haiku club in Fuchû that establishes the coterie journal, *Ashi no Hi* [*Reed Fires*]
1958.01	Chimata Shobô issues Yûji's eighth and most promising collection, *Fue o Fuku Hito* [*Flute Player*], introduced by Ibuse Masuji; 42 poems in 100 pages. Establishes a haiku club in Miyuki; subsequently, this organization absorbs similar clubs in Fuchû, Ekiya, and Arata; Yûji selected the leader
1959.05.08	A cerebral hemorrhage kills close friend Tsunoda Kan'ei (born 1919)
.05	Hiroshima Poets' Association established, Yûji becomes chair (serves for four years); also becomes a member of the *Nihon Shijin Kurabu* [Japan Poets' Club] and *Nihon Gendai Shijinkai* [Association of Modern Japanese Poets]; haiku poets celebrate the fifth year of the *Muikakai* by issuing the collection, *Shunkin* [*Spring Koto*]
.07	Through the magazine *Shuntô* issues his second haiku collection *Enrai* [*Distant Thunder*]
1961	Formation of Hiroshima Shuntô Association; appointed to edit the first issue of its journal, *Shuntô* [*Spring Light*]; becomes a member of the *Haijin Kyôkai* [Haiku Poets' Association]
1962	Japan National Railways commissions Yûji to write verse

DATE	EVENT
	for the regional edition of its centennial brochure
.06	An admirer from a Buddhist temple sets up a haiku stele in Fukusenbô, Numakuma–gun
1963.05	Kubota Mantarô dies; Yûji writes a piece for the *Festshrift* the magazine *Haiku* sponsored in honor of the playwright's contributions to modern haiku
1965.04	The Hiroshima Prefectural Poets' Club solicits poems nation–wide for a collection on the 20th anniversary of the atomic bombing of Hiroshima; Yûji serves as a judge
.05.12	X-Rays reveal blockage of the colon; enters Okayama University Hospital
.05.17	*Chûgoku Shinbun* [a primary newspaper serving western Honshu] requests a poem on the 20th anniversary of the atomic bombing of Hiroshima
.07	Sends off last poem, *"Dômu ni Yosete—Nagai Fuzai* [For the Dome—Gone So Long]"
.08.04	Dies at 0130 from cancer of the colon
.08.05	Funeral service at 1400 in his Miyuki home
.08.07	Ibuse Masuji participates in the commemorative service in Fukuyama Public Hall, sponsored by the Fukuyama Bunka Renmei, Hiroshima Prefectural Poets' Club, and the Hiroshima Shuntô Association
1966.08	On the first anniversary of Yûji's death Bokuyôsha issues his collected haiku; supporters also set up a haiku stele at the site of his birthplace in Kami–Iwanari, Miyuki
.11	Bokuyôsha publishes *Teihon Kinoshita Yûji Shishû* [Col - lected Poetic Works]
1967.01	*Collected Poetic Works* wins the Eighteenth Yomiuri Literature Prize for free verse and haiku
1971	The city of Fukuyama sets up a haiku stele in Takayama Toda Park
1972.05	Bokuyôsha issues under one cover a collection of Yûji's free verse and haiku
1973.03	Kadokawa Shoten issues all Yûji's haiku as Volume 12 of *Gendai Haiku Taikei* [*Outline of Modern Haiku*]
1979.11	A collection of Yûji's verse in English shares the First Japan–United States Friendship Commission Prize for Literary Translation
1981.05	Fuchû High School sets up a haiku stele honoring Yûji

NOTES

Specialists can readily locate—if they do not already know—the cultural or regional information in these notes. The student or comparatist lacking control of Japanese, however, might not be able to check into many of these items. These notes assume an urbanite unfamiliar with but curious about the rural images—whether related to flora, fauna, or culture—that fill Yûji's verse.

Primary sources of this data include the late Professors Ôhara Miyao of Hiroshima and Nishihara Shigeru of Onomichi. Over many years, they provided through interviews and correspondence answers to a host of questions. I also treasure their hospitality. Professors Ben Befu and Okimoto Jirô made significant contributions; I am extremely grateful for their help, as I am for data that Mr. Haraguchi Saburô provided. None should be held responsible, however, for how I have shaped and presented provided information.

Most italicized Japanese words in the translations appear among the poem titles in ABC order. A square (□) before an entry indicates that this poem closely resembles or is a rewrite of another piece. The pointing finger (☞) means, Please refer to the note (in small caps) or poem (in quotation marks followed by the page number in the text). An angled arrow (✔) indicates a new, different, or—an often gratuitous if—related aspect of the entry.

※   ※   ※

ADOLESCENCE—Yûji later presented this work as a poem titled "That Hill." The poem duplicates the prose until after the first sentence (line) of the third section (stanza); there Yûji inserts the sentence, "Eulalia still glitter in the wind." ☞ EULALIA. ✔ Knotting eulalia fronds suggests an out–of–awareness act that one becomes aware of while absorbed in thought.

AFTER DINNER SONGS (i)—(1) Yûji presents the twenty–seven calendar years he has lived in (*kazoedoshi*). His actual age as we count would be twenty six at this time. ✔ In those days, Mothers usually took a *yukata* apart and sewed it back together after washing and starching; this was truly a labor–intensive task.
(2) Flushing after a sip of saké may demonstrate the efficiency of the Japanese liver. Yûji was extremely fond of alcohol. A painfully diffident and retiring person, he needed a drink or two to loosen up. At poetry gatherings, he laced his coffee with whiskey. He served many a visitor to his study saké instead of the customary tea. ✔ On the loquat, ☞ WINTER CROW; the seed in the center of the tart fruit—that tastes like an apple or pear—is fairly large.
(3) The Nazis occupied Paris 1940.06.14.
(ii)—Phosphorescence appears in Roman letters as Phosphor. ✔ A grass fire resembling a snake's tongue likely relates to *noyaki*, ☞ FEBRUARY.

219

AFTERNOON—Bracken or brake [*warabi*; Latin name, *Pteridium aquilinum*] is a fern with yard–long triangular fronds. It grows wild and in a garden becomes an invasive weed; its fronds will poison livestock. The rootstocks and tender, brownish young shoots (fiddleheads; to the Japanese they resemble a baby's fist) can be boiled and eaten. Boiling and drying removes the toxin from the fronds; the dried, rope–like stalks have a shelf life of about two years. Before eating, the fronds must be soaked overnight, boiled again, and re–soaked in cold water. Japanese and Koreans often use this labor–intensive delicacy (associated with early spring) as a side dish.

The *warabi* in Yûji's poems is invariably soaking on the ☞ ENGAWA. This implies it will soon be ready to prepare for a meal. He uses this image to emphasize feelings of cold loneliness and isolation—the more intensely felt because it contrasts with the expected warmth and camaraderie of a family meal and of spring. ✒ The graphs for jonquils [*kizuisen*; "yellow water hermit"] mean yellow daffodil. A bulb of the narcissus • daffodil family, jonquils have long strap–like leaves and small, six–petaled yellow flowers.

AFTERNOON AT THE CHALET—Azaleas [*tsutsuji*; members of the vast rhododendron family] can be evergreen or deciduous shrubs. Many grow wild in hilly areas, others serve as ornamentals. Yûji could refer to the popular Japanese variety, *yamatsutsuji* [mountain or wild azalea]. This semi–deciduous shrub grows 3 to 9 feet high and in spring produces lush five–petaled purple or bright red flowers. In May, a different Japanese variety produces flowers 2 or 3 inches wide in clusters of 5 to 25 blooms; the colors run from salmon red through reddish orange to orange.

AFTERNOON LETTER—The fig image pulses beneath the surface to affect the entire work. Since ancient times, the fig has suggested fertility and abundance. People have, moreover, regarded it the "vaginal fruit," perhaps because of the way the freshly–opened fruit resembles the vulva. The erotic nuances of this flowerless fruit imply frustrated sexual impulses that the cool tone and white color of the titles soothe. ✒ When Adam and Eve left Eden, they concealed their sexuality behind fig leaves. Fig trees also relate symbolically to death and rejuvenation. ✒ For plane tree, ☞ PASSING AUTUMN. ✒ Yûji here uncharacteristically writes *mélancholie* in ☞ KATAKANA.

AKEBIA—Latin name, *Akebia ouinata*, a shrubby, deciduous vine native to hilly areas in East Asia. The *akebi*'s clusters of dull mauve or red flowers appear among five–leafed twigs around April. Its fruit resembles fat lilac–colored oval, thick–skinned sausages about 4 inches long. In autumn, these mature and split open to expose their white, sweet, semi–transparent meat. ✒ In Yûji's day, country boys gathered unripe *akebi* and buried them 2 to 4 inches in the soil. Depending on how hard the fruit was when they picked it, they figured it would mature and become edible in three to ten days.

APPLES—Japanese peel apples and other fruits before eating them. ✒ "Home altar" renders *Butsudan*, "altar for the *hotoke*," the departed ones (*butsu* in compounds). Death makes people Buddhas (i.e., "enlightened ones"). Autumn is also the time poetic Japanese—traditionally attuned to seasonal changes in nature—pay special attention to thoughts of death and dying.

AT A GRADE CROSSING (i)—Yûji detested interruptions over which he had no control. ✔ Throughout Japan, streets cross railroad tracks in countless places. Since a mountainous terrain squeezes the populace into less than 20% of the land area, in many areas (even in the country) it is difficult to walk very far without confronting a railroad crossing. Some claim Japan has more such crossings [*fumikiri*] than any other nation. ✔ Because the female mantis (mantid), the only predatory member of that order, often consumes the male who has fertilized her eggs, this insect suggests cruelty and voraciousness.
(ii)—For the rape flower [*nanohana*], ☞ INTERURBAN IN SPRING. ✔ "Ghosts" renders *bôrei*, "dead spirit[s]."

AT A TRAIN STOP—Train stop renders *teishaba*, which means "where the car stops." The term raises the image of a small and humble country depot. ✔ For "inbound [*nobori ressha*]", ☞ MY HOMETOWN (ii). ✔ On the citron, ☞ JOURNEY'S END.

AT AN INN IN SHINJI—Shinji is a small town in Shimane Prefecture (in the ancient area of Izumo; ☞ ON THE IZUMO ROAD). Situated at the southwest corner of Lake Shinji, across from Matsué, Shinji lies on the San'in Trunk Line serving cities along the Japan Sea coast. For centuries, Shinji has been known for its large Shinto shrines and comfortable inns. Lake Shinji, the sixth largest in Japan, is some 31 miles in circumference.
　　As the subtitle, Yûji quotes a verse by Kubota Mantarô (1889–1963; ☞ TEN YEARS), his haiku teacher: "*Mijikayo ya omowanu kata ni urakôshi* [Short night. / An unexpected / Backyard lattice]." One presumes that the hot night seems short because the poet cannot sleep. The lattice suggests a cool arbor; finding one unexpectedly implies a joy that might compensate for lack of sleep. ✔ The fish, the pond smelt [*wakasagi*], is a special delicacy of Lake Shinji. ☞ LAKESIDE— TÔGÔ SPA. ✔ For another example of the image of a stamp pasted to the brow, ☞ "Wharf" (ii) (page 82).

AT HINOMISAKI VILLAGE—Hinomisaki, a cape and village on the Japan Sea, is situated at the extreme western tip of Shimane Peninsula, Shimane Prefecture. This village, due north of Hiroshima City, is the site of a celebrated lighthouse that, at 128 feet, once boasted being Japan's tallest man–made structure. Now designated a national monument.

AT HIROSHIMA'S MEMORIAL PEACE PARK—The atom bomb exploded over Hiroshima at 8:15 A.M., 1945.08.06. The blast instantly flattened virtually the entire city, taking over 200,000 lives. ✔ The park, slightly over a mile southwest of Hiroshima Station, is the site of the Memorial Cenotaph dedicated to A-Bomb victims. The Cenotaph (designed by Dr. Tange Kenzô, born 1913) frames the Atomic Bomb Dome (i.e., the remains of the Industry Promotion Hall directly below the epicenter of the blast); ☞ UNDER SHARED SKIES, Parts II and III. The park also contains Peace Memorial Hall (built 1955) and an auditorium. ✔ The "slight hopes" to which Yûji refers echo lines in the Hara Tamiki poem he quotes in Part IV, VISIONS OF A FLOWER, from "Under Shared Skies" (page 149).

AT KATSUYAMA STATION—Katsuyama (more precisely, Chûgoku–Katsuyama to differentiate it from a town with the same name near Fukui in Hokuriku) lies in the northwestern section of Okayama Prefecture, 77 miles from Himeji (north by northwest from Okayama). A former castle town on the Izumo Road (☞ ON THE IZUMO ROAD), its present population is ca. 25,000. Famous for wild monkeys and agricultural products, especially cows. Celebrated Kanba Falls can be reached in 15 minutes by bus from this station. For "inbound" [*nobori ressha*], ☞ MY HOMETOWN (ii).

AT OUMISHIMA—Yûji quotes lines that Horiguchi Daigaku (1892–1981) translated from "*Cannes* 5" (in *Poésies*, 1920) by the French poet Jean Cocteau (1889–1963). ✒ Oumishima [i.e., "blue–sea island"], Yamaguchi Prefecture (western tip of Honshu), located 265 yards into Senzaki Bay, the Sea of Japan, just north of Nagato. Circumference about 25 miles; the precipitous cliffs along its north shore are especially breathtaking. The island features scenery typical of the enchanting seascapes in the state park along Nagato's northern shoreline. ✒ "Turbo tankard" registers *sazae no tsubo* ["turbo–shell bowl]."

AT SANDAN GORGE (i)—The Japanese government designates Sandankyô an "Outstanding Scenic Spot." Located in the upper reaches of the Ôta River, 45 miles northwest of Hiroshima, Sandankyô is famed for the riveting series of waterfalls that dot its ten mile–long gorge.
(ii)—Dead beetles are invariably supine, that is, on their backs facing up; for other works using this image, ☞ "Hotel in the Foothills" (page 168) and "Luna Park" (page 166). Reference to the coed implies that a group of students is sightseeing in the area.

AT TABLE—The plaster is an analgesic preparation to alleviate the stiff shoulders that tenseness causes. ✒ Greenfinch (green linnet or goldfinch; *kawarahiwa*; i.e., "riverbed siskin") are very small seed–eating birds.

AT THE PARK—Cuneiform [*kusabigata moji*, "wedge–shaped writing"] refers to ancient Babylonian graphs pressed into clay tablets with a wedge–shaped stylus. This creates words and designs that look like assemblies of three–dimensional isosceles triangles. ✒ Whitish bird droppings on the bronze statue would be three dimensional and, under the sun, their "sparkle" probably caught Yûji's eye. ☞ "Squall" (page 87) that describes bird droppings as "fresh medicine."

AT THE TEMPLE—Many Buddhist temples offer economical hostel services for travelers. ✒ For cuckoo, ☞ JUNE SKETCHES. ✒ Bamboo shoots [*takenoko*], widely coveted for use in foods, can grow as much as 4 feet in a single day. The noises refer to their splitting skin.

AUTUMN DAY (iii)—Until American–inspired post–World War II reforms, the father (or his family) both by custom and legal right had first claim on any children when a marriage failed. ✔ This work dates from 1956. But despite the 1947 Civil Code's comprehensive legal reforms, Yûji's extremely conservative rural milieu makes it unreasonable to expect single–generation changes in conventions or people's attitudes.

Why books by these particular poets and why keep them at the bottom of the shopping bag? The ☞ SYMBOLIST emphasis on emotion and intuition appealed to Japanese poets. The conformist Confucian ethos of Yûji's provincial area, however, made Bingo an unwise place to flaunt the morality these French poets advocated.

Jean–Nicholas Arthur Rimbaud (1854-1891) wrote most of his verse before the age of twenty, when he was proud of being a hellion. He insisted on creating his own forms and refused to work within "accepted patterns." He sought to transcend good and evil by refashioning his world on amoral principles. His work and thought influenced the ☞ SYMBOLIST movement. After he gave up poetry, he led the life of a vagabond. ✔ Verlaine (☞ FIRST LOVE), with whom Rimbaud earlier had a presumed homosexual affair, published in 1886 a collection of Rimbaud's prose poems and poetry titled *Les Illuminations* (date of writing uncertain).

Charles–Pierre Baudelaire (1821–1867) may be the greatest modern French poet; he was also an important art critic and the translator of Edgar Allan Poe. Baudelaire rejected the morals of his day as well as every formal and conventional stricture on poetry. For many Japanese, he was the epitome of the contemporary amoral writer dedicated to modern objectives. He aimed to discard reactionary elements in convention, free himself from the past, and push the language and content of poetry to the limits. Prosecuted for obscenity because of his *Les Fleurs du mal* (1857 and 1868) [*Flowers of Evil*; in Japanese, *Aku no Hana*], it is understandable that he might have a strong appeal to artists in a chokingly conservative milieu.

AUTUMN ETCHED IN ME—Characterizes autumn: Skies are clear and blue; from ancient times, the cricket has been the preferred insect, ☞ GROVE (ii); fall is time also to contemplate endings, especially death.

AUTUMN SONG—Judged by the popular picture of Marcel Proust (1871–1922), his droopy mustache suggests the acme of relaxation.

AUTUMN'S EDGE—FRAGMENTS—Yûji renders the word "fragments" in English. ✔ In his prewar milieu, high school [*kôtô gakkô*] was an elite course restricted to male students from seventeen or eighteen through twenty or twenty one; the content of the classes compares favorably with what we consider college–level studies. Summer break occurred between the first and second terms; homework projects might include gathering insects for biology class. ✔ On the golden olive [*kinmokusei*], ☞ FRAGRANT OLIVE.

Anton Pavlovich Chekhov (sometimes spelled Tchekhov; 1860–1904), Russian novelist and playwright, began studying medicine but invested most of his energies in short stories that depict life in Russia. ✔ One scholar writing of Chekhov's work says, "the frustrated longings of...provincial intelligentsia blighted by life's emptiness...symbolizes a universal modern malaise"; this suggests one of the charms Chekhov's work held for Yûji and other intellectuals in his rural milieu.

Marigolds [*marîgôrudo*] have no Japanese name, nor do they appear in most dictionaries. Various varieties grow from 6 inches to 4 feet tall, but in Japan they range from 18–24 inches. This scented plant belongs to the chrysanthemum family [*senjûgiku*; Latin name, *Tagetes erecta*] and blooms double flowers from early summer through the first frost. ✔ On the smartweed, ☞ SMARTWEED SPIKE.

BACK GATE—The sound of a comb running through a woman's long hair has an eerie effect on Japanese. ✔ On bath water, ☞ HEATING THE BATH WATER. ✔ "Round little red lanterns" [*hôzuki jôchin*] are miniatures that children use as toys. Red paper pasted over the windows casts a festive light that recommends their use also in parades, to mark sales at stores, and for festivals.

BEAUTIFUL MAN—Takamura Kôtarô (1883–1956) was a sculptor and the son of a sculptor. Though his poetry is more impressive and abundant than his sculptures, he regarded himself more a sculptor than a poet. ✔ Many admire the passionate love songs he wrote to his young wife, Chieko (née Naganuma, 1886–1938), whom he married in 1914. Like Yûji, Kôtarô found the severity and sparseness of winter more interesting than spring and fall, the traditionally honored seasons. ✔ The Japanese commonly believe that those who die become enlightened Buddhas • *hotoke* or spirits • *kami*.

BEFORE KUMAHIRA TAKEJI'S POETRY STELE—A regional poet (1906–1960) from the Hiroshima area. Italicized words indicate the inscription on Kumahira's poetry stele (written in Chinese). At the dedication of his stele, he rejected the ritually correct water oblation and instead used wine. Takeji died of leukemia, an indirect victim of the atom bomb.

BINGO CITIES • POETRY ... DREAMS—① Bingo is one of the eight ancient provinces along the Inland Sea. It once comprised the nine districts now included in Hiroshima Prefecture. ✔ The *Chûgoku Shinbun* [*Western Honshu News*], which commissioned this work, often features articles that encourage pride in local customs, landscapes, institutions, and writers.

② Fukuyama (ca. 365,000), former castle town, is four hours and twenty minutes west of Tokyo on the Bullet Train; a Kodama stop. The major urban area in the eastern section of Hiroshima Prefecture, just over the border from Okayama Prefecture and some 64 miles east of the city of Hiroshima. ✔ The Yamanokawa flows ca. 8.5 miles north of Yûji's home in Miyuki; the Ashidakawa, fed also by the Kamo River near Yûji's place, flows southeast through Fuchû and Fukuyama before emptying into the Inland Sea.

③ Situated on a small plain, Mihara (ca. 86,000) faces the Inland Sea at the junction of the San'yô Trunk and Kuré Lines; it lies 13.5 rail miles west of Fukuyama and 45 miles east of Hiroshima. Originally a castle town famed for saké production, it is now one of the industrial centers of the area. Mihara's factories make cement, manufacture rolling stock, and produce rayon and ramie. The Nutagawa flows through the city.

④ For Onomichi, ☞ TO TSUNODA KAN'EI. ✔ Matsunaga lies east of Onomichi and in 1966 merged with Fukuyama. Matsunaga Bay is bordered on the southwest by Mukôjima, ☞ ¶ ⑥. ✔ For Senkôji Hill, ☞ HARBOR FESTIVAL and TO TSUNODA KAN'EI. ✔ For Fuchû, ☞ SLAUGHTER HOUSE.

⑤ Miyoshi (ca. 40,000), originally a castle town, is a commercial and industrial hub, transportation and distribution center, and the chief city in the Miyoshi Basin. Miyoshi can be reached via either the Geibi Line (59.5 miles northeast of Hiroshima) or the Fukusen Line (58 miles from Fukuyama). Nearby, the confluence of three lesser streams creates the Gônokawa; the longest river in the area, it empties into the Japan Sea.

⑥ For the Ashida and Yamano Rivers ☞ Fukuyama, ¶ ②. ✔ For the Nuta River, ☞ Mihara, ¶ ③. ✔ For the Gôno River, ☞ ¶ ⑤. For Miyoshi, ☞ ¶ ⑤. ✔ Mukôjima ("yonder isle") lies in Onomichi Bay, directly south of the city of Onomichi (☞ TO TSUNODA KAN'EI and ¶ ④); it can be accessed from the mainland by bridge. Innojima, larger than Mukôjima, lies to its southwest and connects to that island by bridge.

⑦ Laver [*nori*; a type of *Porphyra*—sloke or sloak] consists of thin sheets of dried, edible seaweed. Since the early 17th century, Japanese have grown this dark brown alga in sheltered shallows. Gathered and washed in fresh water, makers placed the thin sheets on frames to dry. The mechanized process now produces thin and brittle 7 by 8 inch sheets. ✔ The *nori* may be toasted and seasoned, cut into strips, shredded, wrapped around rice crackers or ☞ SUSHI, ad infinitum. It adds flavor and nutrition to many a native dish.

⑧ The gingko [*ichô*; or maidenhair] is a stately deciduous tree imported from China. Tolerant of low temperatures and little water; it grows to 90 feet. Often regarded as sacred, the *ichô* frequently appears around temples and shrines. The carpet of fan–like brilliant yellow leaves it spreads in the fall is particularly dazzling. So is the way they seem to drop all at once. The *ichô* flowers in spring, then produces edible fruit. ✔ On the plane tree, ☞ PASSING AUTUMN.

BLACK FLIES—For background on this Fuchû scene, ☞ SLAUGHTER HOUSE.

BLANKS IN SUMMER NOTEBOOKS—For bugs pinned to wooden cases, ☞ "Autumn's Edge—Fragments" (page 92) and "Seashore Town" (page 110).

BONJOUR—Yûji writes the title in capital Roman letters. ✔ Images of the parachute (also ☞ SONGS OF EARLY SPRING [i]), carbon paper, and laundry powder were arresting in poetry written those days.

BOREDOM—The nun [*ama–san*] could be Buddhist or Christian, though Yûji usually means the latter. For other poems that refer to a nun, ☞ "Youthful Days— Prologue" (page 65) and ☞ "Thoughts while Sick" (page 72).

BUTTERBUR STALKS—Belongs to the *Compositae* family; related to the chrysanthemum [*kiku*]. *Fuki*—sometimes called bog rhubarb or coltsfoot (Latin name, *Tussilago farafara*)—is a perennial herb most people regard a weed. In Japan, a summer image. ✔ *Fuki no tô* [stalk] is a strong spring image. Butterbur stalks (short and stout) are among the first in late winter to poke through the snow. They consequently symbolize the vitality, promise, and potentials of the new season. By April the plant develops large, broad, fleshy and vaguely heart–shaped leaves that measure some foot across. Like the rhubarb the butterbur resembles, both stalks and leaves are edible.

Western folklore identifies the coltsfoot with maternal love and care. Since at least the time of the Romans, Westerners have considered this plant a water marker; where the coltsfoot grows, a spring runs underneath.

CALLER (i)—For aralia [*yatsude*], ☞ JUNE POEM—FRAGMENTS.

CAMPSITE—ON HIRUZEN PLATEAU—This plateau lies 1800 feet above sea level in the southern foothills of Mt. Hiruzen, ca. 3500 feet high—due north of Okayama in Daisen National Park. On the border of Tottori and Okayama Prefectures, the area provides camping grounds in summer and skiing in winter. Reached by bus in under two hours from Chûgoku–Katsuyama Station, ☞ AT KATSUYAMA STATION.

Mt. Daisen, a dead volcano in Tottori; the tallest peak (over 5,000 feet) in the Chûgoku region. ✔ Bellflower [*kikyô*; Latin name, *Platycodon grandiflorum*], also called balloon flower (at times mistakenly the Chinese bellflower, actually the *Abutilon*, a viny, evergreen shrub). The *kikyô*, a perennial the Japanese regard an autumn plant, grows about 3 feet high. Light olive–colored leaves 2 or 3 inches long contrast with five–pointed, blue–violet (sometimes white or pink) star–shaped flowers reminiscent of the morning glory.

Wild pinks [*nadeshiko*; Latin name, *Dianthus superbus*] belong to a large family of small herbs that contains ornamentals, weeds, and wildflowers (including the carnation). Pink refers not to the plant's color—which can be white to pink to purple—but to its notched or "pinked" stems. Many bloom from summer through the first frost. ✔ Ferruccio Tagliavini is a bel canto tenor born 1913 in Reggio Emilio, Italy; he graduated in 1938 from the Parma Musical Institute and debuted in Florence the following year. Internationally famous since; known to Yûji through 78 r.p.m. shellac recordings.

CHANSON D'AMOUR—Yûji writes the title in capital letters. ✔ It may prove a challenge to discern exactly how certain parts fit the designation "songs of love." ✔ In the fourth section of this 1958 work, Kinoshita's sense of the body existing in two separate places resembles a similar idea Maruyama Kaoru stated in his 1957 poem "Autumn Dreams."

CIGARETTES—Yûji here very likely refers to himself; he began to smoke sometime toward the end of middle school (*chû gakkô*), that is, in his late teens. In those days, *chû gakkô* covered five years, roughly from the age of twelve through seventeen. ☞ JUNE POEM—FRAGMENTS. ✔ On blue October skies, ☞ SKY.

❑ **CITY SHOWER (i) (ii)**—Virtually identical poems. Yûji writes (i) (page 144) for children and uses only ☞ HIRAGANA in the title—"*Machi no Shigure*." In (ii) (page 201) he uses the customary graph for *machi*.

CHRISTMAS NIGHT—In Yûji's rural milieu, reference to Christmas was exotic.

CORDATA—The Latin is *Houttuynia cordata*, from which I take this designation. Cordata registers *dokudami* (*doku* means poison or venom; the current graph loses this connection with a subsequent image). This foul smelling weed–like perennial grows throughout Japan, especially in damp areas. ✔ Counted among the ten most effective medicinal plants that poets celebrate, it is invariably associated with summer. Since around the seventeenth century, Japanese have used the deep green *dokudami* leaves to reduce swellings.

COUNTRY TABLE—After the title, Yûji writes in English, "To my T. Niwa," doubtless a friend from the Nagoya College of Pharmacy and possibly the same "N" mentioned in "Diary Excerpts" (page 183).

CREAKY CHAIRS—The rainbow's red band, its most dominant color, lies at the top of the bow; the bands below in order are orange, yellow, green, blue, indigo, and, at the bottom, violet.

DAWN OVER THE SETO INLAND SEA—Inland Sea usually registers *Setonaikai* [Seto Inland Sea]. Yûji here writes only Seto, however, which in a different context might refer to the well–known porcelain center in Aichi Prefecture. ✔ This poem—doubtless solicited by an editor—appeared in the central Japan edition of the *Asahi Newspaper*. ✔ I convert Yûji's *kamigami* [gods • spirits] to Nereids, sea nymphs. ☞ SONGS OF OLD—FRAGMENTS.

DAY AFTER DAY—Re the fragrant olive [*mokusei* or *kinmokusei*], ☞ FRAGRANT OLIVE. For *miso* soup, ☞ MISO.

DAY IN THE CITY—Attending the Nagoya College of Pharmacy, Yûji has possibly withdrawn money from Miyuki. He found the profit motive "dirty" so he detested banks; ☞ "Bank" (page 159). On the olive, ☞ FRAGRANT OLIVE.

DAY OF A JOURNEY— ☞ FRAGRANT OLIVE. ✔ In pre–1945 days, a red ticket signified third class, the cheapest way to travel. Boarding passengers have their tickets punched at the wicket; when they detrain, they surrender their tickets as they exit through a wicket. ✔ Yûji elsewhere compares such a ticket to the tongue of a cow; ☞ "Black Flies" (page 158).

DELUGE—"Families wiped out by murder and suicide" renders *ikka shinjû* [the *shinjû* of a whole family], an event that occurs more frequently in Japan than in the West. *Shinjû* translates "love suicide" or "double suicide"; it implies a wish to die together, most often to avoid social, economic, or moral problems. As a rule, the male kills the consenting female before committing suicide.

In *ikka shinjû*, the parent (usually the father) kills the children. Japanese law does not regard *shinjû* as murder but as an act of compassion; the surviving children would not fare well in that society.

DEPARTED, THE— ☞ THE DEPARTED.

DIARY EXCERPTS—Most buildings were made of wood in Yûji's day. Since many had thatched straw roofs, and since the houses stood close to each other, the fear of fire was always real. It is easy to understand why for centuries Japanese regarded arson a capital offense. ✓ For lilac, Yûji writes *rira* (from the French *lilas*); most Japanese now use *rairakku*, derived from English.

"Onion–headed" renders *negibôzu* ["onion shaved head" (as of a Buddhist priest or little boy)]; such stars likely result from atmospheric conditions. They remind of "Starry Night" that Vincent Van Gogh (1853–1890) painted in 1889 at the asylum in Saint–Rémy. ☞ BUTTERBUR STALKS. ✓ "N" could refer to the T. Niwa, to whom Yûji dedicated the poem ☞ COUNTRY TABLE.

EACH CHILLY GUST—On the significance of reeds, ☞ SONG OF THE REED.

EARLY SPRING (i)—Plum (*ume*, actually apricot) blossoms often bloom in the snow, so they suggest hardiness and serve as harbingers of spring.

EARLY SUMMER—Candyman [*ameya*] refers to the peddlers who once pushed their carts through residential areas; they blew a flute or whistle [*fue*] to inform children (eager to buy their rice jellies) of their presence. ✓ "Young sweetfish" registers *waka–ayu*, a trout variety found widely in East Asia. *Ayu* hatch in streams in the fall and soon go out to sea; they return to the stream in the spring and lay their eggs in an area they protect from other fish. It is hence not clear why Yûji describes these spring fish as "young." ✓ Traditionally, Japanese have associated the *ayu* with good luck; in some districts, women fish for them early in April to tell their fortune: catching a good *ayu* augurs well for the coming year.

EN ROUTE—Two *sen* was worth about two cents. A bamboo bank corresponds to "piggy bank." ✓ Radish refers to *daikon* [the *nerima daikon*, the giant white radish or "great root"]. Introduced from China in ancient times, it's a *Crucifer* belonging to the rape or cole family. In spring the *daikon* produces cross–like, delicate mauve flowers that bloom on stems reaching some 3 feet high. Its long white root (symbol of poorly–shaped female legs and items difficult to extract) grows more than a foot long (in contrast to our far smaller variety). *Daikon* are also sharper than our radish and thus used widely to flavor dipping sauces, etc. Fresh *daikon* leaves are also edible.

ENGAWA—Too narrow to justify the rendering veranda or porch, the wood–floored *engawa* (usually some 3 to 4 feet wide) serves as a hallway that runs along the sunny south side of traditional Japanese homes. Sliding glass doors separate the *engawa* from the yard or garden; these doors are usually shuttered at night with sliding panels [*amado*—rain doors]. ☞ SHÔJI doors customarily allow entry to the *engawa* from the family's living space.

EULALIA—This is my rendering of *susuki* (Latin name, *Miscanthus sinesis*— native to East Asia), more often translated "pampas grass" (Latin name,

Cortaderia selloana—native to Argentina). The word *susuki* appears in Japanese poetry from very early times; Japanese always associate it with autumn and admire especially its plumes. This ornamental grass grows 8 or more feet high; its highly–valued whitish or ecru–hued plumes, rising from a spurt of saw–toothed leaves, reach from a foot to a yard in length.

EVENING FOX— ☞ NANDINA.

EXACTA TICKET—Sometimes called perfecta, the exacta is a system where to win the bettor must pick the first and second place finishers. ✦ Dr. Kinoshita Takuji gave me a copy of this poem in manuscript, discovered among Yûji's effects after his death; to my knowledge, it has yet to be published in Japan. Because a race track opened in the Fukuyama area around 1950, Dr. Kinoshita guessed that this work dates from about that time.

FAMILY—After the title, Yûji writes in English, "To Mr. S. Hamamura," a friend from the Nagoya College of Pharmacy. ✦ Crucifers [*jûjibanaka*] refer to cabbage, radish, rape (mustard), etc. They have flowers shaped like small crosses. The description "cheerful" [*akarui* could also be rendered "bright"] derives from the early spring array of enjoyable colors these edible plants produce. ✦ Yûji may have adapted the merino wool image from French poets read in translation.

FEBRUARY— ☞ EULALIA. ✦ "Burnt–over fields [*noyaki*]" refers to the ancient custom of preparing for new growth. Reference to *noyaki* appears in Japan's most ancient poetry. Controlled burning of grass and weeds in the fields provides ash that acts as fertilizer, thus facilitating the growth of spring grasses. By signaling spring's advent and the burgeoning of every growing thing, *noyaki* implies potentiality and hope.

FINGERS OF A NEW SEASON—Duralumin, a modern building material, is an alloy. It contains 90% aluminum, 4% copper, 1% magnesium, and less than 1% manganese; its tensile strength and hardness—both superior to aluminum—make it most suitable for use in airplane manufacture. ✦ Yûji's text on organic chemistry [*Organische Chemie*] is written in German because in prewar Japan that was the language of science and medicine. By the end of the 1960s, medical schools had switched to English. ✦ Brownian movement or motion refers to the zigzag movements of small particles of matter in colloidal suspensions. The effect operates independent of external conditions.

By pretending he has a friend, the persona amplifies his sense of isolation and meaninglessness. This conceit appears frequently in Yûji's earlier work. ✦ People widely regard ripened pomegranates as images of the brain. ✦ The shrike or butcher bird [*mozu*—"bird of a hundred tongues"] is a predatory songbird. The designation "butcher" derives from the way the *mozu* impales on twigs or thorns the small birds, mammals, and large insects it catches; it then tears them apart with the hooked tip of its notched beak.

FIRST LOVE—Yûji here uses English, written in ☞ HIRAGANA (not the expected ☞ KATAKANA) as *fuasuto • râbu* (not the usual *hatsukoi.*). ✦ I don't know how the lamb's belly connects with Verlaine. The surrealistic figure of sheep in the stomach elicits an image of Pan piping among flocks in the field. He is the patron of pastoral poets and shepherds, as well as the mythical inventor of the syrinx, the panpipe or shepherd's flute. ✔ Yûji probably reads Horiguchi Daigaku's translations of Verlaine (first published 1927.02).

Paul Verlaine (1844–1896; ☞ AUTUMN DAY), French poet who attempted with the Romantics to develop a personally unique style at odds with the tradition. The poet Rimbaud (☞ AUTUMN DAY and SYMBOLISTS) urged Verlaine to be more innovative. ✔ After a violent 1873.07 quarrel, Verlaine shot Rimbaud in the wrist, an act that cost him two years in prison. Once released, he recommitted to Catholicism and his art became decorous. He actively resisted Romanticism and urged clarity and classic order. Much late work deals with tensions between spiritual aspirations and carnal enticements.

FRAGRANT OLIVE—This renders *mokusei* (or *kinmokusei*) [sometimes called the sweet olive; Latin name, *Osmanthus fragrans*], imported from China. In *Treelike* (1982) and elsewhere I consistently mis–translated *mokusei* as daphne. This evergreen of the magnolia family has glossy, leathery leaves, grows to a height of 10–12 feet, and sports inconspicuous but fragrant flowers that bloom most densely in October. In milder climates, *mokusei* flowers may still be scattering in mid–winter.

Japanese differentiate the two varieties—*kin* [gold]–*mokusei* or *gin* [silver]–*mokusei*—mainly by the color of the flowers; the former has orange, the latter white blossoms. The silver variety also has slightly serrated leaves.

FRESH AUTUMN LYRIC—Using the term "Gillette blade" in a poem constituted a fresh and modern image. For other references to a Gillette blade, ☞ "Invitation to a Trip" (page 196), "Songs of Old—Fragments" (page 103), "Summer Sketch Book" (page 88), and indirectly, "June Chanson" (page 84). ✔ The image of white teeth—sometimes described as fangs or tusks [*kiba*]—reflects, first, the bite of colder weather and, second, one traditional color of autumn, white, that further links with low temperatures.

"Water–sprinkled pavement" refers to a practice, especially in the heat of summer, to keep down the dust. The wet pavement suggests coolness, thus giving the passerby a feeling of release from the heat and a palpable sense of re-freshment. ✔ For other references to a flower blooming from a stone embankment, ☞ "Invitation to a Trip" (page 196), "River" (page 133), and "Song of the Stream" (page 182). ✔ Addressing himself as "friend" is one of Yûji's standard conceits.

GLITTERING PEOPLE—This 1964 assembly of poems Yûji wrote on the eve of the 1964 Olympics (the XVIIth Olympiad) held in early fall in Tokyo.

GOING HOME—When he wrote this poem, Yûji was studying pharmacy in Nagoya and felt very homesick; he returns home only imaginatively. ✔ ☞ SOUR SORREL. ✔ Ainu, an aboriginal Caucasoid folk now limited to Hokkaido and mostly absorbed by the Japanese, stain their lips with mulberries for ceremonial and ritual purposes (hunting, etc.). ✔ For reed flutes, ☞ YOU ON THE FLUTE. ✔

The knife image intensifies Yûji's feelings of sadness and frustration at being forced to desert his study of French literature in Tokyo so he could take over the family apothecary. The familiar landscapes of the countryside continue to exert a pull on him.

GONE SO LONG—The *Chûgoku Shinbun* [*Western Honshu News*] a major regional newspaper, commissioned this work 1965.05. The editors asked for a piece commemorating the 20th anniversary of the atomic bombing of Hiroshima (1945.08.06). ✈ Going down a spiral staircase calls to mind the descent into Hades, the darkness of the kingdom of the dead. For these spiral stairs, ☞ UNDER SHARED SKIES (Part II. THE ATOMIC DOME).

The title *Twisted Memories* comes from line eight of this poem (page 207). That line reads, *watashi wa nejireta kioku no kaidan o orite yuku*. As happens in countless Japanese relative clauses, one cannot properly render in English the expression's possible ambiguity. Does *nejireta* [twisted] modify only *kioku* [memories], the phrase *kioku no kaidan* [steps of memory], or both? I think both; English forces one to choose.

GROVE (ii)—Note the famous Matsuo Bashô (1644–1694) haiku, which Yûji means to echo: "*Shizukesa ya / iwa ni shimiiru / semi no koe* [How serene / Cicada voices / Soak the rocks]."

HANIWA—In antiquity, the death of a highly–ranked Japanese forced his soldiers, servants, and equipment to be buried with him. Two notions supported this practice: first, a retainer could serve but one lord; second, in the next world, the lord required vassals to serve him. Included in the burial were horses—symbols of leadership—and related gear, as well as weapons and implements; later items include replicas of buildings. ✈ Legend states that this practice ended two thousand years ago when the mythical Emperor Suinin (said to have ruled 100 years) ordered *haniwa* [earthen or clay statuettes] made and buried in place of live retainers; this later included the lord's horses, as well as the retainers' weapons and equipment. ✈ Others aver that humanistic Buddhist thought, which entered Japan several centuries later, encouraged the Japanese to end this barbaric custom of sacrifice and instead inter *haniwa* with deceased personages.

HARBOR FESTIVAL—Senkô Temple [*Senkôji*, i.e., "Temple of 1000 Lights"] is a Shingon Buddhist temple founded in 806 A.D. on a high hill (Senkôji [Temple] Hill), a three minute ropeway ride. The site offers a superb view of Onomichi harbor and the Inland Sea. For Onomichi, ☞ TO TSUNODA KAN'EI. ✈ "Portable shrines" renders *omikoshi*, which house local tutelary deities • spirits taken out for an "airing" during the festival. ✈ For another reference to box lunch, ☞ "My Hometown" (ii) (page 163); for another image of a protruding parsley sprig, ☞ "Hotel in the Foothills" (page 168).

HARBOR TOWN—The canna [*kanna*], Latin for "cane," is a perennial tropical or subtropical plant from India and Malaysia that entered Japan during the Tokugawa era. A tuberous rootstock used in the Tropics for starch, its stems reach 4 to 6 feet high; its large leaves run from a rich green to bronze red. The brilliant

spikelike scarlet flowers (some ca. 4 inches wide) produce a showy blaze bloom-
ing from late summer into fall. Japanese regard canna an early autumn bloom.

HEATING THE BATH WATER (i) (ii)—This activity was once a chore assigned
to youngsters. The traditional bath is a deep wooden tub with a small furnace at
one end. Family members wash up outside the tub, then soak in the hot water
(usually around 112° F, though some prefer temperatures closer to 120° F!). The
entire family, and sometimes neighbors as well (☞ "Late Autumn" [ii], page 79),
can thus economically soak in the same tub of water.

Shriveled corn and bean stalks suggest the variety of combustible scraps that
the frugal Japanese used in the furnace. Some baths were in a shed outside the
house proper; in many other cases, the small furnace projected outside the house.
Feeding the furnace from the outside, the lad finds himself distracted by the
natural surroundings where he is used to playing.

HEIGHTS—Both domesticated and wild *cha* [tea, a type of camellia] produce tiny,
five–petaled fragrant white flowers with bright golden stamens that dominate the
centers. The wild plant grows 6 or more feet high, its leaves shiny and tough. Tea
derives from the young leaves of the 3 foot high domesticated plant, plucked in
spring. For Japanese, *cha* flowers announce the coming of winter because they
bloom from late fall into early winter.
      Tsuwabuki [rock butterbur (*fuki*) or coltsfoot; Latin name, *Ligularia tussi-
laginea*] is the Japanese silverleaf; ☞ BUTTERBUR STALKS. Its stem grows some 2
feet high and produces multiple yellow daisy–like flowers. Its shiny deep green
edible leaves resemble the heart–shaped butterbur (and bring rhubarb to mind).
Flourishes in mild western Honshu, Kyushu, and along the coast of the Inland
Sea; Japanese regard *tsuwabuki* a spring plant.

HILLS IN EARLY SPRING—For the white–faced bunting [*hôjiro* or *hohojiro*,
"cheek white"], ☞ VALLEY.

HINOMISAKI VILLAGE— ☞ AT HINOMISAKI VILLAGE, which explains the
lighthouse figure. ✔ For Izumo, ancient name of the area now called Shimane
Prefecture, ☞ ON THE IZUMO ROAD.

HIRAGANA—The cursive syllabary. In Yûji's day, children learned *hiragana* only
in the second or third grade after having mastered ☞ KATAKANA (block letters).
American schools similarly switch from printing block letters to cursive writing
(penmanship) after at least the first grade. The child Yûji depicts here is probably
in second grade.

HIRUZEN PLATEAU—AT A CAMPSITE—"Strung–up tobacco leaves" refers
to the way tobacco farmers hang the leaves to cure after harvesting. Using straw
rope, they tie together about ten leaves and hang them under the eaves or in other
shaded places until they turn the proper shade of yellow.
      Though it does not sing at night, some translate the bush warbler [*uguisu*] as
nightingale because of its lovely chirping [*saezuri*]. The *uguisu*, the size of a

sparrow and a most inconspicuous brown, lives in forests and among tall grasses feeding primarily on insects. It makes a plate–shaped nest on the ground. ✔ On bracken as a food, ☞ AFTERNOON.

HORSETAILS—Are *tsukushi* (Latin name, *Equisetum hyemale*). Japanese also call this plant *sugina*, the "field horsetail." Its brownish stem resembles rushes and has pointed, spore–bearing cones at the top. Edible but invasive, this coarse–textured plant likes moist sites and grows from 12 to 18 inches high. Japanese use it in cooking. ☞ HEATING THE BATH WATER.

HOTEL IN THE FOOTHILLS—Born in Algiers, Albert Camus (1913–1960), French novelist, essayist, playwright, and journalist, led the postwar disillusionment movement. Showing ardent interest in nihilism, the absurd, and moral problems, Camus won the 1957 Nobel Prize in Literature. Perhaps his most discussed work in Japan is the 1942 novel *l'Etranger* [*The Stranger*], translated into Japanese as *Ihôjin*.

Jean–Paul Sartre (1905–1980), French novelist, playwright, critic, and philosopher; refused to accept the 1964 Nobel Prize for Literature. Many Japanese are especially intrigued by his novelistic trilogy, *Les Chemins de la liberté* [*Paths to Freedom*], translated as *Jiyû e no Michi* (1945–1949).

Beetles that have died turn over on their backs; for similar beetle images, ☞ "At Sandan Gorge" (ii) (page 196) and "Luna Park" (page 166). For an identical parsley image, ☞ "Harbor Festival" (page 187).

HOUSE WHERE I WAS BORN (i)—Silk tree [*nemunoki*; Latin name, *Albizzia julibrissin*] is a very tall and beguiling deciduous tree that belongs to the legume family. It prefers hilly or riverside habitats and blooms red in June or July. Its flower clusters consist primarily of long, slender stamens that spread out from a yellow stem; this gives the appearance of a dense silky–red fan. *Nemunoki* flowers lie on leafy fronds that resemble intricate ferns; its leaves fold up at night. The bean–like fruit consists of 5 or 6 inch long pods containing flat seeds. Haiku poets associate this tree with autumn.

(ii)—Yûji loved the family's visits to a cottage by the sea when he was young but always hated being interrupted by routines originating beyond his control. ✔ In his own home, his widow Miyako reports that he rarely ate with his family; the two meals he had each day he ate alone.

I CAN MAKE IT—Chinese cabbage stalks [*hakusai*; Latin name, *Brassica pekinesis*] are sometimes called white rape; this plant was brought into Japan from China during the last half of the 19th century. ✔ Yûji's image here may derive from the fact that *hakusai* is a hardy plant that resists cold; it associates therefore with winter and survival.

IN A LITTLE PORT TOWN—Marcel Pagnol (1895–1974), French playwright and cinema director, is well known for a film trilogy that dealt with life on the waterfront in Marseilles. The works Yûji mentions constitute the first two of these scripts: *Marius* (1929) and *Fanny* (1931), which in 1945 the American playwright S. N. Behrman adapted as a musical comedy (the third was *César* [1936]). These earthy, sentimental comedies faithfully depict simple lives; sometimes, however, critics claim that vulgar caricature erodes the plays' vitality, humor, and pathos.

INTERURBAN IN SPRING—Scarlet vetch renders *akai genge*, Chinese milk vetch [*rengesô*], a leguminous herb belonging to the Pulse family. Its stems grow from creepers that farmers plant in their fields for fertilizer. Common vetch blooms in spring with purple or pink flower clusters; the stems measure 4 to 12 inches high. ✔ Rape [*nanohana*] is a hardy annual herb of the *Cruciferae* family (Latin name, *Brassica napus*), related to cabbage and turnip. Its seeds valued for oil content and as a component of bird feed.

INVITATION TO A TRIP—For a flower growing from a stone embankment, ☞ "Fresh Autumn Lyric" (page 85), "River" (page 133), and "Song of the Stream" (page 182). ✔ For other references to a Gillette blade, ☞ "Fresh Autumn Lyric" (page 85), "Songs of Old—Fragments" (page 103), and "Summer Sketch Book" (page 88); indirectly, "June Chanson" (page 84).

JAPANESE FALL—This work catalogs natural features that Japanese traditionally associate with autumn. Mustard plants are the same as rape [*nanohana*], ☞ INTERURBAN IN SPRING. ✔ Bush clover [*hagi*—the Chinese character combines graphs for grass and autumn; Latin name, *Lespedeza bicolor*] is a legume that grows 3 to 5 feet tall. The tips of its twigs nearly touch the ground when its spikes bloom several layers of delicate red, butterfly–like flowers. ☞ EULALIA [*susuki*]. ✔ The line, "cricket chirrups saturating rocks" refers to a common classical conceit most famously captured in a famed Bashô haiku, ☞ GROVE (ii).

JOURNEY'S END—The citron [*yuzu*; Latin name, *Citrus junos*, the Chinese lemon] features a prominent bump that suggests the nipple of the female breast. In autumn this tart fruit exudes a very pungent odor. ✔ For "inbound [*nobori ressha*]," ☞ MY HOMETOWN (ii).

JULY—"Sans eyebrows" refers to the ancient custom among Japanese women of having their eyebrows shaved or plucked to mark the onset of puberty or entry into womanhood [*mayu–harai*]. Heian court ladies customarily applied makeup to create false brows slightly above where nature placed them. The poem's expression refers also to contemporary entertainers or courtesans who find it chic to imitate ancient courtly traditions.

JUNE CHANSON—Yûji consistently writes French words like *chanson* in capital Roman letters. For plane tree, ☞ PASSING AUTUMN.

JUNE POEM—FRAGMENTS—Aralia registers *yatsude* ["eight hands"; Latin names, *Araliaceae* or *Fastia japonica*], a plant that Japanese associate with winter. Dictionaries describe the *yatsude* as an evergreen shrub with shiny leaves but offer no English term. I derive the name from the Latin. ✔ Pallid neck and paleness suggest that this girl suffers from TB; reference to the neck, by connecting with sex, also could imply that she may never know love. Japanese have long regarded the female neck as extremely erotic. ☛ Yûji began smoking when he was in middle school (no smoking allowed on campus, however) and never gave up the habit; ☞ CIGARETTES.

JUNE SKETCHES—The cuckoo [*hototogisu* or *kakkô* after its call] is a long–tailed, thin bird slightly smaller than a dove; it summers in Japan, arriving between mid–April and mid–May and leaving in mid-August. The *kakkô* announces the coming of summer—a time of heavy heat—so it associates with weightiness and can convey a tinge of pensiveness.

The cuckoo has obnoxious habits. The female lays each of her four or five eggs in the nests of smaller birds (she prefers the shrike [*mozu*, ☞ FINGERS OF A NEW SEASON] or bunting [*hôjiro*, ☞ VALLEY] because their eggs most closely resemble hers). She makes sure to replace an existing egg with hers; this guarantees that her larger chick will dominate its surrogate mother's feeding energies. ☛ ☞ BUTTERBUR STALKS; for gardenia [or jasmine; *kuchinashi*], ☞ YOUTHFUL DAYS—PROLOGUE.

KATAKANA—The "square" syllabary resembles our block printing and contrasts with the cursive syllabary, ☞ HIRAGANA, comparable to longhand. Before 1946, schools taught *katakana* in first grade; after 1946, teachers introduced it in second or third grade.

KATYDID—These singing, winged, nocturnal insects are a species of horned grasshopper, usually green. What we hear as *katy–did, katy–didn't*, the Japanese hear as *suichon–suichon*, so they call it *suitcho*. Some call it *umaoi* [horse chaser] because its song supposedly resembles the cry of a colt looking for its mother. ☛ Japanese associate katydids with autumn, when the insects often enter buildings, especially at night, attracted by the light. Japanese conventionally connect autumn with the joys of reading. ☛ A. G. Eiffel designed this 984–foot iron tower for the 1889 Paris Exposition; for decades it was the world's tallest man–made structure.

KIN—Yûji was going on six when his father was killed; the extended Kinoshita family then pitched in to help the widow care for her children. Since his mother re–married two years after this event, it is not likely this aunt "raised" Yûji. ☞ SASANQUA. In the Japanese context, a "moss–covered yard" conveys positive nuances of good taste and antiquity.

KIND TAGGER—This poem was put to music and performed for the first time on 1961.03.19 at the Takanashi Middle School in Onomichi (on this city, ☞ TO TSUNODA KAN'EI); ☞ SASANQUA; ☞ NANDINA; for another reference to playing tag, ☞ the children's poem, "Hide and Seek" (page 143).

KOTATSU—Consists of a charcoal brazier [*hibachi*] under a blanket–covered table or frame; one sits around the table where the trapped heat can warm hands and legs. A built–in *kotatsu* consists of a table over a *hibachi* sunk in the ground; this allows one to sit on the mats (☞ TATAMI) with legs dangling. Most city dwellers now use a low table with a built–in heating lamp.

LAKESIDE—AT TÔGÔ SPA—This hot springs in Tottori Prefecture, due north of Okayama City, cures female diseases, nervous disorders, skin problems, and so on. Located on the south shores of Lake Tôgô, it is close to Matsuzaki Station on the San'in Trunk Line that runs along the Japan Sea coast. Kurayoshi is the nearest large city. ✔ For reed, ☞ SONG OF THE REED.

Smelt registers *amasagi*, a regional name for pond smelt [*wakasagi*], a small slender fish of the salmon family with tasty and fragrant meat. Some swim up streams to spawn and some exist in landlocked lakes. ✔ "Savory pear" registers *Nijusseiki nashi* [20th century pear], a delicious round Japanese variety, crunchy like apples—both taste and shape unlike our pears.

LATE AUTUMN (i)—On the white season, ☞ PASSING AUTUMN. ✔ A sedge hat [*sugegasa*] now suggests an outdoor worker doing manual labor; in former days, however, anyone desiring protection from the sun might wear one. These hats, which look like large upside–down, shallow bowls, very effectively keep sun and rain off the wearer's face and neck. ✔ Grasslike sedge [*suge*], a marsh herb that resembles bulrushes, has solid, angular stems that distinguish it from true grasses. A white sedge hat might suggest fading because of continued exposure to the bright sun.

(ii)—On the bath, ☞ HEATING THE BATH WATER. ✔ "Sunken hearth" registers *irori*, often in the center of a room; a hook hangs from a rafter to hold vessels over the fire. Universally symbolic of family unity.

(iii)—For reference to fall's white hands, ☞ SUMMER'S END. ✔ "Sounds of water" doubtless refers to paddies being drained; ☞ SONGS OF THE FOOTHILLS.

LATE NIGHT WHISTLER—Giuseppe Verdi (1813–1901) finished the tragic opera *La Traviata* [woman led astray] in 1853; it abounds in the lush, romantic motifs and arias many Japanese find appealing. The same could be said of the melodies of Peter Tchaikovsky (1840–1893). ✔ In winter, Orion appears late at night. Among the brightest and most conspicuous, this constellation reaches its zenith in late January.

LATE SPRING (ii)—Yûji writes *Juglans Sieboldiana* in Roman letters. It's one of many plants the German naturalist Philipp Franz van Siebold (1796–1866) named. He spent over a decade in Japan studying plants, history, and language.

Yukiyanagi [snow willow; a spiraea] is a deciduous shrub of the rose family. It grows along riverbanks; flowers and leaves appear simultaneously. The name comes from the plant's drooping willow–like branches and delicate snowflake–like flowers. ✔ "Blue cat" refers to Hagiwara Sakutarô's second poetry collection (1923; ☞ MORNING POEM) and elicits thoughts of a sad tomcat roaming night streets in search of companionship and sex.

LATE SPRING FLUTE—On the flute, ☞ YOU ON THE FLUTE.

LATE SUMMER—Squash and millet [*kabocha* and *kibi*] mature in autumn; they frame the poem with an anticipated fruition that contrasts with the scene's static ennui. ✔ A section of the second stanza of Horiguchi Daigaku's poem "Sanitarium Nocturne," in *Moon and Pierrot* (1919), may have partially inspired

Yûji: "Tooting its lonely whistle, / the night train stops / at the foothill station. / (No one gets off.) / (No one gets on.)" Daigaku would feel honored, not that his work had been plagiarized.

L'ESPOIR—Yûji writes the title in capital Roman letters. ✒ "Moon mushroom" renders *tsukiyotake* [moonshine mushroom], a deadly poisonous half–moon shaped fungus of the *matsutake* family indigenous to Japan; it thrives in the fall. ✒ The average Japanese kitchen in those days, invariably on the north side of the house, was a dark and dank place.

LIGHTNING (i)—For water draining from paddies, ☞ SONGS OF THE FOOTHILLS. ✒ The zelkova [*keyaki*; Latin name, *Zelkova serrata*] is a massive deciduous tree related to the leek [*nira*] family. Reaching from 60 to nearly 100 feet in height, it flowers in spring and produces small serrated leaves resembling those of the elm. In autumn, these leaves turn brown and fall with tiny berries attached to their short stems. Zelkova wood serves equally well for construction, or to make soaking tubs and utensils. ✒ These trees prefer hilly areas but also may be found planted as windbreaks around farmers' homes (cf., the Musashi Plain, west of Tokyo).

❏ **LITERARY FRAGMENT**—Both (i) and (ii) describe the same experience, if with noticeable differences in expression. In (i) the final image features cabbages, in (ii) it is onions.
(ii) Dahlias [*dariya*], native to Mexico, are perennials of the chrysanthemum family that bloom in most colors but blue. Japanese varieties produce bushes that reach from 4 to 6 feet high. They grow from tubers that resemble sweet potatoes. The puffy flower reaches 6 inches or more in diameter.

LITTLE HARBOR TOWN—For another work with the image of ice cream melting on a coach windowsill, ☞ "Seaside Town" (page 206).

LUNA PARK—In those days, *Runa • pâku* served as the name for amusement parks, the way Kodak long meant camera. The original Luna Park opened 1906.09.10 in the Asakusa entertainment quarter of Tokyo. It emulated the Luna Park (one of two amusement areas on Coney Island; the other was Dreamland) located south of Manhattan Island, New York City. ✒ After the Tokyo Asakusa park burned in 1911.04, another Luna Park—the one Yûji refers to—opened 1912.07.03 in Osaka. Fire bombs destroyed it 1943.01.
　　Warbler registers *uguisu*; ☞ HIRUZEN PLATEAU—AT A CAMPSITE. ✒ Beetles habitually turn over on their backs when they die; this figure suggests a youth lying on a field and dreaming of the future and its rainbow of hope. For related uses of this image, ☞ "At Sandan Gorge" (ii) (page 196) and "Hotel in the Foothills" (page 168). ✒ Hagiwara Sakutarô (1886–1942; ☞ MORNING POEM) wrote the poem "At Luna Park," first published in 1931 and included in his 1934 collection, *Isle of Ice* [*Hyôtô*]; it features the persona "alone together" with his girl friend on the airplane ride.

MEADOWLARK NEST—Larks [*hibari*], robin–sized birds with brownish feathers and speckled breasts, make their nests on the ground.

MÉMOIRE—Title in capital Roman letters. For fava (or horse) beans, Yûji writes
☞ SORAMAME in ☞ KATAKANA. ✔ The buckwheat plant [*soba no hana*; Latin
name, *Eriogonum*], an annual of the smartweed family, grows from 1.5 to nearly
3 feet high. Its flowers are petite and delicate white blooms that lack true petals.
In early fall they blossom in clusters and look like stamens rising from among a
ring of five very small leaves (on stems that grow from the plant's far larger
heart–shaped leaves).

MEMORIES OF FIRE—MOURNING HIROSHIMA VICTIMS—"That form
burnt into..." refers to the shadow of a human being etched on the sidewalk in
front of the main Sumitomo Bank in downtown Hiroshima; the atomic blast had
vaporized an individual standing there. ☞ AT HIROSHIMA'S MEMORIAL PEACE
PARK; ☞ UNDER SHARED SKIES, II. ATOMIC BOMB DOME.

MEMORIES OF SNOW—Wagtail [*sekirei*], the size of a sparrow, is a long–
tailed, insect–eating terrestrial songbird related to the pipit and lark. The wagtail
incessantly bobs its tail; it prefers to settle near water.

MISO—A fermented paste—long a staple of the Japanese diet—derived from
soybeans. This paste creates a dish with a high level of gas–producing B vitamins
(and reasons to belch). ✔ Makers crush boiled soybeans, add another grain
(barley, rice, or wheat), then a mold that acts like yeast. This mixture ripens from
several months up to three years.
  This soup [*miso shiru*] is not only extremely nutritious—the usual serving
contains ca. 16% of an adult's daily protein requirement—but very quick and
easy to prepare. This makes it a favorite for breakfasts, though it may be served at
any meal. Cooks add such vegetables as button mushrooms [*nameko*], bean curd
[*tôfu*], eggplant, or whatever is in season.

MOCHI—Makers first use a large wooden mallet to pound hot, steamed glutinous
rice into a viscous mass. They then form the sticky paste into balls or cakes to be
used in various dishes or eaten separately. Sometimes *mochi* is toasted and
included in soups, sometimes made into confections. *Mochi* has had special
associations with New Year's festivities.

MORNING POEM—Blue cat refers to *Ao Neko* [*Blue Cat*], the well–known 1923
poetry collection of Hagiwara Sakutarô (1886–1942). Hagiwara specifies that, in
the English sense, blue means melancholy. Cat calls up images of the tomcat
seeking love on darkened streets. ✔ Dutch lipstick [*Oranda beni*] refers simply to
a Western cosmetic; for many years the word "Dutch" signified exotic European
imports or non–Asian items.

MOUNTAIN INN—Of course, Yûji read these works in Japanese. "Hudson on
natural history" refers to the work of William Henry Hudson (1844–1922),
naturalist and novelist born in Argentina of American parents but naturalized a

British citizen. His works focus on nature or the natural world. It is difficult to know which translation Yûji was reading.

Katherine Mansfield (Kathleen Beauchamp) (1888–1923), British writer born in New Zealand, wrote mainly short stories and produced a collection of poetry. Yûji may have been reading *The Garden Party* (1922; *Enyûkai* in Japanese translation), her best–known short–story collection in Japan. ✔ For sweetfish [*ayu*, which could also be rendered smelt], ☞ EARLY SUMMER.

MOUNTAIN PATH— ☞ EULALIA, a variety of pampas grass.

MY FATHER—Contrast this mid–1950s work with the first two stanzas of the 1948 Maruyama Kaoru children's poem, "*Asa* [Mornings]": "Whenever Father opens his newspaper, / morning sun quickly floods / every article. // Fresh print reeks / in morning sun. / How pleasant the smell of newsprint."

MY HOMETOWN (ii)—On bracken, ☞ AFTERNOON. ✔ "Inbound" registers *nobori ressha*, which refers to a train headed for Tokyo or the nearest main town, in this case Fukuyama. The correlative is "outbound" [*kudari ressha*], a train headed away from Tokyo or any important regional city. ✔ Before the American Occupation (1945–1952), Japanese usually used the term "up train" (correlative: "down train"), translated directly from British English. ✔ For another reference to box lunch, ☞ "Harbor Festival" (page 187).

MY LIFE (ii)—"In deep shade" or a "lone tree" echoes the poet's family name, Kinoshita ["under the tree"], suggesting shade.
(iii)—Re the candyman's flute, ☞ EARLY SUMMER. ✔ The image of an older woman's hidden teeth suggests the traditional reluctance among Japanese females to open the mouth very widely, smile broadly, or laugh openly. It is considered proper for a well–mannered female to smile or laugh only behind a hand held in front of her mouth.

MY WAY (i)—This first poem in the collection *Flute Player* determines the mood for the entire book and my rendering (the Japanese title is "*Michi*").
(ii)—For "deep in my shade," ☞ MY LIFE (ii). I think "tramping my shadow" might consequently suggest something beyond the obvious meaning.

NANDINA—A winter plant, the nandina [*nanten*; Latin name, *Nandina domestica*] is an evergreen of the barberry family that grows to a height of 6 feet. Its cane–like stems earn the description "sacred bamboo." Red berries develop in late fall; leaves redden during the coldest part of winter. If only the berries are red, the time is late autumn or early winter.

❑ **NEW LEAVES ON CHERRY TREES (i) (ii)**—These words register the Japanese title, *hazakura*, which refers to cherry trees that have finished blooming and started to leaf. The English in no way communicates the sense of evanescence over the blossoms' brief but now scattered glory.

NIISAN CRICKET—Yûji writes, *niisan* [big brother] *mushi* [bug]. Professor Okimoto believes the *niisan mushi*, a regional term, is a cricket.

NIKOGORI—Dictionaries identify *nikogori* as jelly or congealed food and sometimes render it "meat jelly." I have translated it "aspic" in the past, but though the image of a cold jelly associated with meat approaches *nikogori*, it may present a misleading nuance. When certain fish—and the juices they were cooked in—cool down, they congeal. Those cold, jelled leftovers the Japanese call *nikogori*. ☛ Yûji also refers to *nikogori* in: "At Table" (page 114), "Evening Fox" (page 203), and "I Can Make It" (page 202).

NIGHT ON THE COUNTRYSIDE—Storehouses [*dozô*; godown] invariably have very thick white walls; they exist throughout the countryside and serve as nearly fireproof warehouses to store family treasures and products. Note that Japanese ☛ TôFU [bean curd] is very white.

NIGHT SCHOOL STUDENT— ☛ KATYDID.

NOCTURNE—Yûji registers this word in capital Roman letters. ☛ On the significance of the *kuchinashi* [gardenia or jasmine], ☛ YOUTHFUL DAYS—PROLOGUE. ☛ Mortuary and other images of death relate to the fall season.

NOTES ON EARLY AUTUMN—Fresh bean curd is white; *tôfu* strained through silk [*kinugoshi*] has an especially fragile delicacy; ☛ TôFU. ☛ "Sword beans" registers *katana mame*, an annual tropical Asian legume cultivated for centuries in Japan. Even writing the graph for sword [*katana*], Japanese usually read *nata* (Mr. Haraguchi reports, however, that in one anthology containing this poem an editor inserts the designation [*rubi*] *katana* by the sword graph). ☛ The bean's proper name, *nata mame*, derives from its curved, flat, and thick pod that brings a hatchet [*nata*] to mind. ☛ Long rows of butterfly–shaped flowers, mauve or rose pink, appear in the summer. The 4 inch long pods yield deep red or purple beans that (like the pods) are edible. Another variety produces white flowers and white beans.

ODE— ☛ EULALIA (pampas grass).

OLD HOUSE—This poem supposedly depicts a house where Yûji stayed in Nagoya while attending the college of pharmacy. He roomed in Tokyo with his brother, Takuji, who was attending medical school.

ON A SUNNY DAY—Yûji's poor sense of direction caused him to get lost, even within a block of his home. For reeds, ☛ SONG OF THE REED. ☛ For fragrant olive [*kinmokusei*], ☛ FRAGRANT OLIVE. ☛ Quartz renders *suishô*; the persona hunted rocks with embedded glittery crystals common to that area.

ON THE IZUMO ROAD—Izumo—the ancient name for the eight provinces along the Japan Sea (the *San'indô*) that now comprise Shimane Prefecture—boasts many ancient and famous Shinto shrines. ✒ ☞ BUTTERBUR STALKS. ✒ For the warbler [*uguisu*], ☞ HIRUZEN PLATEAU—AT A CAMPSITE. ✒ For Mt. Daisen, ☞ CAMPSITE—ON HIRUZEN PLATEAU.

ONE DAY, ONE MOMENT—Larks nest and feed on the ground; many regard them morning birds. For reed, ☞ SONG OF THE REED. ✒ "That distant cloud" refers to the atomic bomb's mushroom cloud over Hiroshima (detonated 1945.08.06 at 8:15 A.M.); ☞ "At Hiroshima's Memorial Peace Park" (page 206) and "Under Shared Skies—Hiroshima Reportage" (page 147 ff.).

The whirligig is the *mizusumashi*, a water beetle of the *Gryinidae* class; haiku poets regard it a summer insect. Regional names include *uzumushi* (whirl bug) and *mai–mai–mushi* (likely, "dance–dance bug"). These shiny beetles feed mainly on small bugs near the surface but sometimes dive for their food. They spin, usually in groups, over sheltered water. Some three–fourths of an inch long, they are oval in shape and dark brown to blue–black. ✒ Note that the forelegs of the whirligig are noticeably longer than its other legs but far shorter than those of the pond skater or waterstrider.

OSPREY—ON OUMISHIMA—For this island, ☞ AT OUMISHIMA. ✒ The osprey [*misago*] or fish hawk belongs to the eagle family; this sleek–looking bird of prey, slightly larger than a raven, has a 5 to 6 foot wingspan. Invariably found near water, the osprey feeds exclusively on fish it catches live with its claws.

The idea that osprey "taught" Japanese how to make ☞ SUSHI may derive, Professor Okimoto informs me, from *misagozushi*. The hawk "makes" this when it stores caught fish among shaded rocks. Salt water splashing on the fish soon gives it the special taste of *sushi*.

PARK—Noon cannon refers to the custom of marking the noon hour, much as fire sirens once announced noon in many small towns across America. ✒ Reference to the "lanky Italian" conveys little more than a striven–for romantic mood. ☞ SKY.

PASSING AUTUMN—Associated with spring when their flowers bloom, plane trees—often called platanus, as Yûji knew them [*puratanusu*]—are tall (reaching 90 feet) deciduous trees belonging to the sycamore family. Their large, lobed leaves resemble those of the maple. ✒ The dry fruit of the plane tree consists of hard brown seed pods that encourage the regional term *suzukakenoki* [bell–hang tree]; these pods invite some in the West to call the trees buttonwoods. Since introducing them as ornamental shade trees during the last half of the 19th century, Japanese have planted platanus along many city streets. ✒ The figure of a "white hearse" matches conventional images of fall. The hearse associates with the death of the year and whiteness with the glare of cloud–free skies that characterize the season.

PASSING SHOWER—Carniolan (presumed from Yûji's ☞ *katakana*, *kânioran*) bees come, I am guessing, from Carniola, a historic region in Slovenia (the northwest area of what was Yugoslavia).

PENSÉE—Aside from being exotic, it is not clear why Yûji uses the French word for thought or idea (*pensée* also means pansy). The foreign vocable may imply that the persona's thought processes in this instance are more objective than normal Japanese terms might suggest. Note the possible echo of man as a "thinking reed"; ☞ SONG OF THE REED.

PHEASANT—Bamboo grass [*kumazasa*; Latin name, *Sasa albo–marginata*] belongs to the rice family; its narrow, whip–like stems grow to a height of from 1 to 3 feet. The edible leaves dry up in late fall and turn chalky—another reason poets connect white hues with this season. ✔ *Kumazasa* prefers hillside habitats, but people love to plant it in their gardens as an ornamental.

PLAYGROUND—"Picture story man" renders *kamishibaiya* ["paper theater man"], someone who biked around local neighborhoods before the days of television to tell stories. He beat wooden clappers to inform children in the area to gather behind his bicycle. After selling them candy, he used pictures mounted in a frame on the back of his bike to tell mystery or adventure stories; many *kamishibaiya* also used a drum for dramatic effects. ✔ I italicize the stanzas that Yûji encloses in parentheses.

POET OF THE RUBAIYAT—Omar Khayyam (1048?–1131) was a noted poet, philosopher, mathematician, and astronomer of Persia. As a poet, Khayyam is known for his collection of quatrains called the *Robâ'îyât*, which his translator Edward FitzGerald (1809–1883) rendered freely into English under the title, *The Rubáiyát of Omar Khayyam* (1859). ✔ This poem appeared in a publication of Higashi [East] High School in Fukuyama.

PORT—IMPRESSIONS OF "O" CITY—"O" is the Inland Sea port of Onomichi, a lovely city built on steep hills; it lies 12.5 rail miles west of Fukuyama (toward Hiroshima); ☞ TO TSUNODA KAN'EI. ✔ "Longshoremen" registers *ninpu*, usually translated coolie or laborer.

PORTRAIT OF THE CITY—Portrait registers *dessan*, for the French word *dessein* [design, purpose, scheme, plan]. ✔ On plane trees, ☞ PASSING AUTUMN. ✔ "Caged animals" refers to the small zoos often found on the roofs of metropolitan department stores.

PRELUDE TO AUTUMN— ☞ SMARTWEED SPIKES. ✔ Mulberry leaves provide feed for silkworms fattening up before they spin their cocoons.

QUIET EVENING—On "fields being burnt over," ☞ FEBRUARY.

RAILS—Yûji writes *rêru* (derived from English) in ☞ HIRAGANA rather than the expected ☞ KATAKANA.

RAINBOW AND SNAIL—On silverberry leaves [*guminoha*], ☞ SONGS OF THE FOOTHILLS, 1. MORNING. ✔ On the rainbow's red band, ☞ CREAKY CHAIRS.

RECOLLECTIONS OF FATHER (i)—When an accident killed Tsuneichi on 1920.07.22, Yûji was going on six. The claim that his father died "in late fall" creates a resonance with the season and enhances the sense of loss.
(ii)—Magnolias usually flower in early spring, but some late–blooming varieties blossom in late spring or early summer.

RED MOON—A butterbur leaf is as large as rhubarb; ☞ BUTTERBUR STALKS.

❏ **RIVER**—Source of the superior ☞ SONG OF THE STREAM (page 182), which lists poems with the image of flowers blooming from a stone embankment.

SALVIA—*Sarufuia* [or *sarubia*; Latin name, *Salvia officinalis*], an aromatic shrub, is a mint family herb, a type of sage imported from southern Europe. Many varieties exist; flowers run from deep blue through bright red and purple. Japanese use its leaves to season Western foods, its seeds for beverage or flour. Salvia has summer associations.

SAND BATH—AT YUBARA SPA—A hot springs located in the mountains of northwestern Okayama Prefecture, adjacent to the border of Tottori Prefecture and due north of Okayama City. Yubara lies almost 13 miles north of Katsuyama Station (☞ AT KATSUYAMA STATION). Used as a spa since the 11th century, designated a "National Hot–Spring Resort." Some 300,000 visit annually. Known for large salamanders.

Miho–no–Matsubara [i.e., "Miho's pine groves"]. The Miho sandbar juts into Suruga Bay from east of Kuno Hill to form a natural breakwater for the port of Shimizu, Shizuoka Prefecture. Old pine groves line the spit, a two–mile long stretch of white sand. Poets and artists since ancient times have celebrated the natural beauty of this place and treasured its view of Mt. Fuji, directly to the north.

The "nymph…at Miho–no–Matsubara" refers to the legend of the feathered robe [*hagoromo*] made famous by the Noh play of that name. A nymph (variously described as an angel or a goddess; Yûji writes *tennyo* [heavenly maiden]) visiting Miho–no–Matsubara hung her magic robe on a pine tree and went for a swim. The fisher Hakuryô discovered it, stole it, and kept the *tennyo* from returning to heaven. He promised to return the robe if the unclothed goddess would perform for him the dances of heaven (doubtless erotic). ☛ Spas issue robes (☞ YUKATA) marked to identify the inn; guests wear them to the baths, to bed, and on strolls around the inn.

SASANQUA—The graphs "mountain–tea–flower" identify the *sazanka*, seen as a winter plant. The sasanqua is a broad–leafed evergreen of the camellia family; another name is "*hime tsubaki* [princess camellia]." Sasanqua vary from tall trees (some grow to a height of 30 or more feet) to dense bushes.

Japanese who live in warmer areas like Kyushu, Shikoku, and the Inland Sea cultivate the *sazanka* in their yards as an ornamental; its big seeds yield oil. Large five–petaled clearly flimsy white, rose, or deep blood–colored flowers appear lushly from early fall into winter.

SCENES—Yûji had earlier published three of the four parts that comprise this poem; he gave each the same title, "*Fûkei* [Scene]": 1—1954.02. ✔ For Yûji's attitude toward crossing gates, ☞ "At a Grade Crossing" (i) (page 138) and "Quotidian Seat" (page 158). The latter indirectly hints that the crossing gate may have symbolized for Yûji the way fate short–circuited his hopes. ✔ For another work that deals with a train whistle having an invisible tail, ☞ "Winter" (ii) (page 135). ✔ 2—1956.07. On reeds, ☞ SONG OF THE REED. ✔ 3—1955.11. Warbler registers *uguisu*, ☞ HIRUZEN PLATEAU—AT A CAMPSITE. ✔ 4—Cattle tongues resemble red third–class tickets, ☞ DAY OF A JOURNEY.

SCHOOL—Professor Befu reports that Japanese customarily say acacia [*akashiya*, actually the pseudo–acacia, *niseakashiya*] when they refer to the honey locust [*saikachi*; Latin name, *Gleditsia*], a deciduous shade tree that grows from 35 to 70 feet high. Acacia designates many related evergreen shrubs and trees. ✔ ☞ HIRAGANA.

The black kite [*tobi*; class *Accipitridae*] is a compact dark brownish bird slightly larger than a crow. Long regarded a second–class relative of eagles and hawks, this kite inhabits much of central and East Asia—often living within city limits or near the shore. It feeds chiefly on frogs, insects, and reptiles but also scavenges small animals.

❑ SEA TRIP—The first part is virtually identical to ☞ "Wheat Harvest" (page 110). ✔ For why I render *aogashi* "camphor trees," ☞ WHEAT HARVEST.

SEASIDE TOWN—ON THE KURÉ LINE—The Kuré Line runs east from Hiroshima, south through Kuré along the Inland Sea through Takehara to Mihara, and terminates at Itozaki. Kuré was a famous naval base on the southeast edge of Hiroshima Bay. ✔ For another image of ice cream melting on a window ledge in a train, ☞ "Little Harbor Town" (page 144). ✔ Oleander [*kyôchikutô*; Latin name, *Nerium indicum*] is a late summer flower that resembles the rosebay. Some identify it as phlox, the "starfire" (Latin name, *Phlox paniculata*). Hot summer weather causes its flowers to droop, giving the impression they are weary of blooming.

SHISO—From the mint family, an edible aromatic annual imported from China. Thanks to the entry common to most Japanese–English dictionaries, people often translate *shiso* "beefsteak plant" after the red variety used for making pickled plums [*umeboshi*, i.e., apricots]; its fragrant leaves turn a delicate purple. The more common green variety is called perilla (after its Latin names, *Perilla frutescens* or *Perilla crispa*). ✔ Green *shiso* leaves customarily garnish food, appear in *tenpura* and *sushi* dishes, etc. *Shiso* usually has summer associations. Many connect it nostalgically with mother's cooking.

SHÔJI—These uniformly–sized sliding divider doors paneled with translucent paper invariably face the corridor (☞ ENGAWA) along the southern exposure in traditional homes throughout Japan. In general, *shôji* doors separate living quarters from hallways. They sometimes serve as interior window coverings.

SHOWER—Comparing an old farm woman to a guinea hen [*horohorochô*, a fowl native to Africa] is an inspired description. This bird has a smallish white head and a medium thin neck that attaches to a plump—even dumpy—silver or pearl-gray body. Its 45º back line ends in a short tail and matches the bent spines of countless older women in Japan's rural areas.

SHÛHÔ CAVE • AKIYOSHI PLATEAU—Also called Akiyoshi Cave, designated a Special Natural Monument; 18.5 miles west of the depot in Yamaguchi, near the western tip of Honshu. Among the largest such caves known; roomiest by far of the several stalactitic caverns on the Akiyoshi Plateau. This karst plateau—an irregular limestone region—features many sinks, underground streams, and caverns.

Shûhô Cave [*dô*] is shaped like a two–tined pitchfork; the long "handle" corresponds to the entrance tunnel. The opening to the cave is over 70 feet high and 24 feet wide. Inside it averages 120 feet in width; it is 450 feet at its widest. A guided tour takes about two hours. ✔ An elevator from the cave floor takes the visitor up 240 feet to the Akiyoshi Plateau; a science museum there features the cave's natural wonders.

SINGING—This poem depicts Yûji helping the teacher during music class (NB: his family name suggests tree shade). Yûji composed the lyrics, written on a large piece of paper attached to an easel or to the blackboard. He holds the page down so it will not roll up. For him, the song's crucial points—as the points of his poetry—relate to life and living as a human being. ✔ Gadfly, sometimes translated horsefly, registers *abu* (which includes a wide variety of large hairy flies). These flies attack livestock and have a painful bite. The female sucks blood and can infect her victims with diseases.

SKY—Autumn weather in Japan suggests cloudless blue skies, thus the special term "clear autumn days [*akibare*]."

SKY—VAGRANT—Vagrant renders *runpen* [German *Lumpen*], which suggests an unemployed loafer, hobo, or tramp. ☞ SKY.

SLAUGHTER HOUSE—Yûji labels this work "No. 1" but no No. 2 exists. ✔ "F" refers to Fuchû (ca. 49,000), a city on the Ashida River that also flows through Fukuyama (☞ BINGO CITIES • POEMS ... DREAMS ¶ ②) before emptying into the Inland Sea. Fuchû—about 12.5 rail miles (on the Fukusen Line) inland from Fukuyama—is the provincial city Yûji commuted to during middle school (in those days, a round trip took an hour). Fuchû's textile industry is salient; agricultural products include tobacco leaves, grains, silkworms, and cattle. ✔ The beef I assume were shipped from the slaughter house in Fuchû, ☞ the 1958 poem "Black Flies" (page 158).

SLEEP—Yûji writes in English, using a capital "U," the words "upas tree" [*upas* in Malay means poison; Latin name, *Antiaris toxicara*]. This gives the poem an exotic cast; few readers outside friends from the college of pharmacy would be familiar with the word. The upas—native to the East Asian tropics—produces a latex that resembles strychnine; Malay natives use it for arrow poison. People have long made its fibers into cloth and paper.

The upas tree belongs to the red mulberry family, which has an unsavory reputation in folklore. The Chinese view the red mulberry as the tree of sorrow. Others see it as a symbol of tragic, unhappy love (notice, for example, the Greek tale of Pyramus and Thisbe).

SLOTH—Following the title (*Namakemono*, written in ☞ KATAKANA), Yûji writes in English, "To my H. Mogami." Mogami Hachihei was a close friend at the Nagoya College of Pharmacy.

SMARTWEED SPIKES—This registers *tade no ho* (Latin name *Polygonum cuspidatum*), called also nettles, jointweed, knotweed, and sometimes water pepper. This tough perennial grows in clumps of wiry stems that reach from 4 to 8 feet in height; the plant produces green–white blooms in late summer or early fall. Juice from the stems serves in summer to prevent insect bites. These spikes symbolize summer's passing and the coming of autumn.

SNIPPETS FROM AN AUTUMN SKETCHBOOK—Camellias [*tsubaki*, sometimes called the Japanese rose; Latin name, *Camellia japonica*]—boast several thousand varieties. These evergreen shrubs grow usually from 6 to 12 feet tall; their extremely delicate flowers fall so readily—not only the petals—that they have long symbolized for Japanese an early, sudden, or untimely death. ✒ Acorns symbolize life and potential.

Ivan S. Turgenev (1818–1883), Russian short story writer, dramatist, and novelist, often dealt with social problems that interested Japan's rural intelligentsia. His 1862 masterpiece, *Fathers and Sons*, confronts problems of tensions between the generations, rebellion against convention, and nihilism.

SOIRÉE—The title means "evening performance • party." Yûji customarily writes French words in capital Roman letters; I add the diacritical mark. ✒ Magnesium burns with an intense but dull and eerie white glow.

SONG OF THE REED (i)—Japanese associate the reed warbler [*yoshikiri*] with summer, for it arrives in May and leaves in August. This bird also frequents reed fields far from water's edge. ✒ Yûji surely had in mind the smaller (about 5 inches long) of the two *yoshikiri* varieties; this type is more often visible and has a more rhythmical call. These sparrow–sized birds, dark brown with black and yellow or white markings, nest on reeds 3 to 6 feet tall. The larger type resembles the bush warbler, ☞ UGUISU.

(ii)—A re–working of (i), written eleven years earlier. Reeds [*ashi* or *yoshi*, also rendered rush or bulrush] are a type of tough but pliant and weavable grass that can reach a height of 6 to 9 feet. ✒ Reeds grow in shallow water or very moist soil; from their jointed, cane–like stems they sprout leaves that resemble those of the bamboo. The single rigid flower spray—rusty red in color and attached to the top of the stem—can exceed a foot in length. Sometimes reed heads bend slightly, giving the impression of humility or of being deep in thought. ✒ One ancient name for Japan was "Land of the Reed Plains."

The ancients used the hollow reed to make music (cf. the panpipe or syrinx; ☞ FIRST LOVE). Reeds accordingly relate to the artist, especially the poet. Though they symbolize resilience in the face of a stormy winds, reeds also imply weakness and vulnerability because they may break easily.

This quality associates the plant with humans, described as "reeds that think." The statement that "man is a thinking reed" comes from the *Pensées* (VI:347; the W. F. Trotter translation) of the French philosopher Blaise Pascal (1623–1662), which Yûji likely learned of through the poetry of Horiguchi Daigaku. The context of Pascal's utterance is that man, though as feeble as a reed, can think. That makes him more noble than the unthinking universe that can so easily crush him. Through his powers of thought, man commands the world. This ability gives him a dignity far more valuable than ability to control space and time.

❑ **SONG OF THE STREAM**—A re-write of ☞ RIVER (page 133), written eleven years earlier. ✔ Flowers that bloom from a stone embankment entranced Yûji, who may have seen them as a figure of his poetry. For other uses of this image, ☞ "Fresh Autumn Lyric" (page 85), "Invitation to a Trip" (page 196), and "River" (page 133).

SONGS OF EARLY SPRING—*Mélancholie* appears in Roman letters with no diacritical mark. ✔ Copper sulfate is a blue crystaline substance.

SONGS OF OLD—FRAGMENTS—Yûji writes the word "fragments" in English. ✔ Rainer Maria Rilke (1875–1926) died of blood poisoning from a scratch he got while tending roses. Rilke's work and poetic theories had a profound effect on many Japanese writers, especially those associated with *Shiki* [*Four Seasons*], whose poets Kinoshita closely identified with; he was never officially a member of their group.

Dryads (wood nymphs) renders *kamigami* [gods • goddesses; Yûji certainly refers to sylvan deities]. In the usual Japanese context, the specific referent of *kami*—the only term the language has for such beings—remains marvelously vague. Japanese can also refer to *tama* • spirits, but the Greeks, by contrast, invented terms for the spirits of mountains, woods, water, etc. ☞ DAWN OVER THE SETO INLAND SEA. ✔ For other references to a Gillette blade, ☞ "Fresh Autumn Lyric" (page 85), "Invitation to a Trip" (page 196), "Summer Sketch Book" (page 88), and indirectly, "June Chanson" (page 84).

SONGS OF THE FOOTHILLS—1. Morning—The deciduous *akigumi* [autumn silverberry] shrub grows to a height of 9 feet or more. Clusters of small red edible berries (with white dots) appear in the fall among green leaves with streaks that hint of silver. Prefers a mountain habitat. ✔ The usual silverberry [*gumi*; an oleaster] is an evergreen with leathery leaves containing streaks of silver; this shrub grows to a height of 15 feet.
2. Noon—Yûji refers to a variety of deciduous magnolia [*hônoki* (*hô* tree); Latin name, *Magnolia hypoleuca*] that grows to a height of 60 feet. Haiku poets associate most fallen leaves, including those of the *hô* tree, with winter. The *hô*'s large leaves grow in clusters at branch ends, where fragrant white, nine–petaled flowers also bloom; each has a triple sepal.

Cypress registers *hinoki*, a Japanese variety of white cedar that grows 90 to 120 feet high. ☛ Water flowing from paddies refers to water being drained near the end of the rice growing cycle; ☞ also "Late Autumn" (iii) (page 118) and "Lightning" (i) (page 134). ☛ The "catch" refers to song birds being netted; like canaries, they will be sold for their beautiful singing voices (not killed or eaten). They include, for example, the *uguisu* [bush warbler, ☞ HIRUZEN PLATEAU—AT A CAMPSITE] and the *mejiro* [white eye].

3. Night—Vladimir Klavdievich Arsen'ev (1879–1930) was a Russian–Soviet researcher and explorer recognized especially for his anthropological and geographical studies of the Soviet far east between 1902 and 1910. ☛ The 1912 Arsen'ev book Yûji mentions (the 1921 Japanese translation is titled *Usurî Kikô*) was a strategic, geographical, and statistical study of the Ussuri region. The work offers minute details about the landscapes of the area, as well as the flora and fauna along the Ussuri River; I suppose this information drew Yûji to its pages. Thanks to its many natural resources, the Ussuri area boasts a comparatively dense population.

One of the region's chief resources is the Ussuri River (which Chinese call the Wushuli) that flows north from Lake Khanka into the Amur and defines part of Manchuria's northeastern border. This 557–mile long waterway—ice free for at least five months—is a rich source of fish and facilitates the transport of lumber, other goods, and people. A city called Ussuri (not found on modern maps) was once situated east of the northern half of Lake Khanka. ☛ For draining paddy water, ☞ second ¶ above under **Noon.**

SORAMAME—Literally, "sky bean," the fava or horse bean is also called broad bean (Latin name, *Vicia faba*). This bushy annual, cultivated in East Asia since ancient times, originates in the Mediterranean area. The large bean turns black as it matures; may be cooked and eaten green. Unlike the usual bean, this is a cool season plant.

SOUR SORREL—*Sukanpo*—popularly called *suiba* in Japan and wood sorrel or shamrock in the West (Latin name, *Oxalis acetosella*)—is related to the buckwheat and smartweed families. In springtime, country children peel the skin from the stem and eat it raw; used as greens in salads.

❏ **SOUTHWIND (i) (ii)**—The second version is fuller.

SPRING—Larks nest on the ground, so it is easy for children to find one and pick up a lark chick. ☛ Few poets in Yûji's milieu would have dared in 1940 to use the technical term "semicircular canals" [*sanhankikan*]. Note that Yûji's mentor, Horiguchi Daigaku, used *sanhankikan* in "Mother's Voice," the opening poem of his 1947 collection, *Ningen no Uta* [*Songs for Mankind*].

SPRING BELL—Yûji wrote this poem in honor of the Takada family, manufacturers of bells in his region.

SPRING VALLEY— ☞ BUTTERBUR STALKS. Aside from the erotic notion of the tumescent butterbur stalks, the idea of a growing butterbur bud [*tô ga tatsu*] implies being past one's prime or left behind.

SQUALL—An ampule is a vial holding the solution for a hypodermic injection or a small glass vessel resembling such a vial. ✔ *Pensée* [thought, idea] Yûji registers in Roman letters; ☞ PENSéE and SONG OF THE REED (ii). He elsewhere compares bird droppings with cuneiform, ☞ AT THE PARK.

SUMMER MOUNTAIN—Gentians [*rindô*], bellflowers [*kikyô*], and the ant [*ari*] appear in ☞ KATAKANA, which compares to underlining or using italics. ✔ Japanese schoolchildren learn that gentians or autumn bellflowers (Latin name, *Gentiana mainoi*) bloom on November hillsides when most other plants have dried up. Their dull brownish habitat thus emphasizes the beauty of their five-petaled, blue–purple flower clusters; these attractive blooms look straight into the sky on stems about 20 inches high. ✔ For bellflowers, ☞ CAMPSITE—ON HIRUZEN PLATEAU. ✔ I render as "oxydol" the word *okishifuru* (oxyful) because Dr. Kinoshita told me that in those days it was a brand name for oxydol, a liquid bleach used sometimes as a disinfectant.

SUMMER SKETCHBOOK— ☞ SOUR SORREL. ✔ For Yûji, middle school was a five–year course for boys between the ages of twelve and eighteen. ✔ Shepherd's purse [*penpen–gusa* (grass) or *nazuna*; Latin name, *Capsella bursa–pastoris*] is an annual herb belonging to the rape family (crucifers—they bloom small, star-shaped flowers). It originated in Europe and western Asia, but Japanese long regarded it one of the seven major spring plants.

The English name comes from the triangular seed pods that people once thought resembled a shepherd's purse. Many regard it a weed. ✔ The stems of the *nazuna* radiate about a foot from the center; edible leaves spread along the ground and in March produce on tall stems tiny, four–petaled white flowers. They no sooner bloom than below them the plant produces flat, deltoid seeds that resemble the plectrum of a *samisen* [Japanese banjo; one regional name is *samisen–gusa*]. Indeed, the *penpen* in this popular designation derives from the "plunk–plunk" sound of the plectrum on samisen strings.

Boys could easily write the straight lines of the ☞ KATAKANA (☞ HIRAGANA) syllabary with this soft green, deltoid seed. ✔ For other references to a Gillette blade, ☞ "Fresh Autumn Lyric" (page 85), "Invitation to a Trip" (page 196), and "Songs of Old—Fragments" (page 103); indirectly, "June Chanson" (page 84).

SUMMER SONG—Herman Hesse (1877–1962), German (later, naturalized Swiss) novelist and poet, recipient of the 1946 Nobel Prize in Literature. The body of his Romantic poetry is inconsequential. In novels that combine Indian mysticism with a Jungian approach to psychology, however, he poignantly probes childhood memories and the dream world of the adolescent; these characteristics of his work appealed to Japanese readers like Yûji. ✔ For cuckoo, ☞ JUNE SKETCHES.

SUMMER'S END—Autumn's "white hand" stands for glaring fall skies; ☞ LATE AUTUMN (iii). For associations of white and autumn, ☞ FRESH AUTUMN LYRIC and PASSING AUTUMN.

SUSHI—This dish consists of bite–sized patties of vinegared rice topped by a strip of raw fish, shellfish, and the like, over a dash of horseradish. Some varieties contain vegetables or fish mixed with the rice and wrapped in thin strips of laver (*nori*, dried seaweed; ☞ BINGO CITIES • POETRY ... DREAMS, ¶ ⑦). Japanese use the best vinegared rice for *sushi*; ☞ OSPREY—ON OUMISHIMA.

Sushi originally consisted of pickled fish eaten between layers of cooked rice. The fish tasted more delicious after the rice had fermented and turned slightly sour. During the Edo period, someone sped up the fermentation process by adding vinegar to the cooked rice; this enhanced the taste. The dish soon became popular. Some shops around Lake Biwa still serve *funazushi*, a variety made according to the ancient method. ☞ OSPREY—ON OUMISHIMA.

SYMBOLIST—Among other aims, such poetry preoccupies itself with the inner life of emotional experience and feelings. It stresses intuition over logic, equates words with magic, and prescribes that the musical qualities of verse be integrated with its imagery.

TATAMI—These mats woven from rice straw have for several centuries been uniform in size (roughly 3 by 6 feet; two *tatami*—6 by 6 feet—make one *tsubo*, the traditional area of measurement). Japanese describe room sizes by the number of *tatami* they contain. A standard room of six *tatami* [*roku–jô*] thus equals a 9 by 12 foot rug, or 108 square feet.

TEN YEARS— ☞ SMARTWEED SPIKES. The teacher Yûji refers to was doubtless Kubota Mantarô (1889–1963), the well–known playwright and novelist who was also a skilled amateur haiku poet. ✦ Tu Fu (712–770), who many call China's greatest poet, was a lifelong wanderer who suffered endless setbacks. Wars, rebellions, and famines (especially one in 754 A.D.) caused him and his family constant misery and forced him to wander through bleak regions simply trying to find enough to eat.

Reference to monkeys wailing for him at high noon reflects an experience in 759 when Tu Fu and his family fled again to escape famine. The context is the poet's lament for a widowed younger sister he had not seen for ten years; he wants to visit her but fighting in the area prohibits his journey. Despite the trials he endured, however, Tu Fu continued writing poetry. I am grateful to Professor Shirleen Wong of UCLA for helping locate these citations.

Japanese call the Milky Way "river of heaven [*ama no gawa*]," which connects with the smartweed in Japanese but not in English. ✦ Pomegranates, a fall fruit, boast rich symbolic associations—their shape recalls the brain, their seeds suggest many children and thus familial longevity.

THE DEPARTED—Reference to the cape, commonly worn on campuses in those days, makes one imagine the subject of this poem was a college friend; ☞ "Winter" (i) (page 123).

THOUGHTS WHILE SICK—If the nun's pale neck is visible, her habit must be "modernized." Perhaps hers is a teaching order (Yûji has a Roman Catholic sister in mind) that requires something less than the usual medieval hooded garb. For other references to nuns, ☞ BOREDOM and YOUTHFUL DAYS—PROLOGUE. ✔ This image also may contain a possible erotic reference and double meaning. In Japan the female neck has long been the focus of erotic interest, and, as in Shakespeare's day, a nun can refer to a prostitute. ✔ On jasmines [or gardenias; *kuchinashi*], ☞ YOUTHFUL DAYS—PROLOGUE.

TO A FRIEND IN THE CAPITAL—Yûji grew rice during the war years. On making rope, ☞ "To Tokyo—For Ômi Takuji" (page 126).

TO SOMEONE—For loquat [*biwa*], ☞ WINTER CROW. Yûji is probably addressing one of his talented haiku followers.

TO THE FAR–OFF CAPITAL—Brambles registers *hanaibara*, a seasonal poetic designation for *ibara* [thorns, brambles], a plant of the rose family that appears in the fields and blooms early in the summer. This deciduous shrub grows some 3 feet tall and in autumn produces thin, vine–like prickly stems, white, five–petaled flowers, and edible red druplets.

TO THE SOIL—This commissioned work originally appeared in the *Chûgoku Shinbun* [*Western Honshu News*], a major regional paper.

TO TOKYO—FOR ÔMI TAKUJI—This childhood friend (1917.03.24–1977.06.29) from Miyuki died of pulmonary tuberculosis; he was bedridden for most of the last seven years of his life. Ômi's given name has a different second graph from the name of Yûji's older brother. ✔ The inflation rate during the years immediately following Japan's 1945 surrender was horrendous. The yen started at a rate of less than twenty to a dollar. By early 1949, it was nearing 400 to the dollar. Occupation authorities hence adopted, as part of an economic stabilization plan, the austerity program that Detroit banker Joseph Dodge proposed. The Dodge Line fixed the yen's value at 360 to the dollar, where it stayed for almost twenty–five years.

Yûji's daughter Akiko attended a Catholic school in the area, so he was familiar with Christian festivals. He wrote this poem well before people in his region showed interest in celebrating Christmas. ✔ By rail, it is 492 miles from Fukuyama to Tokyo and almost another 560 from Tokyo to Hokkaido.

TO TSUNODA KAN'EI—(1919–1959) Amateur poet friend of Kinoshita and director of programs on the arts for *Nihon Hôsô Kyôkai* [Japan Broadcasting Company (NHK)], Onomichi. Tsunoda arranged radio broadcasts that Kinoshita made on Japanese poetry; he died of a cerebral hemorrhage at forty. ✔ On Senkô Temple [*Senkôji*], ☞ HARBOR FESTIVAL. The park surrounding the temple contains a playground, an observatory, and a planetarium; it is known for its splendid cherry blossoms and many fine trees and rocks. Because of the height of Senkô Hill, NHK maintains a transmitter and studio there.

Onomichi (ca. 102,000) lies on the Inland Sea some 52 miles east of Hiroshima. Famed since the 15th century as a major commercial and trading port on the Inland Sea. Hub of ferry traffic to outlying islands, including Shikoku, and a shipping and fishing center.

TÔFU—This soybean curd is extremely rich in vitamin B and proteins, easily digested, cholesterol free, low in carbohydrates, and often considered "the poor man's meat" because it is inexpensive. It appears in countless Japanese dishes, spring to winter. ☛ The Japanese introduced this food, which has existed in China for at least two thousand years, around the eighth century. Over the years, Japanese developed a more delicately–flavored, softer, and whiter variety than what the Chinese manufacture.

First the maker softens the dried soybeans in water, crushes and boils them, and finally extracts the soymilk (the pulp provides the stock for *okara*). A coagulant separates the whey from the curds, which end up in a mold. The *tôfu* maker then soaks the settled curd in water; this not only cools and firms it but keeps it fresh. Changing the water often helps keep bean curd fresh.

TOWN IN THE DISTANCE—Obon or the Bon Festival began as a Buddhist service that families held to honor their departed. The lunar calendar called for celebrating Obon on the fifteenth day of the seventh moon; historically, a late summer holiday.

In Japan, the festival commemorates the annual return of all dead spirits to their families (thus Obon is sometimes called the Festival of the Dead). To guide the spirits on their return, people light white–paper lanterns (another term for Obon is the Festival of Lanterns). ☛ In most places, people demonstrate their joy that the entire family—present and past—has gathered by dancing [*odori*]. Rural districts still celebrate *Bon–odori*, a holiday for farmers throughout Japan.

TRIP THROUGH THE INLAND SEA—Probably commissioned for inclusion in a travel brochure.

TWILIGHT—SONG OF "F" TOWN—Refers to Fuchû (☞ SLAUGHTER HOUSE) where Yûji commuted to middle school. ☛ Moonflower registers *yûgao*, a vine that produces a long, funnel–shaped fragrant white flower (Latin name *Calonyction aculeatum*) reminiscent of the morning glory; native to Africa and the Tropics. Frequently seen on an arbor or trellis, the moonflower blooms after sundown but often remains open during overcast days.

UNDER SHARED SKIES—HIROSHIMA REPORTAGE— By rail, 556 miles west by southwest of Tokyo, Hiroshima was originally the site of a castle built at the end of the 16th century. Now a major metropolis of over one million inhabitants, it is the focus of Japan's Chûgoku ("central" but implying western Honshu) Region. The city lies at the head of Hiroshima Bay on the delta of the Ôta River, which splits primarily into the rivers Tenma, Motoyasu, Kyôbashi, Enkô, and the Ôta drainage canal—all of which empty into the Inland Sea.

I. From Hijiyama—The atom bomb exploded over Hiroshima 1945.08.06. With the exception of the rise called Hijiyama [Hiji Hill], not quite a mile south of the main railroad station (of the San'yô Trunk Line, five hours by *Shinkansen* [bullet train] from Tokyo), the area is very flat. Most of the city is visible from the observation point on the southern tip of Hijiyama. ☛ Hiroshima Bay lies to the south of the hill, the City Hall due west, the ABCC Laboratory Building directly south; the Atomic Bomb Dome and other structures associated with Memorial

Park are west and slightly north of Hijiyama.

II. Atomic Bomb Dome—This refers to the gutted ruins of the Industry Promotion Hall, which lay under the epicenter of the blast. The Dome is the only bombed building city officials allow to stand. ☛ Because he was unwilling to give banks—which he detested—free advertisement, Yûji writes only "S," which Japanese readers know stands for Sumitomo. For the "shadow of death," ☞ AT HIROSHIMA'S PEACE MEMORIAL PARK. For another reference to the spiral staircase, ☞ "Gone So Long" (page 207).

III. Before the Cenotaph—The Memorial Cenotaph for A–Bomb Victims features a great vault that imitates the shape of a ☞ HANIWA saddle found in ancient tombs. ☛ A stone chest under the vault contains a list of all bomb victims. On front of the chest is the inscription, *Rest in peace; the error shall not be repeated*. The architect Dr. Tange Kenzô (born 1913) designed the Cenotaph and its location so that the Dome is visible when one faces the vault; directly to the viewer's rear is Peace Memorial Hall. ☛ On the park, ☞ AT HIROSHIMA'S PEACE MEMORIAL PARK.

IV. Vision of a Flower—The precincts of Hiroshima Castle (to the north and west of the sites described above) serve now as a city park. They once were a parade ground for the Japanese Army. The castle's five–story donjon, registered as a national treasure, was not rebuilt until 1958. When Yûji wrote this work in 1956, only ruins existed at the castle site.

Hara Tamiki (1905–1951) was born in Hiroshima Prefecture and graduated in 1932 with a B.A. in English literature from Keiô University in Tokyo; he loved Russian literature and the work of the poet–novelist Murô Saisei (1889–1962). Hara's wife died of illness in 1944; he was exposed to the atomic bomb while visiting Hiroshima to observe the first anniversary of her death. The bombing therefore affected him deeply. ☛ Hara published in 1947 the highly–regarded short story "*Natsu no Hana* [Summer Flower]" about this experience. He committed suicide by jumping in front of a train.

Satô Haruo (1892–1964) was an eccentric and multi–talented artist, poet, novelist, and critic; sometime amateur painter and designer of his books' dust jackets; lifelong friend of the poet and translator Horiguchi Daigaku (1892–1981). Awarded the Culture Medal in 1960; works issued in 12 volumes between 1966 and 1970.

V. Atomic Maidens—Refers to the twenty–five disfigured Japanese girls who, accompanied by two Japanese doctors, left Haneda International Airport on 1955.05.05; doctors at Mount Sinai Hospital in New York City treated their radiation sickness and keloids. ☛ Ms. Helen Yokoyama, their interpreter, informs me that the names of several of these girls began with "H"; Yûji' may refer to Hirata Sadako, who died not long after returning from New York. "N" doubtless refers to Nakabayashi Tomoko. ☛ Keloid scars result from the intense heat of radiation; they are particularly large, thick, and disfiguring. The word comes from the Greek term for "claw," which suggests their ugliness.

"Dog Day Cards" registers *shochû mimai*—the long–standing Japanese custom of sending condolences during the hottest season (dog days) of the year. ☛ For canna [*kanna*], ☞ HARBOR TOWN. ☛ Citizens of Bochum, Germany, donated the four bells in the belfry that towers before the three–story ferroconcrete cathedral. The bells peal daily at 7 A.M., noon, and 6 P.M.

VI. Cathedral Scaffolding—Refers to the Memorial Cathedral for World Peace built in 1954. It began as the dream of the German Jesuit Fr. Hugo Lassalle, present at the bombing. Its pipe organ, presented by the people of Cologne, Germany, is the largest in Japan. ✦ Black rain [*kuroi ame*] refers generically to radioactive precipitation, specifically to what fell in Hiroshima after the atom bombing. The term has been immortalized in world literature by the 1966 Noma Prize–winning novel of that title (English translation 1969) by the late Ibuse Masuji (1898–1993). ✦ "White box" is the Japanese military or civilian equivalent of a casket. It is customary that the deceased's cremated remains, including parts of several larger bones, be interred in such a box. ✦ Purgatory renders *rengoku*, which also might be translated "hell."

USHIMADO—OLIVE GROVES—Yūji's description suggests that he faces southwest. Ushimado ["cow window"] lies on the Inland Sea in Okayama Prefecture, north by northeast of Takamatsu (on Shikoku) and southwest of Okayama. Views of the Inland Sea waterway through olive groves at Ushimado are particularly famous. ✦ Yashima (Kagawa Prefecture), formerly an island but now attached to Shikoku by a narrow land strip, is less than a half hour east by public transportation from Takamatsu. Nanrei [South Summit], accessible by cable car, allows a magnificent view of the Inland Sea.

The Yashima Buddhist Temple on the summit contains historic relics of medieval battles between the Taira and Minamoto clans. Nanrei towers over Shodôshima (Shodô Island) and an associated isle that lie partially in the line of vision from Ushimado. ✦ Awajishima (Hyôgo Prefecture) lies off Kobe between Shikoku and Honshu. Largest island in the Inland Sea (229 square miles), lots of rain, mild temperatures; famed as the birthplace of the puppet play (*bunraku*). ✦ Shodôshima (Kagawa Prefecture), second biggest island in the Inland Sea (60 square miles, population 50,000), sandwiched between Honshu and Shikoku, northeast of Takamatsu. Olives a primary product.

VALLEY—Plum [*ume*] is actually the apricot, which sounds less "poetic" than plum. ✦ The pussy willow [*nekoyanagi*; Latin name *Salix discolor*], sometimes called river willow, is a deciduous shrub growing to a height of 3 to 6 feet and found mainly along streams or in dry riverbeds. Its silky soft, pearl gray buds resemble kitten tails; its budding early spring branches serve in flower arrangements and for decoration.

The mountain bunting [*yama hohojiro* (or *hôjiro*)] is one of many varieties representing the plump finch family. The customary *hôjiro* is a wren–sized bird that feeds on the ground, eating grass seeds, insects, and the like. Japanese buntings are brownish and appear to have black speckles; some have white facial markings. Its song is very short but lovely; ☞ HILLS IN EARLY SPRING. ✦ For butterbur, ☞ BUTTERBUR STALK.

VIEW OF THE SANITARIUM—Pulmonary tuberculosis was long the leading cause of death among Japanese young people; TB was a virtual death sentence. Before effective drug therapies, people regarded it the way many think of AIDS today. ✦ ☞ CORDATA emits an unpleasant sour smell.

VILLAGE—"Acne lotion" renders *Kumumerufuerudo–shi eki,* i.e., "Mr.

Kummerfeld's [cleansing] liquid" [*Kummerfeldisches Waschwasser*], which Dr. Kinoshita Takuji identified as an antibiotic for acne because of its alcohol content. Like rose water, it also served as an eau de cologne.

VILLAGE—FRAGMENTS—For the fig tree, ☞ AFTERNOON LETTER. ✔ In Shakespeare's *Hamlet*, the hapless and insane Ophelia, Hamlet's frustrated love, floats down the river to her death. This image, which resonates with the sunset, darkens the superficially bright figure of Ophelia's glowing cheeks.

VISIT TO A GRAVE—Water in the bucket refers to the graveside ritual of pouring a water libation over the tombstone.

WHARF (ii)—This poem appeared in the 1932.10 edition of the Tokyo journal *Wakakusa* [*Young Grass*] (Yûji was eighteen at the time). Horiguchi Daigaku (1892–1981), the poet and noted translator of French poetry, chose it to appear in his poetry column. ✔ For another reference to a stamp sticking to his forehead, ☞ "At an Inn in Shinji" (page 206).

❏ **WHEAT HARVEST**— ☞ "Sea Trip" (page 197), includes almost the same imagery as Part 1. ✔ Throughout *Twisted Memories*, I render *mugi* as either wheat or barley, depending on context and rhythm. Strictly, wheat is *komugi* and barley is *ômugi*. Yûji uses only *mugi*, though he most often means barley. ✔ The graphs for *aogashi* imply it is the "green oak"; Professor Befu suggests, however, that the *aogashi* is a type of camphor tree [*kusunoki*; Latin name, *Cinnamomum camphora*]. This evergreen grows to 50 feet; when crushed, its aromatic leaves exude a camphor smell. Its early spring foliage can be bronze, pink, or red. ☞ SEA TRIP.

WHO'S THERE?—The deciduous wisteria [*fuji*] vine readily entwines trees or a trellis. Because this flower dangles in bunches from its branches, it is vulnerable to the slightest breeze. *Fuji* belong to the legume (Pulse) family and grow wild in fields and hills. They prefer full sun. ✔ Japanese invariably associate *fuji* flowers with late spring and cultivate the delicate and fragrant, four–petal pea–like wisteria flowers in arbors. Most *fuji* clusters are violet or blue–violet, but they may be pink or white. Streamers of the Japanese *fuji* usually reach 1.5 feet but can be 3 feet long.

WINTER (i)—College students in those days frequently wore capes instead of overcoats over their school uniforms. ✔ Fyodor Mikhaylovich Dostoyevski (1821–1881), Russian novelist whose leftwing activities resulted in a conviction of conspiracy against the government. A last–minute reprieve saved him from execution; instead, he received four years of hard labor in Siberia, where he began suffering from epileptic seizures. Dostoyevski's psychological search for truth and meaning stimulated Russian–reading Japanese to make early translations that compellingly affected readers. ✔ Japanese adore giving their shops exotic names like *Café Automne* [Café: Autumn], which Yûji writes in Roman letters. ✔ Yûji avoided dentists as though they had AIDS.

(ii)—For another reference to the image of the tail of a train whistle, ☞ "Scenes" (i), Number 1 (page 160).

WINTER CROW—The crow serves in Japanese culture as the messenger of death. Few references to crows can entirely escape this nuance, underlined here by the connection with winter, the "dead" season. ✐ The evergreen loquat [*biwa*; Latin name, *Eriobotrya japonica*], sometimes called a medlar tree, belongs to the rose family. This ornamental plant reaches heights of 15 to 30 feet; its crisp, leather–like leaves are a deep, glossy green; 3 to 6 inch clusters of tiny dull–white, modest–looking, and slightly fragrant flowers appear in autumn. On its fruit, ☞ AFTER DINNER SONGS (i) #2.

WREN'S SONG—Bramble druplets registers *ibara no mi*, not actually berries but clusters of red, edible fruit. For brambles, ☞ TO THE FAR–OFF CAPITAL. ✐ Drying racks, made of lashed–together bamboo poles, can hold two or three tiers of rice sheaves. ✐ For flute, ☞ YOU ON THE FLUTE.

YARD AT NIGHT— ☞ AKEBIA.

YOMOGI—Also called *mochigusa* [mugwort or wormwood; Latin name, *Artemisia princeps* or *indica*]. A perennial aromatic herb of the chrysanthemum family, its sprouts come up when the last snow melts. *Yomogi* blooms in autumn and appears often in very early Japanese poetry. Housewives use its leaves in cooking or for decorating dishes; this accounts for associating *yomogi* with the foods mother makes.

YOU ON THE FLUTE—For centuries, the flute has stood universally for poetry (or the spirit of poetry), the flute player for the poet. Note that Euterpe, the Muse of lyric poetry, carries a flute (Erato, the Muse of erotic poetry, usually carries a lyre). Flutes symbolize the explosive imagination that, in direct opposition to science, would maximize ambiguity and free association. ✐ In "*Les Collines* [The Hills]," from *Calligrammes* (1918), Guillaume Apollinaire (1880–1918) wrote, "…it is myself / Who am the flute I play upon. / A whip to punish other men."
  Sein (German for "to be," what exists) refers to the world that is, present conditions. *Sollen* ("shall be," what should exist) refers to the ideal state—what man or society ought to be, do, or become. ✐ In Yûji's day, German was the language for medicine, science, and philosophy; educated people naturally used these terms, Japanized from the original.

YOUTHFUL DAYS (i)—"Grayed eulalia" refers to the fronds' fading color, which implies it is late fall; ☞ EULALIA.

YOUTHFUL DAYS—PROLOGUE—In Western folklore, gardenias [*kuchinashi*], also called Cape jasmine, indicate secret love; they are good gifts to men. Their stems can grow to 6 feet; they produce shiny evergreen leaves and six–pointed flowers that begin to bloom in May or June and emit a strong fragrance. *Kuchinashi* fare best in warmer climates. ✐ Re the nun's habit, ☞ THOUGHTS WHILE SICK and BOREDOM.

YUKATA—Short for *yukatabira*, the *yukata* is a bath [*yu*] robe [*kata* = *koromo*], a cotton kimono–like garment worn after a bath, to bed, or for leisure wear around the house and yard in summer. ✔ Originally, people only wore *yukata* in the privacy of their homes, but now they often go outdoors in them. In fact, around spas and hospitals it is customary in warmer months to see guests from inns or ambulatory patients seeing visitors off on railroad platforms or strolling the streets dressed in *yukata*. ✔ Unfortunately, some hospitalized Japanese equate pajamas with *yukata*.

YUKI SPA—Located in a quiet valley of the Minochi River southeast of Sandan Gorge (☞ AT SANDAN GORGE), nearly two hours by bus northeast of Hiroshima. This spa is famed for the croaking frogs and flashing fireflies that enchant its summer evenings. Popular area for hiking.

YUSURAUME—Neither plum nor apricot (despite containing the word *ume*), *yusuraume* (Latin name: *Prunus tomentosa*) belongs to the rose family. Imported from China, it grows to 9 feet. Very sweet ruby–like fruit ripens among fresh green leaves in June, when they become a favorite target of children. ✔ The class *prunus* comprises both deciduous and evergreen trees and shrubs, including the laurel. This class also contains the so–called "stone fruits," such as cherries, peaches, plums, and the like.

YÛZÔSÂSAN—"Higo pocket knife" renders *Higo no Kami* [Governor Higo], a famous brand name that Professor Okimoto informs me continues to enjoy good sales around Hiroshima. The name possibly derives from an ancient sword maker in that area. ✔ Higo is the ancient name of the twelve districts that now comprise Kumamoto Prefecture, in the center of Japan's southern–most island, Kyushu.

Sakurajima [Cherry Island] once floated in Kagoshima Bay, on the southern tip of Kyushu. Lava from the 1914 eruption, to which Yûji refers in this work, filled in the gap between the island and the shore to make Sakurajima a peninsula. Yûji's town lies some 270 miles west by northwest of the volcano. Note that Yûji was born in 1914.

From the distance, Sakurajima looks like a single volcano though it actually consists of a cluster of three cones. The highest (nearly 3,400 feet) is on the northern side of the cluster, but only the southern cone is now active. The first recorded eruption of this volcano occurred in 708 A.D.

"Second childhood" may refer to the age of 60, which Yûji would have reached in 1974 (this poem was published in 1963). At that age, it has been the tradition for men to mark their return to childhood by wearing a red hat, a red jacket, or red vest to signal the freedom of old age. ✔ Many details in this work are clearly fictional despite Yûji's writing as though he is in the poem.

ZÔRI—Sandals (thongs) made of woven straw; in Yûji's milieu, country families made in their homes these standard footgear for children.

ENGLISH TITLE INDEX

F ollowing the title in small caps, I add the designation (P) if the work is prose. The small Roman numbers [(i), (ii)—sometimes (iii) or (iv)] indicate poems with the same translated titles; these numbers do not exist in Yûji's original. The collection in which the poem first appeared (in bold italics; its date in parentheses) follows. If not a collected poem, the known date of first publication—most often in a local magazine—appears in parentheses (a question mark follows the unknown); the late Professor Nishihara Shigeru provided this data. The last numbers indicate the page.

GS refers to *Ganshu no Shijin: Kinoshita Yûji* [*Diffident Poet: Kinoshita Yûji*] (Fukuyama: Bunka Renmei, 1975), published on the tenth anniversary of the poet's death (twenty–five poems). Other page references key to *Teihon Kinoshita Yûji Shishû* [*Poetic Works*] (Tokyo: Bokuyôsha, 1966).

MS indicates a poem translated from a manuscript; there are more than two dozen. The poet's late brother, Dr. Kinoshita Takuji, supplied most of these. Dr. Kinoshita hand copied some for me from originals, others were copies in Yûji's hand. Although several had been published earlier, none exists in the *Poetic Works*. These necessarily include some verse in *Late Spring* (1950) and *Poems for Children* (1955), for example, which were not available. Other works include "Wharf" (ii), which Yûji published in the 10.1932 edition of the Tokyo magazine *Wakakusa* [*Young Grass*].

YC refers to the unpublished youth collection, titled *"Watashi no Bunshû"* [*Collection of My Writings*], which Yûji's widow Miyako kindly allowed me to photocopy. I include fifty poems from this work. The Kinoshita family did not care to make public what Yûji would not show to others. I nevertheless find that many of these lovely lyrics show the promise of the mature poet and therefore beg for inclusion in a collection of his work. My pagination is often only approximate because many pages are not numbered and some appear missing.

Full data on the poetry collections may be found in the appendix titled COLLECTIONS (page 211). I include also nearly forty separately–titled sections of longer poems; each of these can stand as an independent work.

JAPANESE TITLE INDEX

The designation (P) indicates a prose work. I add the numbers (i), (ii) and sometimes (iii) or (iv) to indicate poems with the same translated titles; these numbers do not exist in the original. YC refers to Kinoshita's unpublished youth collection; he titled it *"Watashi no Bunshû"* [*Collection of My Writings*]. Yûji's widow Miyako kindly allowed me to photocopy this work many years ago; I include fifty poems from it; note that the pagination is often only approximate because many pages are not numbered and some appear to be missing.

GS refers to *Ganshu no Shijin: Kinoshita Yûji* [*Diffident Poet: Kinoshita Yûji*] (Fukuyama: Bunka Renmei, 1975), published on the tenth anniversary of the poet's death (twenty–five poems). All other page references key to *Teihon Kinoshita Yûji Shishû* [*Poetic Works*] (Tokyo: Bokuyôsha, 1966).

MS indicates a poem translated from a manuscript (twenty two). The poet's late brother, Dr. Kinoshita Takuji, supplied most of these. Dr. Kinoshita hand copied some for me from originals, others were copies in Yûji's hand. Although several had been published earlier, none existed in *Teihon Kinoshita Yûji Shishû*. Several appeared in the 1949 work *Banshun* [*Late Spring*], not available to me. Yûji published "Wharf (ii) [*Hatoba*]" in the 10.1932 edition of the Tokyo magazine *Wakakusa* [*Young Grass*].

The English Index contains the dates and the names of the collections in which most poems appeared. Not all Japanese titles appear in full; any interested in locating the original work, however, should have no difficulty. I have shortened some English titles to fit the space. For the complete version, please refer to the translation or to the English Title Index.

I am much indebted to Professor Okimoto Jirô for substantive help with many details in this index.

❖   ❖   ❖

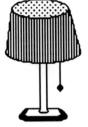

Yakusha

Box #666, Stanwood, WA 98292–0666
U. S. A.

Hagiwara Sakutarô, *Rats' Nests* (1993.03)
Collected poetry (365 works)
$30 Postpaid, Boards
ISBN 1–880276–40–2

Horiguchi Daigaku, *Rainbows* (1994.07)
Selected poetry (550 works)
$30 Postpaid, Boards
ISBN 1–880276–50–X

Kinoshita Yûji, *Twisted Memories* (1993.11)
Collected poetry (360 works)
$30 Postpaid, Boards
ISBN 1–880276–25–9

Maruyama Kaoru, *That Far–Off Self* (1994.03)
Collected poetry (460 works); 2nd edition
$35 Postpaid, Boards
ISBN 1–880276–34–8

Mushakôji Saneatsu, *Long Corridor* (1995)
Selected poetry (250 works)
$30 Postpaid, Boards
ISBN 1–880276–70–4

Sekine Hiroshi, *Cinderellas* (1994.11)
Selected poetry (200 works)
$30 Postpaid, Boards
ISBN 1–880276–55–0

Tsuboi Shigeji, *Egg in My Palm* (1993.07)
Selected poetry (290 works)
$30 Postpaid, Boards
ISBN 1–880276–61–5

—— *Translations from the Japanese by Robert Epp* ——